Kristina's Cache in Alaska

A Memoir of Adventure and Survival

By
Kristina Ahlnäs

Olympus Story House

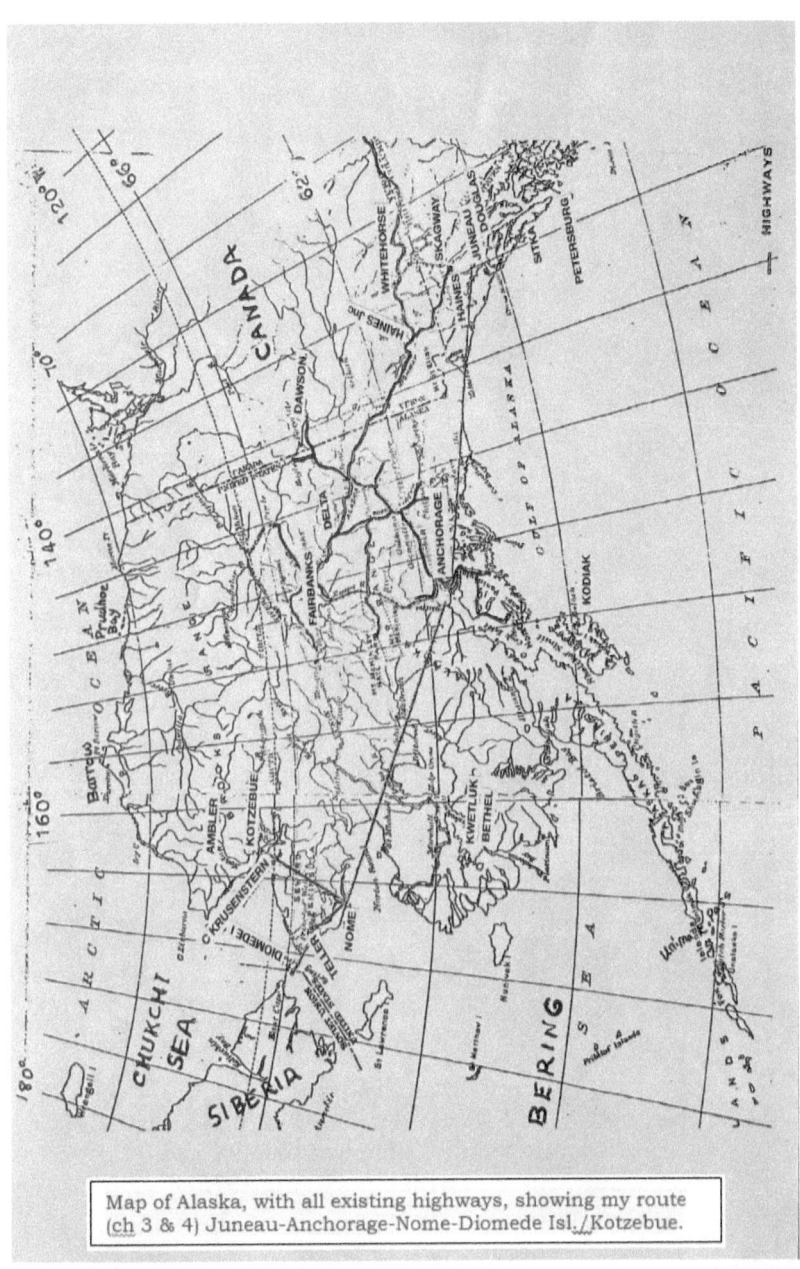

Map of Alaska, with all existing highways, showing my route
(ch 3 & 4) Juneau-Anchorage-Nome-Diomede Isl./Kotzebue.

Kristina hand-drilling to attach logs
in cache wall with rebars, Aug 1975

The finished cache in August 1976.

Aurora lit sky behind cabin and cache in December 1985.

First floor of cabin addition with winch truck, September 1991.

Acknowledgments

I praise the Lords, God and Jesus, for safely leading me through an interesting life so far. Without heavenly protection I might not be alive to tell these stories. I am grateful for all the apparent coincidences and amazing appearance of helpers when needed for my lengthy construction project. I am thankful to all the volunteers who dropped by, some numerous times to help me build my cabin. Keeping me employed for 26 years at the University of Alaska against serious economical odds, I attribute to heavenly mercy.

I am deeply thankful to the members of the Community Writers Group in Fairbanks, lead by Janet Baird. For three years I turned in 10 pages for critique every month. The diverse critique by multiple readers greatly improved the manuscript. Dave Listoe and Larry Pacquin were particularly helpful. Libbie Martin, Edward Hoch, Lee and Betty Higbie, and Cat Whitney, gave detailed critique on a couple of chapters. Rachael Kvapil, Ulyana Korotkova, Betty Robinson, Jack and Katherine Ferguson, Mike McGee, Steve Anderson, Dick Ourada, Liz Gill, Joyce Freeman-Clark, and Walter Rutherford gave good pointers and encouragement.

Marieanna Lowe critiqued my work related chapters from Douglas Marine Station. Marilyn Gentleman helped me scan my family pictures. A consultation with Debbie Miller was helpful in preparation for publication. My heartfelt thanks also goes to Neil Davis, a colleague and science editor, who reviewed the whole manuscript. He understood what I wrote about and knew most of the scientist.

Contents

Acknowledgments vii

Foreword xi

Introduction xii

1 Come to Alaska 1

2 Douglas, my new home 5

3 Winter Visit in Eskimo Land 13

4 Day-tour to Tomorrow 22

5 Norwegian Celebration in Petersburg 29

6 Chief Scientist at Sea 33

7 Work at Douglas Marine Station 37

8 Prisoner of Clouds 47

9 Juneau Icefield 59

10 Closing the Icefield for Winter 73

11 Traveling by Train 82

12 Moving to Fairbanks 90

13 Whaling Celebration in Barrow 100

14 Winter Chores in the Interior 107

15 Harvest Dinner 128

16 Trading by Radio 133

17 Fur Seals on the Pribilof Islands 138

18 Encounters on the Way to Work 147

19 On Thunder and Ice Patrol 155

20 Power Outage. 163

21 Side Effects of the Oil Rush 174

22 Camping and Building on my Own Property. 181

23 Hiking the Chilkoot Trail. 197

24 Building My Cache 210

25 Rescued by the US Coast Guard. 225

26 Building My Cabin 241

27 Silver Anniversary for Gold State 273

28 Pleistocene Bison on the Menu. 276

29 Visit by President and Pope. 282

30 Finding the Perfect Ice Floe. 287

31 Fishing Bears 293

32 Meditations in Storm 302

33 Mission with Dates 310

34 In Anna's Shoes Through The Gold Rush 315

35 U Da Naa - Long Ago. 323

36 Slavig in a Yup'ik Village 333

37 Kobuk Sand Dunes. 344

38 Cape Krusenstern 358

39 Addition with Running Water. .371

Bibliography 385

Index 387

Foreword

I didn't plan to write a book but things seem to happen to me and people I meet soon say: "You should write a book!"

Alaska is a land of mystery and beauty where things out of the ordinary do happen. How we respond determines our quality of life. I lived four years in a 49-square foot cache I built as a practice house, flew with NASA, and I ate part of an ice age bison now in the Museum.

Why did I title my book "Kristina's Cache?" Cache is a hidden store of things out of reach of wild animals. Moving into a forest I felt a cache with a 16-foot ladder was a safe place to live. I thought I could build it quickly and so learn what I needed to know to build a cabin. I also like to think about the cache as the collection of stories I share with the reader.

My book deals with selected experiences of my life in Alaska during 33 years from 1969 to 2002. Work related chapters from my 30-year employment at the University of Alaska and chapters from my 20-year construction project are interspersed with stories depicting everyday life in extreme weather, experiencing Native culture, and outdoor adventure.

The collection of 40 chapters are chronologically arranged to show my personal development and the changes in Alaska during more than a quarter century.

Kristina Ahlnäs Fairbanks,
May 2012

Introduction

Parts of this book, titled "Bopålar i Alaska," were originally published in Swedish in 1998 by Schildts in Finland. On a book tour through the Swedish speaking parts of Finland, I addressed a question I thought might be of interest to the reader:

How did I become the kind of person I am?

People who read my book might think I am weird. I end up in strange situations most normal people wouldn't even dream of. Whatever molded me? This is a difficult question to answer. Heritage and environment are not enough; else sisters and brothers would end up rather similar. I believe our thoughts, dreams and experiences are important in shaping our lives.

In this introduction, I will relate selected events and experiences that influenced the development of my character. Things happen but we choose how to respond, and so learn to handle life. I gradually develop a strong-minded determination to dare to try, believing I will succeed. The spirit of adventure and the soul of an explorer urge me to visit new places.

Kristina at age 4 with my parents Tua and Uno Ahlnäs
and baby sister Benita in Finland. Uno is on temporary
leave from the war in 1941.

I became a big girl at age four when my little sister
Benita was born. We lived on an island in a seven-
story apartment house on a large field where cows and
sheep grazed. On the other side of the strait was one
of the harbors in Helsinki, Finland. At age six, I was
big enough to run out in the woods, on a cold winter
morning in 1944, to investigate craters made by bombs.

All windows in our house were broken. My father
was fighting in the war and couldn't help. I can still
remember tall houses on fire that we passed going to
the railway station. My mother, sister, and I took the
train to Grandmother, who lived in a small, safer town
to the north. When snow started to melt we moved from
Grandmother's crowded house to an abandoned mice-
infested bakery without electricity and water.

When school started in the fall, the war was over. We
were back home. When I grew up, there were large forests
on the island. I had one girlfriend. We played with the
boys, climbing trees and exploring the island. When I fell

on a big ski hill, one of the older boys commented that it was a shame to be a coward and sit down. I conquered my fears, bent forward, and improved my skiing.

Candy was not available. I picked salty leaves from the meadows and dug up roots that tasted like licorice. When we scratched our knees, we healed them with plantain leaves so mother didn't need to know. When we wanted a weather report, we sang to a slug that showed its horns when fair weather was in sight.

Sometimes my father took me along on his bicycle to pick blueberries. He would locate some good bushes where he left me alone. It never occurred to me to be afraid in the forest.

When I was 10 years old, my mother had a lady make me corduroy slacks since clothing could not be bought. The navy blue slacks were so beautiful that I did something daring and shocking. It was not customary for girls to wear pants but I wore them to the movie theatre.

"School is your job," my father told me. "I expect you to do better than average." He paid me for excellent grades in exams. It helped my bicycle savings. When I turned 12, I had saved half the money and my father gave me the rest.

When the Finnish national hero, Field Marshal Mannerheim, died in February 1951, I had been a Girl Scout for three months. On a cold winter day, I had the honor to stand proudly freezing at attention along the funeral procession. My patriotic feelings became stronger that day.

After a year in the Girl Scouts, I was sent to patrol leader training. Generally I was very shy, but the Girl Scouts was an exception. I did well which strengthened my self-esteem. I took the scout promise and law seriously and expected everybody else also to put our duty to God and country first. My belief in God was founded early. Prayer before sleep was a habit. Later I realized I could pray for more than protection.

At the annual Saint George Scout parade in the spring I graduated from High School, I was awarded the Mannerheim clip. This is an appointed honor that made me beam with pride as I marched out from the Senate Square carrying the flag of Finland. That summer I participated in a work camp and leadership training in Lapland north of the Arctic Circle. We used drawknives and axes to peel huge logs for a cabin.

Kristina going to girl scout leadership and work camp in Lapland in 1955

At my last Girl Scout camp in Finland, I was in charge of the kitchen. Every morning I gave the 16-year-old girls in the kitchen crew the ingredients and responsibility to prepare them. I trusted them to use their judgment and do their best. The girls did fine without disturbing me. This method of leadership, by giving responsibility and not meddling in the performance, worked well for me also in future work. Through the Girl Scouts I learned the power of positive thinking, to appreciate nature, to improvise, and to use my imagination.

What I wanted to do when I grew up was an enigma that took me a long time to solve. I went to the University of Helsinki and started to read bulletin boards. I saw a familiar name, Shakespeare, with a time and a place. Later I saw my name on the bulletin board. Congratulations, I had passed the entry exam to an advanced class in English. After a year and a half of studying English, French and Psychology, I realized this track would lead to teaching, something I didn't want.

Then I found a catalog from the department of Natural Sciences with subjects that interested me. I was the only girl in those classes and didn't know women couldn't become oceanographers, and nobody told me. Oceanography required practice at sea.

"There's an opportunity for two students to come out with the research ship, Aranda, next summer," Professor Hela announced in the fall.

"Can I come?" I was the first, and only one, to ask after class.

"It's still too early to make that decision, but come back later," the professor replied. The third time I asked, it was too late. The positions had been filled — with two men! I had to have a summer job. The student job service only had waitress jobs.

"I am studying oceanography. Don't you have anything more suitable?" I asked. The job service lady thumbed through the pile of cards once more and pulled out the bottom one.

"Mess girl on the R/V Aranda." I couldn't believe my good luck to get a second chance to come aboard.

This was really an answer to my prayer. Scared that the job wouldn't wait, I searched out the ship in dry dock. The Captain and Stewardess were desperate to fill the position. The workday was 10 hours. The salary was half of the meager pay I made at a bank the summer before but I signed on. My Mother was horrified. I had two weeks to get my sailor's passport. "Impossible," said the snobby lady at the passport office, casting a condescending glance at such scum as me. Nice girls didn't go to sea.

"But I am studying at the University and I am required to get my practice at sea." The lady re- evaluated me and I got my sailor's passport in two days.

On the day of departure I was standing at the rail dressed in a blue-white checkered cotton dress and a white apron. I was very nervous when professor Hela approached the gangplank.

"It's nice you could arrange to come along," he said while shaking my hand. That's how I started my career in oceanography, through the galley door.

Galley crew on R/V *Aranda* Summer 1959: Kristina, mess girl of Captain and scientists, "Ville," mess boy of officers, Olga, cook, "Kalle," mess boy of crew, Santu, cook's helper.

In the winter, professor Hela offered me a temporary job at the Finnish Institute of Marine Research. After getting my master's degree in geophysics on the oceanography line, I wanted to visit the USA. I needed funding. An ASLA-Fulbright scholarship gave me the opportunity to study oceanography for a year at Scripps Institution of Oceanography in San Diego, California. ASLA is a scholarship fund created by USA from the money Finland paid back on its loan from USA after WW2.

I believe these early experiences helped mold my character to make me the person I am who believes I *can*. It is just to find the way.

1

Come to Alaska

"What on earth are you going to do in Alaska?"

"You must be crazy to even think about going to Alaska."

"What will you find there but snow and ice?"

"Can't you find anything sensible to do a little bit closer?"

"Can you hide me in your suitcase?"

These are some of the comments I encounter from people in Finland and Sweden when I announce my intention of going to Alaska in 1969. Most are skeptical and few encouraging. What makes people in general fear the unknown? I won't speculate. Instead, I will tell how I happened to end up in Alaska, what I do, and what it is like to live here.

Initially, even I consider going to Alaska a joke. I have jested to my boss, Dr. Stig Fonselius, at the Royal Fishery Board of Sweden in Gothenburg, that I am going to Alaska if he cannot extend my contract funding. I know a scientist there that might provide work. Somehow my joke gradually matures to seriousness during one and a half years as a lab assistant in marine chemistry. While I do the lab work my boss accomplishes his goal of finishing his Ph.D. thesis. Although my job situation in Sweden appears to stabilize, with a promise of a 5-year contract and a raise in salary, I have made up my mind. Thoughts of Alaska have whetted my appetite for adventure. Then I get a telegram from the Alaskan scientist.

"Come within two weeks!"

My boss is disturbed when I give notice. Still, this is less sudden than his job offer by radiophone as "my" Norwegian freighter passed Greenland on a misty winter morning in December 1967. I was returning to Scandinavia from Seattle by the cheapest conveyance, since my American marriage was on the rocks and I had given up my career there. I had mailed many requests for work to Scandinavia but received few replies before leaving USA.

You have to be insane to choose Alaska, I think, but I pack my bags. Eight boxes of my belongings go by ocean freight from Gothenburg via Seattle to Juneau.

Finally I am ready for departure. First I fly to Helsinki to say good-bye to my parents and family. They are concerned, but never surprised over my decisions. From Finland I fly to Holland. The KLM DC-8 takes off from Amsterdam at mid-day in June 1969. The beautiful sunshine seems to accompany us as we soar across the ice fields of Greenland and the sea ice of the Arctic Ocean.

We enter Alaska from the north. The Brooks Range rises impressively from the flat coastal plain, dividing the waters of the big rivers between north and south. The mighty Yukon is the largest river on the southern side. It is very distinct from the air as it winds through plush velvet looking greenery for 2000 miles to the Bering Sea. The almost total absence of roads and habitations is striking. I have a feeling of flying across a desolate, still undiscovered land, as I look down over tundra followed by mountains and forests.

One hour before take-off from Amsterdam, we land in Anchorage. The sun is still up. It is strange to land before I started on the same day although I had spent eight hours in the air. Including stopovers in Hamburg and Amsterdam, I have been under way for 15 hours and crossed a dozen time zones from the start in Helsinki, Tuesday morning, to the landing in Anchorage around noon the same day.

I spend the night in Anchorage, so I can see a little of the largest city in Alaska. In 1969 it has a population of 45,000. Including surroundings, it totals 113,000. The scenery around the airport reminds me a little of northern Finland, but Anchorage looks like any standard American city except for a large polar bear outside a gift shop. Soon the time difference affects me. I crash in bed. When my normal requirement for sleep is satisfied, it is night, a bad time to continue my sightseeing. I spend the rest of the night reading old Swedish ladies magazines I took along as ballast.

From Anchorage it takes one and a half hours to fly to Juneau, the capital of Alaska. The wonderful sunshine continues, as we fly south along the coast, lined with dizzying high mountains and vast snow-glittering ice fields and glaciers. The Golden Nugget jet approaches Juneau between snow covered mountain peaks, and lands at the airport with Mendenhall Glacier as an impressive background. Due to the terrain and water barriers, Juneau can only be reached by air or sea. In 1969, the city population of the capital of Alaska is 7,000 with 13,000 including the metropolitan area.

To my surprise and relief, I discover my new boss, Dr. Y. R. Nayudu with one of his assistants, Charlette Chastain in the welcoming crowd. The comfortable part about my new job is that I already know my closest colleagues from my previous work at the University of Washington in Seattle.

Basalt rocks from submerged volcanoes at the bottom of the Pacific Ocean were part of the marine geologic samples I was curator of at the University of Washington. They belonged to Dr. Nayudu, a marine volcanologist, who at times had contributed to my salary.

3

Dr. Nayudu is now the director at Douglas Marine Station (DMS), an outpost of the Institute of Marine Science (IMS) of the University of Alaska. The University is headquartered in Fairbanks, but the DMS is in Southeast Alaska about 3 hours away by air. When one of his assistants quit, he offered me a job.

Driving the city streets of Juneau is like a roller coaster ride as the city clings to the steep mountainside. A bridge takes us to Douglas Island. The DMS, where I will work, is situated three miles from Juneau. I get housed in "Jumbo", an old abandoned school taken over by the University of Alaska. Lots of other people appear to live here as well.

My first impression of Southeast Alaska is overwhelming. It is June and the sunshine is warm. The clear blue sky frames the three thousand-plus feet high mountain peaks still covered with snow.

To make the first impression even more memorable, my new boss invites me to dinner. I find out later that Mike's is the only restaurant in Douglas and one of the best in the area. I am very impressed. The boss hands me the menu.

"Order anything you want."

"I haven't had lobster for years." It is my favorite food, and I figure this is a one-time offer.

2

Douglas, my new home

When I come to Alaska in June 1969, the rights to drill for oil in Prudhoe Bay on the coast of the Beaufort Sea are being leased. Hour after hour the bids from the oil companies are read on the radio. The final sum for all the leases is 900 million dollars and this is just the beginning of Alaska's income from oil.

The city of Douglas was founded around 1880. The reason was gold. Around 1900, Douglas, with its company town, Treadwell, had one of the largest gold mines in the world and a combined population of 30,000. The mining activity in Juneau, on the other side of the Gastineau Channel, was considerably smaller, as was its population. The Treadwell mine was partly under the Channel. In 1917 the mine caved in and was filled with water. The flooding moved the center of activity to the Juneau side. Before that, the gold mine had produced 65.5 million dollars-worth of gold.

Seward's folly, as the sale of Alaska by Russia in 1867 is called, paid back well. The price for Alaska was 7.2 million dollars or 2 cents per acre. The original price was 7 million but at closing it was noticed that ice delivered from Sitka to San Francisco had not been paid for. The final price was adjusted to include the shipment of ice.

In the early 1970's, Treadwell is just a collection of partly decayed houses in a dense forest. The population of Douglas is 1,200 spread out over the town that is five streets wide and 10 streets long. Douglas has a post office, where every household has its PO box, a city hall with a library open two nights a week, a school, a voluntary fire department, a grocery store, a gas station, and four bars. This sounds very civilized, but I soon discover that my favorite cheese is moldy although it is not Roquefort. Prices are high and the selection limited. This inspires me on Saturdays to take a 7.5-mile round trip hike to the grocery store in Juneau. There is no public transportation. Consequently, I shop lightly, considering how much weight I want to carry home.

The warm and beautiful weather that welcomed me to Juneau causes towering cumulus clouds. They turn into thunderstorms with lightning, igniting forest fires on the Canadian side. Soon the smoke seeps into Juneau and starts to irritate my eyes. Fortunately, there is a wide belt of glaciers between Canada and us. After some time it starts to rain and the air clears up. Soon I discover rain is far more common than sunshine in this area.

I have the VIP room in "Jumbo", the abandoned school, but don't really enjoy it although the rent is free. I am still out of alignment with time or simply jet-lagged. I still feel sleepy in the morning and ready to start my day at night. A bunch of loud, fieldwork students in the corridors and kids playing ball under my open window in the schoolyard at night are not conducive to sleeping. Just because it is light at night nobody seems to go to bed. I grab the first opportunity to move.

I find a furnished one-bedroom apartment in a new three-story house with a fantastic view over the Gastineau Channel and the mountain peaks on the other side. I ask my boss for an advance of $500. The monthly rent of $220 is more than I can afford but I plan to continue searching. The move is rapidly accomplished since I only have two suitcases. The rest of my belongings are still on their way across the Atlantic, through the Panama Canal and up along the coast of the Pacific Ocean. They will arrive in a couple of months.

Compared to the studio I sub-leased in Sweden, this apartment is sheer luxury. My job is close-by so I can walk home on my lunch hour and sit by my panorama window and enjoy the view. Traffic in the Gastineau Channel is busy with two daily ferries and many ocean-going luxury cruise ships each week in the summer. Despite the high rent, I soon discover the walls in the apartment are so thin I can hear everything my neighbors are doing.

Our secretary at work, Julie Isaac, calls the radio's "Problem Corner." Finally, she convinces her neighbor, Edla Cashen, who lives alone in one of the oldest houses in Douglas, to rent her attic apartment. The rent is $125 for a studio with a kitchen, bath, garage, and access to the landlady's washer, freezer, carpentry shop, and garden flowers. The attic is cozy with its steep sloping roof. I still have a view of the Channel and the mountains but they are now further away since I moved from First Avenue by the water to Fifth Avenue by the edge of the forest. From my kitchen table I can sometimes see a bald eagle in a spruce tree on Fourth Avenue. At times I can see dark spots above the tree line on the mountains. With field glasses I confirm some are black bears above Juneau.

Most of the time the mountaintops above Juneau are snow covered. In winter the snow cover can get too thick for the steep slopes. From my window I can see the results of many old avalanches as clean swept slides down the mountain. Broken trees line the slides as matches thrown from a box. Sometimes I can track an avalanche from a small cloud of snow on the mountaintop until the snow masses surge across Thane Road that runs along the coast of Gastineau Channel.

Traffic along Thane Road is light but some cars always end up on the wrong side of the avalanche.

I will scarcely need the garage that is included in the rent, I think, since the job is still within walking distance, as is all of Douglas. The longest road leads 33 miles north of Juneau. It is *The Road*. Later, when I try to scout out people's places for picking berries they just tell me they are out along *The Road*. If you add the lengths of all the roads in the area including the city streets in Juneau and Douglas the result is 140 miles. This is less than half the combined length of all the gold mining tunnels in Juneau.

My colleague, Charlette Chastain, who welcomed me at the airport, lends me her bicycle. I am excited to have wheels. A beautiful Sunday I decide to explore Thane Road on the other side of the sound. First I have to bicycle to Juneau. From there the road leads nine miles to the south. Some distance out of Juneau I come to an uphill and get off the bicycle. I hear a rustle in the brush to my left. I am no longer alone. Fifty feet from the road a large black bear looks at me. The black fur has a beautiful shine. Many thoughts race through my brain, as both of us stand motionless.

- If the bear approaches, I'll turn my bicycle and flee downhill, but it would be disappointing. I want to find out where the road is going.

- I wonder if I'd have the time to get my camera out. With one eye on the bear I dig in my bag, ready to turn around if necessary. Unfortunately, the bear acts faster. It turns around and jumps gracefully over a log and disappears in the shade of the dense forest.

I get to the end of the road but no longer feel the urge to pick blueberries.

Meeting the bear lessens my interest in bicycling. I need a car! There are only two auto dealerships of interest in the area and both are out *The Road*. To get there you need a car.

I call the Volvo dealer. Mrs. "Volvo," brings me a new Volvo to test drive. I take it to north Douglas where the dirt road is rough. The Volvo floats smoothly over the potholes. I would love to have this car. The only deterrent is the price. Mrs. Volvo understands and brings me a used Volvo the next day. The price is affordable. We drive the dirt road to north Douglas, but this car reminds us of every pothole. The next day I get a small Datsun to test. I like the turquoise blue color. The car handles the north Douglas road admirably. While the sales lady makes a phone call I see a paper, not intended for the buyer. It says the car might be difficult to start in the cold. I need to think about this.

I call the Volkswagen dealer. Eero Tetri picks me up. While driving out *The Road* to the dealership he talks about Volkswagen cars. I am interested in a station wagon.

"Have you ever driven one?" "No."

"There is a fast fix for that. Here are the keys. Take your time and drive out and look at the Mendenhall glacier."

I haven't driven much for a long time. When I stop at the glacier a strange man walks up to me.

"Something is smelling burnt," he says. "This concerns your car and it is serious. You shouldn't drive back to the car dealer but call them."

Eero promises to come to the glacier and look at the car. While waiting I look at a display about the life cycle of the salmon.

"What seems to be the problem?" I suddenly hear a calm voice ask in Finnish. I didn't notice a big red-haired man driving up in an old pick-up. Who is he? How does he know to address me in Finnish? Of course, he saw the car by the road. I expect a reprimand. What have you done to our new car?

"Release the hand brake and come back," is all he says.

As with the new Volvo, this car also costs too much. Embarrassed, I accept a ride back to Douglas. This dealership I will never hear from again, I think.

A couple of days later, Eero delivers a used 1966 Volkswagen to my job. I may use it as much as I want. The $1,250 price tag is affordable but the car has already registered 33,000 miles and feels like an old car. With access to transportation I have the possibility to investigate other cars. Charlette has seen a white 1967 Volkswagen in Juneau with a "For sale" sign. It costs 200 dollars more but feels like a new car. It has only been driven 9,000 miles. I ask Eero about it. His used car I was permitted to drive as much as I wanted is immediately picked up.

To pay for the 1967 car I must get a bank loan for $1,000 but it is easily arranged. The president of the bank knows my landlady. It is enough for security.

Although I didn't buy my car from Eero's Volkswagen he gives me perfect service. When I call and ask for service he asks, "Is it a 1967 car?" before I have even told my name. He must recognize my voice with a foreign accent.

Alaska's registration plates are issued from the capital of Juneau. The Governor has number 1. The first 200 plates go to people in the government. I like to have an even number. They promise to contact me when 1300 turns up. It becomes a lucky number. Suspicious people give me plenty of room.

I have brought two pairs of skis from Finland. One afternoon in the beginning of January I plan to try them. The weather is a pleasant 18°F. I haven't seen any ski trails but I should be able to make my own.

I have shoveled a lot of snow outside the garage so there should be enough in the forest. Normally Juneau gets 13 feet of snow every winter.

I put some extra clothing in my backpack, step into my ski bindings and side step up into the forest from

Fifth Avenue. That's as far as I get. The spruce forest is dense and brushy. I take off my skis and squeeze through the branches. The ground slopes steeply uphill towards the top of 3,300-foot-high Mount Bradley. I am mainly climbing. At times I even have to crawl through the brush. The skis are in my way. When the ground finally levels out and the forest thins a little I put on my skis and break my own trail. Now and then I can ski for thirty feet until the forest gets too thick again. I have never seen forests like this. I am accustomed to the open forests in southern Finland where there is room for berries and mushrooms and ski trails between the trees.

After a couple of hours of desperate progress I am no longer sure where I am. The ground doesn't slope noticeable in any direction. It is cloudy so I cannot tell directions. I have eaten everything I brought along. This is no longer fun. Besides, the short January daylight is dwindling. It would be safest to follow my tracks back, but it would be too exhausting. I hope to find an easier and shorter way out. I come to a frozen creek. It must be on its way to the sound and the Douglas road! If I follow it, I will find my way out! The brush is dense along its banks but the ice is smooth. Finally I can enjoy my skis. The creek bed gets deeper, the stream wider, and my glide faster. I hope the ice is strong enough. The creek turns ahead of me and I slow down. In the next blinking of my eye, I glance out over the unfrozen water reservoir of Douglas. Shaken, I realize how close it was that my ski tour had ended up in the public drinking water.

***

Thirty-five years later I visit Juneau and find my way to the water reservoir. It is abandoned leaving a 50-foot-high concrete wall as a strange monument. Hidden in the dense forest I see large white signs with faded red text

11

proclaiming NO SWIMMING, NO TRESPASSING. I saw no signs when I skied down. I guess they didn't expect anyone to slide down on the water from the mountain.

3

Winter Visit in Eskimo Land

Every year I eagerly await the arrival of winter. I appreciate skiing and find a special attraction in the fresh smell of cold, clean, white snow. Coming to Alaska I expect to get my fill but instead it looks like I have brought the Gothenburg weather with me to southeast Alaska. When it doesn't rain, I can see winter on the tops of the mountains. There is a downhill ski area on Douglas Island but after a three-mile climb with my skis on my shoulder, I am not yet in shape to fully enjoy skiing. I have to do something.

On board Alaska Airline's Golden Nugget jet I leave a rainy Juneau in February 1970 to go to Alaska's only ski resort, Alyeska. We fly northwest along the coast of the Pacific Ocean, over the mighty mountain ranges of St Elias and Chugach with peaks of 16,000 feet and some of the largest glaciers in the world.

I have booked a winter package. The ski bus is supposed to wait for me in Anchorage.

"Are you Kristina?" a man at the end of the airline counter asks. "I am your driver, Curly. You are the only passenger." After a 45-minute drive, we arrive at Alyeska.

Next morning my driver comes out with a busload of skiers from Anchorage, but despite that, he keeps me company all day.

"I don't want you to get lost before Monday night when I will bring you back to Anchorage. Let's take the one mile chair lift," Curly says. Despite my attitude of a scared bunny rabbit I feel safe with him in the blowing snow at the top of the lift above the tree line.

"I used to be on the ski patrol," Curly says as he leads me down through knee-deep soft new powder that makes me think of whipped cream. With my ski technique untrained, the descent offers a few surprises. Suddenly we have large snow blocks under our skis.

"A recent avalanche!" We couldn't see it in time, below the thin snow cover in the whiteout. "Let's get out of this area!" Curly shouts.

Towards the end of the day I start to gain more confidence. I am getting accustomed to the terrain and to having ice in my lashes but I don't have the time to overcome my respect for the glistening blue ice mounds at the lower end of the run.

My third day I am ready to conquer the slopes, but the ski lift is closed on Mondays.

"You may use our Scorpio snow machine instead.

The key is in the ignition," a hotel clerk says.

"I have never used a snow machine. How do you start it?"

A man comes out and turns the key. "You can drive to the moose pasture and practice," he says.

Heavy wet snow cascades down covering my yellow goggles and restricting visibility. Through trial and error I manage to progress far enough to be concerned about getting back. I see the trail further on disappear into the forest and worry how far it will go? I try to make a loop to turn around. Apparently I don't know how to manage the loose snow and get stuck. Feelings of panic mix with the heavy falling snow as I try to lurch the machine from side to side while giving it full gas, but in vain.

It might take hours until anybody will miss me; so just sitting here waiting for rescue is not appealing.

Walking back could be a questionable enterprise in the whirling snow without any tools of navigation. I am uncertain how long I could follow my trail. Besides, I imagine I would sink deep at every step and it would be embarrassing to return without the Scorpio.

It is imperative to get the beast back on the trail. After digging it out with my hands, I tramp down the snow surrounding the snow machine and try to lift it from the tips of the skis. It is like tramping down cotton balls except my boots get filled and my mittens wet. What shall I do? The only things I can think of is full gas, lurch, push, and repeat the procedure. The Scorpio is heavy and barely moves but it has to! Dressed in my arctic outfit, since people said it is cold to ride a snow machine, I get over-heated. After persistent repeated tries, the nuisance finally, slowly, let's itself be moved. What a relief!

Back on the trail I don't dare make another attempt to turn around. I am more afraid of getting stuck again than of the unknown ahead. I continue over roots and branches into the forest hoping sooner or later to get somewhere. To my relief, the trail makes a sharp turn and I feel rather than see I am getting out of the forest. After this experience I am ready for the unplowed roads and return to the hotel. Somewhat embarrassed, I give an account of my struggles.

"You may continue one more hour for free," the hotel concierge offers without noticing my exasperated exhaustion.

"Thank you I had enough for now."

Taking a hot shower flushes away the desperation I feel as I relive the adventure with proud satisfaction.

From Anchorage I fly to Nome to find out how the Eskimos live in wintertime. A man with a wolf ruff on his parka hood stands at the bottom of the stairs from the airplane.

"You must be Kristina. I'm your guide, John Andrews."

Again, I am the only tourist on the tour. I don't mind. I love to travel. The fewer tourists I see the better. I like to meet locals and if possible, be considered one myself.

"First we have to get you some warm clothing," John says. "Warm clothing is included in the tour that normally starts in Seattle."

I thought I was warmly dressed in my sheepskin lined suede coat and Norwegian sealskin boots.

The airplane has left and so has my luggage.

"No problem," says John and goes searching. "Is this yours?" he asks as he proudly returns with a large black bag. "A taxi driver had taken it."

On our way to the village of the King Island Eskimos at the edge of Nome, we pick up a lot of giggling Eskimo children. The girls are dressed in flounce trimmed colorful cotton dresses with fur- trimmed hoods. I suppose the dresses are fur lined.

The meeting hall is heated with a big iron stove. We sit down on the only bench in front of the stage. Opposite, a row of small, shy dolls with pigtails look at us with curiosity. The orchestra sits cross-legged on a bench at the back of the stage. Each man has a drum in his hand consisting of a round driftwood frame covered with a stomach of a walrus. The drum is big enough to hide his face behind and is so utilized.

The members of the orchestra start to beat the drums with a wooden stick in an increasing tempo. Some short, more or less improvised dances follow rapidly. It is mainly the older women, standing in line, making simple swaying rhythmic motions with their bodies and arms. They don't move their feet. The motions symbolize a seal hunt and other common activities. The women in the middle of the row know what they are doing while the others discreetly observe and imitate. A man wearing an imposing mask and a lot of feathers performs the dance of the raven. Contrary to the women, the men move their feet in rhythmic stamping with deeply bent knees.

Next morning my guide takes me on a tour of Nome. The surroundings consist of gold fields with abandoned dredges that used to float. Now, from a distance, in the flat arctic light, they look like huge ghostlike contraptions, reminiscent of run-down apartment houses.

In the fall of 1898, the "Three Lucky Swedes:" Jafet Lindeberg, a Norwegian reindeer herder, John Brynteson, a Swedish coal miner from Michigan and Eric Lindblom, a Swedish tailor, discovered gold in the hills outside Nome. This started the Nome gold rush.

Rumor spread fast and people poured in, first from the Klondike. Next summer gold was found on the beach. In two months a million dollars-worth of gold was retrieved. When this gold reached Seattle the gold rush was a fact. Gold valued close to 30 million dollars was retrieved from the Nome area between 1900 and 1904. Many became rich fast by day and poor even faster during the excitement of nightlife with gambling and women. In 1900 the population of Nome was 12,500 with an additional five to ten thousand gold miners spread out along 25 miles of the beach.

Today in 1970, Nome has a population of 3,300 and the gold rush is just a memory. The second largest gold nugget in Alaska, weighing 182 Troy ounces or 12.5 pounds was found here in 1903. Later, in 1998 a 294 ozt or 20-pound nugget was found in Ruby, Alaska.

In the summer at least one gigantic electrically driven dredge is excavating gold. Engstrom, a Swedish descendant, and his son own it. There are still unknown amounts of the golden metal in the ground but as long as the value of gold is frozen at
$35 per ounce, it is not worth retrieving.

After my historic sightseeing, I get more clothing; a pair of heavy insulated navy pants with lots of pockets and buttons.

An Eskimo couple will show me how to ice fish. Sarah, dressed in a beautiful parka artistically made from many different kinds of furs, is waiting for us on the beach by a skin boat called an oomiak. The fur next to her face and around the sleeves is wolverine. Because it contains more oil than wolf it doesn't get frosty in the cold.

Sarah's husband, Jack, is out on the sea ice making a hole with an iron bar. The early February sun on the 65th parallel is still low on the horizon and cannot push the temperature above -10°F.

The fishing tool is a worn string with a triple hook. The top part of the hook is wound with a red thread. The string is attached to a 15-inch long stick with jacks in both ends.

Sarah pulls up a small tomcod to show me how it is done. I get to try.

"There is a jerk in the line!" I announce excited. "Let me help you," John says as he grabs the

string, but too late.

"Can you hold my movie camera?" I ask John as I pull it from beneath the warmth of my parka. With both hands free I can work a lot better. Rapidly I pull up two tomcods and a tiny fish "for the cat." The fish we catch are immediately frozen in the deep freeze of nature.

Kristina with her catch of two tomcods, ice fishing with
Sarah and Jack outside Nome.

Sarah is sitting cross-legged on the ice at another
hole. In one hand she holds the ancient fishing tool of
the Eskimos — in the other a cigarette. She seems to
have lost her luck and starts to watch my method with
curiosity. I do have some fishing experience from the
Grand Banks, but that time the catch of the whole ship
consisted of one Atlantic cod, one Norwegian mess-girl,
and two Spanish deck hands. The last three had hooked
each other.

Twelve miles out of Nome we encounter a rapidly
growing cloud of dust. Traffic seems to consist of just
us. The low rays of sunshine through the dust show a
boiling witch kettle of horns and backs. Three reindeer
herds totaling 2,000 animals are gathered in an
enclosure. Now and then a few reindeer are let into a
smaller enclosure where they sometimes try to climb
the walls, while the brown eddy in the large enclosure
silently continues. Except for the tramping and scraping
of hoofs, the reindeer are silent. One by one the reindeer

are let from the small enclosure into a narrow furrow with a wooden bottom and slanting walls, where their hooves slide. This slows the scared animal enough for a few men to catch it and keep its head still for marking the ears. The reindeer doesn't seem to feel any pain and bolts wildly as soon as it is free again. After marking or presentation to the bookkeeper, the reindeer are separated into herds and let into their own enclosure through one of three gates in the marking enclosure.

The reindeer is not native to Alaska. It was imported from Siberia between 1891 and 1902, when the Eskimos suffered from famine because of a decline in the numbers of wild reindeer, called caribou, and marine mammals. Reindeer herders from Lapland in Scandinavia were invited to teach the Eskimos.

After I have seen the sun sink beyond the pack ice on the Bering Sea, I am introduced to the secrets of building a kayak. We sit down around a kayak in the lobby and Dominique starts to explain. He speaks good English with vigorous hand movements but doesn't understand my accent, so John has to restate my questions.

"Each man uses his personal measures to build a frame from drift wood. All parts are tied together using leather straps or baleen. No nails are used. A walrus hide is split into two layers to make them lighter. One of them is used to cover the middle of the kayak. The split walrus skin is a lot stronger than the lighter sealskin used for the pointed ends. The sealskin will shrink the ends a little."

Dominique sits down in the kayak and pulls his parka over the edge of the cockpit.

"My rain parka is made from waterproof intestines. It keeps the inside of the kayak completely dry," he explains.

In front of him on the kayak he has a frame of driftwood with a long coiled line of leather attached to a harpoon.

"When a seal comes within reach, I throw the harpoon. Then I can either pull it up or attach the other end of the line to an inflated sealskin that acts as a marking buoy. There is room to stuff one seal behind you in the kayak, the others you have to tow. However, you better stuff the seal head first, the elders say. When the elders speak, we have to be quiet and listen, for they know what they are talking about," Dominique, who is not that young himself, says.

The source of this story is rather realistic. One Eskimo had stuffed the seal the wrong way. "The seal revived and started to chew on the rear end of the poor Eskimo," Dominique tells us without unnecessary embroidery.

"Tell us about the time when you stepped through the ice," John urges. I expect a scary story.

"I had tested the strength of the ice with a pole with a metal point. If the pole had a point of walrus ivory instead, this would never have happened because ivory doesn't lie," Dominique says. He waves his arms with exuberance and shows us how he quickly pulled off his caribou socks, turned them inside out, rubbed them dry with snow and pulled them on again.

After this demonstration I pick up the King Island Eskimos' recipe for ice cream:

2   handfuls of reindeer tallow moistened with
     fresh snow
2   cups blueberries or bearberries Season
     with seal oil.

Whip together with your hand in a large bowl until fluffy.

Three decades later, a version of this ice cream becomes my favorite food during a week in an Eskimo village. For now, I am intrigued by the ingenious native life style and the well-adapted Eskimos who live on this windswept shore. My tour is over but I decide to stay another day to explore.

4

Day-tour to Tomorrow

"You are really lucky, we have one seat left," I am told at Munz Northern Airlines in Nome. "It's not every day you can fly to Little Diomede."

Little Diomede is a tiny island in the Bering Strait with a population of 80 Eskimos and 100 dogs. They have been isolated since September, when they got their last supplies and mail by ship. Now it is February 1970. Airplanes can land on the ice when the Bering Strait freezes. The airfield, however, is unstable and can be broken up by waves. It is only 2.5 miles from the Russian watchtower on Big Diomede so it is not advisable to try a landing when visibility is poor.

My heart flutters with excitement when I think about the possibility of flying there on the first flight of the season. My fellow passenger is an Eskimo who will attend to the store on the island for a couple of weeks. The pilot is also an Eskimo with bright squirrel eyes and propeller scratches over his nose. He laughs at me.

"You are so stuffed in that tourist outfit that it will be difficult to get you up in the airplane."

The plane, a Cessna 170, is already over-loaded or so it appears to me. I get strapped on the back seat together with a lot of mail and provisions. We manage to take off. After half an hour we stop in Teller. The pilot jumps out and pulls a heavy comforter over the nose of the plane. I had been sitting on it, that's why I couldn't straighten my back. The wind in Teller is biting but nobody knows how cold it is... We quickly unload part of the freight and get a new passenger, a Catholic priest.

Both of us sit on the back seat fastened with the same seat belt. We get the comforter over our knees. I am more squeezed-in than before with my nose in the wolf ruff of the pilot. I can barely move my toes inside my boots. With two Eskimos and a priest I consider my chances of surviving an emergency landing the best possible and concentrate on the view.

We fly along the southwestern coast of the Seward Peninsula. I see some fishermen's dog teams on Port Clarence bay below us. It is a desolate snow covered scene with rolling hills. Cape Prince of Wales is our last contact with the mainland. The Cape is the westernmost point of the continental USA. It is even further west than Hawaii.

"Let's see now if I can find the island," the pilot shouts through the engine noise and steers out over the frozen Bering Strait between the Bering Sea and the Chuckchi Sea. I am gazing anxiously between the ears of the pilot and the storekeeper. Soon, to our relief, the steep island appears out of the haze. It is only 26 miles from the coast. The pilot makes a turn over the international dateline for my benefit. I manage to snap a shot of the Russian Big Diomede and the next day before my camera freezes. It is cold in the plane. It must be below zero behind the back of the pilot.

The Cessna lands with a few hesitant shakes on the snow covered sea ice between USA and Russia. Eskimos, some of them oriental looking, and a biting, 37 miles per hour wind greet us. Twenty-five below with a breeze like this is colder than I have ever experienced. I jump from the airplane with my movie camera and beat my way against the storm for some pictures.

Unfortunately, our time on the ice is brief. The eyepiece of the camera hits my eye. My contact lens pops out. Fortunately, it gets stuck in the frost on my cheek where I catch it with my bare hand. I walk back to the plane. Soon I lost the feeling in my hand and get concerned I might drop the lens. A flash of genius hits me and I put the lens in my mouth. With a wind chill factor around -90°F, exposed flesh may freeze within 30 seconds.

"Your nose is white," the priest comments as I reach the plane.

"Umm, umm," are the only grunts I can produce with my tongue holding the contact lens.

The pilot lifts me into the plane and pulls his knitted headband over my nose.

"I am OK," I assure the worried pilot as soon as I get my contact lens out of my mouth. The others on the ice watch me with amazed concern. I might be the only visitor they ever saw loose her faculty of speech in the cold.

I move to the copilot seat. Two scientists, who have studied the life style of the islanders, occupy the back seat.

"What do the people eat?" I ask.

"They eat what they can catch, mainly king crab."

"Wow, that's a delicacy! What else?"

"They may eat seal, walrus, blue-cod, whale, and bird eggs. Between half and one third of all raw ivory in Alaska comes from Little Diomede."

The pilot, trying to make the fastest take-off I ever experienced, interrupts my questioning. He pulls off the nose comforter, twirls the propeller, and jumps into the plane. As the plane starts rolling, he simultaneously closes the door, fastens his seat belt, and blows life into his frozen fingers. Now I have enough room to move both my arms and legs although the pilot has to rest his arm on my knee to handle his instruments.

Three and a half hours later we land in Nome after seeing two continents, two seas: the Bering and the Chukchi, and two days. My contact lens is frozen in its case.

In the evening I leave Nome and fly to Kotzebue, the second largest Eskimo community in Alaska. The almost empty jet feels strangely desolate and silent compared to the bush plane. I hear a crackle from the load speaker.

"This is your captain speaking. Fasten your seat belts and secure your drinks. We are approaching the Arctic Circle." The plane makes a skip and we are safely across.

The air terminal in Kotzebue is crowded with well-outfitted tough gentlemen with all the confidence in their glance that money can provide, and a few accompanying elegantly fur-enrobed ladies. I assume they are all polar bear hunters.

No one is there to meet me. Kotzebue is not part of my official tour. After half an hour I, together with a lot of others, manage to squeeze into the only taxi that is in service.

I thought I had chosen an inexpensive hotel above a general store but the price, $25.50, immediately makes me abandon any thoughts about a longer stay. The hotel has ten rooms with a shared toilet and sink in the end of the corridor. There is also a bathtub — filled with tools — but without faucets. The only amenity is a plastic bottle with water in the room. There are no door keys but many guests don't even bother to close their doors.

The next morning the sun is shining as I step out to take a look at Kotzebue. The main street follows the frozen Chukchi Sea, a bulge of the Arctic Ocean, with rows of small airplanes on skis. Steam from cars, snow machines, and burning garbage lingers dense and white over town. The sound of howling dogs carries through the hum of idling engines. The dogs are curled up in groups of at least six wherever there is room along the back streets. To preserve peace, each dog is tied out of reach of its neighbor.

I see some Eskimos on the sea ice and walk out to see what they are doing. It almost looks like they are ice fishing — with a rope! The hole is rather big and the edges look bloody.

"What are you doing?" I ask with curiosity.

"A polar bear hide," the Eskimo woman holding the rope replies. The machinery in the English to Swedish translation department of my brain works poorly in the early chilly morning hour. Is a polar bear hiding under the ice, tied with a rope? I get more confused and take a couple of frightened steps backwards. They must be joking.

"What do you have there?" I repeat my question. "A polar bear hide," the woman shouts for the third time, thinking my hearing is poor.

Some men in large thick down parkas walk out to us. More curious tourists, I think. Boldly they give compliments to the Eskimo lady who is dressed in a red fur-lined flounce-trimmed kuspuk. They ignore me. One of the men starts to pull the rope. Something white and furry emerges. The new "tourists" photograph enthusiastically and so do I in the background. Soon the whole polar bear hide lies on the ice. So, hide meant skin in this case. The salt- water wash has cleaned the fur well. They cover it with snow and the Eskimo woman starts to prance on it. The treatment is not as hard-footed as it might sound since she wears mukluks, which are sealskin boots. The snow gives the fur a final clean-and-dry.

The men pose with the bloody polar bear skull that was on the Eskimos' sled. Finally the situation clears for me. I have shamelessly clambered straight into the final act of a polar bear hunt. Poor little polar bear, is my only thought. The hide isn't too imposing compared to the skin my Swedish boss had from Spitsbergen.

After the hide has been folded on the sled the hunting guide turns to me.

"Your face is glowing red."

It is -31°F and I have been longer on the ice than the hunters dressed in down. Neither they nor the Eskimos are red in their faces from the cold. Maybe my skin is more delicate since I am the only blond in the group. I miss my tourist clothing from Nome. My suede fur coat from Finland isn't as warm here. It has no hood to protect my face.

The rest of the day I wander around town. From time to time I have to drop in to warm up at the cafe, general store, library or senior center.

I run into the polar bear guide and two hunters. "Are you interested in coming along to Charlie's

house to watch ivory carving?" he asks.

We step directly into the only room of the house followed by a cold draft. A large wood stove radiates heat. The kitchen table with chairs stands under a cracked window with a bed by the opposite wall. Charlie's wife sits cross-legged on the bed sewing on a parka. The guide throws a few small lynx skins to her and pulls out the chairs for us to sit on, surrounding Charlie who sits on the floor. Charlie is working on a bracelet consisting of rectangular pieces with an animal on each. With a file he creates polar bears, seals, and walruses in the light of a small flickering lamp.

I am amazed at how fast and seemingly effortlessly the animals take shape under Charlie's skillful hands.

"How long does it take you to make the bracelet and how much does it cost?" one of the hunters asks.

"How do you get the holes through the pieces?" I ask.

"I drill them, two holes lengthwise through each piece." Charlie puts a pointed pin in his mouth and places the point carefully on the edge of the ivory piece. A string is wound around the pin and attached to a bow. It looks as if Charlie was sawing when he rapidly rotates the pin with the bow.

The bracelet looks small but since it fits me one of the hunters buys it for his wife in Los Angeles.

Leaving Charlie's we pass the guide's house that looks a lot larger.

"I hired four Eskimo girls to clean it and they even scrubbed the dog," the guide says.

The sun is setting on my last Arctic day. The sunset and a small fire on the Arctic Ocean make a stunning background for the cabins with their white chimney smokes. The fire invites me for one more walk out on the ice. My spirits are high until I come close enough to discover the garbage from Kotzebue burning out there.

At the check-in counter in Anchorage I get a chilly greeting: "Your plane left this morning. You are a day late! The next plane to Juneau at 5 a.m. is already full."

What a shock! I stayed an extra day in Nome and forgot to change my reservation. "Put me on the stand-by list, please," I say.

My adventures in Eskimo land and skiing at Alyeska feel as dreams but I will treasure and remember them forever.

5

Norwegian Celebration in Petersburg

Keith Miller, the governor of Alaska has been kidnapped from the capital of Juneau — by Vikings! I don't know anything about this until I see the Governor in Petersburg on May 16, 1970.

My idea to go to Petersburg was conceived three months earlier when Ken Nestler from Petersburg visited the Alaska Dancers' square dance club in Douglas.

"Visit me in Petersburg and I'll take you fishing," Ken said as we finished a tip of dancing.

"I rather eat fish than catch them."

"In that case you should come to our May 17 celebration. A large part of the city's population of 2,000 have their roots in Norway. Petersburg is actually called Little Norway. Every May 17 we celebrate the independence day of Norway. We have a "fish-o-rama", a whole smörgåsbord of fish."

"Last year I celebrated May 17 in Norway, without fish. I don't think any Norwegian would discourage me from celebrating with a little fish this year."

I have put in enough over-time to take two days off. On Thursday I buy my first fishing license for

$10. Thinking ahead, I park my car at the ferry terminal and take the bus to the airport.

Since the flight makes a stopover in Sitka, I spend the night there. My room at the centrally located Sitka Hotel, across from the first Pioneers'

29

Home in Alaska, costs as much as my fishing license.

When USA bought Alaska from Russia in 1867, the transfer ceremonies took place on Castle Hill in Sitka. Sitka was the capital of Alaska from 1810 to 1900. Two of the Russian governors, Etholen and Furuhjelm were from Finland. Etholen brought along a pastor and built the first Lutheran church in Alaska. I find the organ from the Lutheran church in the museum that is officially closed but I get permission to enter.

Sitka has a long-standing Tlingit Indian heritage. A tall totem pole stands by the Pioneers' Home. The Tlingits carve totem poles for special occasions, to honor somebody or to tell a story. Normally the poles consist of a row of symbolic animals such as bear, raven, whale, and frog sitting on top of each other. Sitka has a National Historical Park consisting of a spruce forest filled with totem poles. The tall Sitka spruce is Alaska's state tree. I walk the forest trail looking at all the poles painted brightly in red, white, turquoise, and black while the rain is pouring down.

At 10 a.m. I am ready to fly to Petersburg.

"The flight is postponed. Check back in half an hour."

The interval between the check-ins grows. I have time to walk the totem trail completely or partly many more times and to admire the poles and the snow covered volcano, Mt. Edgecumbe, on the other side of the sound.

One crystal clear day the volcano suddenly attracted attention when black clouds of smoke started to rise from the dormant crater. Someone with access to resources and a sense of humor had transported 100 old tires and oily rags by helicopter and set them on fire as an April fools joke in 1974.

At 2 p.m. I go to the airport. Six people still want to go to Petersburg. A small strange looking airplane, a Grumman Goose with two red propellers at the height of the wings above the cockpit, is waiting in the rain. I get the co-pilot's seat on this Alaska Airlines' passenger flight.

An hour later we land at a desolate airfield in Petersburg. To my surprise, my luggage is standing on the field! The other passengers disappear. I stand alone on the airfield wondering what to do when two ladies dressed in Norwegian-inspired costumes approach.

"We didn't notice that your unannounced plane landed. The official welcoming committee, all dressed in Viking costumes, are drinking beer in a back room."

My private welcoming group consisting of Ken Nestler with his friends, Ruth Sandvik and Ethel Bergmann, appear.

Petersburg makes a neat impression with its white single-family houses under tin roofs. I accompany the others to town. We knock on the door to a house but nobody is home. The door is unlocked so we enter and make ourselves at home. When the owners arrive, their house is filled with people but they don't appear surprised. Everyone knows each other here.

On Saturday morning it is pouring rain but Ken takes me on the promised fishing trip. It is more boat trip than fishing. We don't catch anything.

We return to Little Norway in time for the festivities consisting of folk dance and a declaration of independence. A Viking with a long red beard and a silver helmet with horns directs traffic at a street corner with a silver sword and a red shield.

The main attraction, in my opinion, is the fish-o-rama smörgåsbord. Everything is well organized. Ken helps the Forest Service to entertain us with movies while we wait to get in line. While in line we are served small delicious pieces of beer batter halibut. The fishing waters of Alaska supply salmon, halibut, crab and shrimp but also cod, smelt and clams. Everything is well represented in many delicate varieties.

We head for a long table. Alaska's Governor, Keith Miller, and his wife sit down opposite us. A Norwegian sawmill owner sits down next to me. These VIPs happened to stand behind us in line. A select group of Vikings with a private plane had "kidnapped" the Governor from Juneau this morning. Last year, the Norwegian consul in San Francisco was abducted.

The festivities continue with dance in the evening to the music of Sven Anderson's three-man band. They include both Swedish waltz and schottische. The Governor is asked to speak in the wee hours of the night. He walks up on stage, takes the microphone and — sings: "I left my heart in San Francisco..."

The ferry Malaspina makes a brief stop in Petersburg Sunday night. It has room for 750 passengers and 120 cars. I wind myself between the armrests of some chairs on the view-deck and manage to sleep until we approach Juneau after six and a half hours. My car is waiting on the dock where I had the foresight to park it when I left by air. I have time to go home and change before going to work. What an invigorating way to start the day waking up at sea with my spirit filled with lively memories!

6

Chief Scientist at Sea

In two weeks we will go to sea to take marine geological samples from volcanoes on the bottom of the Pacific Ocean in the Gulf of Alaska. That is not the place to go by ship in October. The 200-ton research vessel, Acona, belonging to the University of Alaska, is far too small. Dr. Nayudu, our boss, is a marine geologist but also a politician. We are concerned he wants to go out to prove that the university needs a larger ship. This trip has been postponed for two years but now it appears to materialize.

"Kristina", Dr. Nayudu tells me one day, "would you make sure we get all the necessary sampling equipment on board. You will find most of it in the Jumbo school."

I review the "Observations and Collections at Sea" chapter in my 1000-page book in Physical Oceanography from the University of California, San Diego. *"The Oceans"* by Sverdrup, Johnson, and Fleming was considered the oceanographer's Bible in the 1960's.

"Kristina", the boss tells me as he hands me a list of coordinates. "Plot these station locations on charts. They are for the sampling we might want to do in four inshore bays just in case we need an alternative plan. With your diploma in coastal navigation from Finland, I am sure it won't be a problem for you," he says.

I board the ship late in the evening on October 3, 1970. I haven't had the time to think about my personal preparations and wonder how much I have forgotten. Unconsciously I have, somehow, packed everything I need, to my great surprise. We are to sail at midnight. There is a storm at sea. Captain Ken Turner brings me a message.

"Dr. Nayudu cannot make it. We have to do the first leg without him. He wants Kristina to be in charge of the scientific work." The responsibility falls on my shoulders immediately when the captain asks me:

"Can we postpone the departure to morning, when the storm is expected to subside?" The captain has a good portion of common sense. Everybody gets a good sleep the first night on board.

Before dawn we are underway to Port Snettisham, the first bay in the alternative plan. On the advice of the captain and the U.S. Coast Guard, we stay inshore.

The scientific expedition personnel are all female. My assistants from the lab are Dolly Dieter, marine technician, Marieanna Lowe, marine geologist and Sally Wienke, marine chemist. The crew consists of six men of whom the cook never sets foot on deck. We work around the clock in six-hour watches making the workday 12 hours. For the captain and during the last leg, for me also, the workday stretches to 16 hours per day. It is physically as well as mentally exhausting.

I feel responsibility is the heaviest burden. The sampling equipment is expensive. If I decide to take a sample where the sea bottom doesn't correspond to the sampler I have chosen, we could damage or even lose the sampling equipment. It is important to accurately interpret the echo sounder that gives the depth. For security, we always take a grab sample of the bottom before rigging the core sampler that can take sediment cores up to 33 feet long. In these waters we restrict our sampling to 10-foot cores. The crew, that has more muscle power than us scientists, helps out with the coring.

When the first core is rigged, I notice something is not right. Although I am the chief scientist, I am "just a girl" and cannot tell an experienced seaman he has done something wrong. I need good cooperation from everybody. If I let the corer launch he will certainly discover the error, but if we lose the equipment, the responsibility is mine. I need to use diplomacy. I study the corer with interest.

"How does this work?" I ask. I get a detailed explanation. The error is detected and we get a successful sample.

We return to Juneau to pick up the boss after a short but successful tour to Port Snettisham. I am happy to turn over the command. Despite the feeling of power I had when the ship moved according to my will, the weight of responsibility felt too heavy. It is much easier to take orders than to give them. I understand how power can corrupt. The feeling is pleasant. If power isn't combined with responsibility the result can be devastating.

Dr. Nayudu has gone to Anchorage. He will meet us in Skagway. Disappointed I have to resume command.

Soon we cast off and set course towards the North, up along the Lynn Canal. The weather is beautiful. The bow spray of the ship has an honor guard of porpoise. They play, jump, and dive in the wave formed by the bow. They move with the same speed as the ship. In addition, they have time to weave their trail up and down through the surface layer. They cut through the surface like knives. We get a glimpse of their white sides before they return to their element with the spray flying.

Pastel colored sunrises and sunsets in rose and lavender behind majestic, high, steep, snowcapped mountains reward us as we work around the clock. A small bay is clear as a mirror reflecting the mountains in the water. The scenery is like paintings. With everybody cooperating the sampling goes well and we enjoy our work. After a couple of days we approach the historical Skagway of the gold miners. We wonder if the boss will be there to welcome us? No, he has gone somewhere else. We seem to do well without him.

The rest of the stations I have plotted are south of Juneau. We pass Juneau and set course towards the South. The wind is blowing hard in a sound. The waves hit the windows of the bridge. On a previous voyage to the Bering Sea one window on the bridge was crushed, but this storm is soon over. The guns in their racks on the back wall are safe. Gun racks seem to be standard equipment on boats and trucks in Alaska.

Tracy Arm and Endicott Arm are fjords with active glaciers at the ends. We get to see both of the glaciers in daylight from a distance of two miles thanks to the skill and cooperation of the captain. These fjords are filled with blue glistening icebergs. They are beautiful but dangerous. Most of the icebergs are below the surface. The smallest show so little above the surface that they can be difficult to detect. Here we only sample in daylight.

Although we never managed to get Dr. Nayudu on board, we are proud over the success of our expedition. We took a total of 120 bottom samples of which several were 10-foot long sediment cores.

After the trip, I write the report of the expedition to the headquarters of the Institute of Marine Science (IMS) at the University of Alaska in Fairbanks Diplomatically, I try to explain why we didn't follow the official cruise plan, that was the only one IMS knew about, and why we returned to Juneau twice. I am pleased with myself and feel I did a good job. The only comment from the boss was:

"Did the report have to show I wasn't on board?"

7

Work at Douglas Marine Station

Charlette Chastain and Sally Wienke had long ago checked out the surroundings of Juneau and bought powerful .357 magnum pistols as protection against bears. Since they hadn't had any bad experience, Marieanna Lowe and I decide there is no immediate need for us to get armed. Marieanna joined our team from Seattle slightly after me. Although a gun is not necessary, Dr. Nayudu, whom we call Doc, demands we get telephones. Doc is shorter and has a darker complexion than us women. He wants to be in control but doesn't interfere in how we accomplish our work.

"It's important I can get hold of you any time," Doc says.

Douglas Marine Station, (DMS) looks like an old family home with white painted walls and pale blue trim. It is three stories with a full basement and a small attic under the pitched roof. Large rose bushes guard the front entrance that faces the end of Third Street, which is also the end of the three-mile long Douglas Highway. The large back windows look out over the small boat harbor. To the far right is a vast landfill with mud and old pilings from the time of gold mining. Juneau is on the other side of the Gastineau Channel.

Douglas marine station, the two-story white building to
the right, and Mt Bradley.

Initially, my duties at the DMS consist of measuring
gravity and magnetic susceptibilities in cylindrical rocks
from submarine volcanoes. If the samples really are of
volcanic origin, they are very fine grained with a low
susceptibility. I have problems with the measurements.
The method is new for this laboratory and nobody here
can help me. After many phone calls, I reach a geologist
at the Bureau of Mines in Denver, Colorado and the
problem gets solved.

To get cylindrical samples for testing, I have to use
a rock drill. This is a huge homemade device fashioned
by the station engineer, Len Weimer. Marieanna strokes
her shoulder-length curly brown hair to one side and
adjusts her glasses as she looks at me with concern.

"That drill is awfully noisy. You need to protect
your ears."

That never occurred to me. Bob Rice, the short
and jolly lab accountant, buys me a bright yellow set
of earmuffs.

"These are good enough for me to sight in my
rifle," Bob says.

In my lab one wall is filled with cabinets. Inside are shelves with boxes of rocks and loose rocks. More rocks are spread out on tables in an adjoining room and down-stairs. None are labeled. Doc and Charlette know them all personally by sight. However, these rocks are strangers to me.

"Couldn't we label these rocks?" I ask.

"No, it isn't necessary. Besides, somebody could steal them if they knew what they were," Doc says.

From time to time Doc wants to visit with a special rock. When it comes back, it is left on a table. I group them by seamount. Gradually, most rocks, organized by seamount, are out on a long table. One day Doc notices the arrangement.

"Kristina, why don't you put these rocks back in the cabinets and organize them by seamount," he says to me.

I chose a different color stick-on dot for each seamount. Next time when we have visitors, Doc proudly opens the cabinet doors to show his color coded seamount samples.

Each technician performs specific duties as part of our research team. Marieanna starts the process of rock analysis by grinding up the samples. Sally determines the chemical composition by atomic absorption spectrophotometry. Doc and Charlette identify minerals in specimens under the microscope. I do the petrographic calculations for percentages of different minerals in the samples and draw the results on triangular diagrams. Finally, Charlette prepares colorful diagrams for publications and seminars. Doc writes the publications and makes presentations at scientific conferences.

One exotic rock analysis is especially meaningful to me. The return of Apollo-11 from the moon in July 1969 with the first rock samples generates intense interest and excitement among scientists. It is disappointing that Juneau is one of few places on earth that cannot watch the moon landing in real time. The analysis of the minerals in the moon samples is published and I can calculate the weight proportions. The results are similar to our basalt samples from the Pacific Ocean. However, the moon samples have much higher values of titanium.

The moon landing made a lasting impression on some people. A year after the landing, a friend of mine found an orphaned black bear cub in the woods outside Juneau. He put it in his backpack and took it home. They named the cub Apollo after the moon-lander.

When I visit the family, Apollo is three months old and tries to climb up my pant leg.

"He will stop if you tap him on the nose," says the daughter, who has become Apollo's new mother.

"Apollo is smarter than our family dog," her father says. "Apollo only makes a mistake once." Apollo becomes so smart, he goes to the Juneau- Douglas high school for one day with his adopted mother. He even gets his picture in the paper when he takes a drink from the water fountain. After that schooling, he is released in the wilds of Canada.

Charlette quits and goes to California for her Ph.D. in geology. Her drafting jobs for Doc are taken over by the draftsman of the U. S. Coast Guard. One night he is working late in preparation for a conference Doc is going to the next morning. About 2 a.m. my phone rings.

"I can't see clearly anymore," the draftsman says, "but the job is almost finished. It will be done by the time you get here."

Reluctantly I get up from bed and drive to Juneau. The draftsman hands me a large roll of transparent Mylar sheets.

"Everything should be there. I'm going to bed, but look them over carefully," he says.

I drive to the lab and spread the sheets out on a long table. Everything is neatly drafted with large numbers and letters in India ink. When they get photographically reduced, the result will be perfect. As I compare the figures to the originals, I find a few errors. The draftsman doesn't want to be disturbed anymore. Any necessary corrections must be made by me. I erase the mistakes with an electric eraser and take out Charlette's drafting set. I have tried it out once with resulting blurs, but never done any drafting. I am too tired to be nervous and too scared not to keep my hand steady. To my surprise, the correct numbers take shape without any blurs. Doc arrives at 8 a.m.

"Good, you got everything finished," he says. "I need one more diagram. Bring it to the airport. I'm leaving now to be on time. I'll tell them to hold the plane until you arrive."

Urgent jobs like these put butterflies in my stomach. Racing along the narrow winding Glacier Highway to the Juneau airport, does nothing to calm those butterflies.

As my reward, I am assigned to do the future drafting, since I am cheaper and more readily available than the professional draftsman. I also replace Charlette as Doc's confidante. However, it is seldom we see him. Being the scientific advisor of Alaska's Governor William Egan, he spends most of his days in the Governor's Office. Sometimes he comes to the lab at night and leaves notes for us of work he wants accomplished.

One morning in August 1970, Bob Rice announces that IMS has hired a new marine station manager.

"IMS is planning to close the station," Bob says. "You know, the ship operations have already been moved to Seward. It's cheaper for the University to operate vessels from there, because you can drive there from

Fairbanks. It's too expensive to work out of Juneau where you have to fly."

What will happen to us I wonder?

The wheels of bureaucracy move slowly. Our work at the station continues for more than another year.

Doc continues to attend conferences and give presentations. The night before he leaves for a conference I stay late, skipping dinner to finish a job. It takes longer than I think. I work through the night drafting. When Doc arrives in the morning, I am just wrapping up the job.

"Good you got it finished. I have another job you can continue with," Doc says.

"Now I'm going to bed, I can't see clearly anymore," I blurt out, tired and hungry but also a bit embarrassed to contradict Doc despite a 24-hour work day.

Doc is often gone.

"What is going on?" Sally, Marieanna, and I wonder. We hardly ever see Doc. We seldom see the new station manager. Both travel a lot. Wonder if they even have met? We have never seen them in the office at the same time.

One day Marieanna, Sally and I are called to meet Doc in the Governor's Office.

"The Atomic Energy Commission (AEC) wants to do an underground nuclear test on Amchitka Island in the Aleutian Chain," Doc tells us. "I have to advise Governor Egan and need your help."

"That's dangerous. They cannot just detonate an atomic bomb in Alaska," I say with horror in my voice.

"The AEC says it's perfectly safe, since they will only detonate five Megatons and do it at a depth of a mile," Doc answers. "Unless we can find serious evidence about possible harm, they will go ahead. I have a lot of material to read and want you to help me by underlining and making notes of what is essential," Doc says as he leaves us with a stack of papers.

Despite the important task at hand, we feel very small seated around a large oak table in a huge room with a very high ceiling in the Capitol Building in Juneau.

We hope to come up with enough ammunition for Doc to deliver to the governor, so he can stop the blast. We are alarmed, because we know the physical shock of an underground blast can affect the unstable geology of the Aleutian area. The fragile ecosystem of the local coastline might suffer from radiation. Other points of concern include the possibility of an earthquake with resulting tsunami, radioactive pollution of the groundwater, and harm to sea otter transplants that were extinct once before. In the end of May 1971, an Alaska hearing is arraigned to inform the public and answer questions. It is decided that the concerns for national security with a strong nuclear force outweighs the environmental concerns. The AEC sets off the nuclear charge in the fall of 1971.

Although Doc almost lives in the Governor's Office, it doesn't improve our job security at the Douglas Marine Station.

"You better take your vacations, but don't spend any money, since you may not have a job to return to," Doc tells us in the middle of the summer. Sally travels to Hungary and I get stranded on the Juneau Ice Field. Doc is least displeased with Marieanna, who only takes two weeks off and stays in town. She becomes Doc's new confidante and is called to the Governor's Office on September 27, 1971.

"Doc is trying to decide whether he should terminate us on October 1 or 15, but he cannot pay wages up to October 15," Marieanna tells me afterwards. "Doc must obtain permission from his funding agents, the Office of Naval Research and the National Science Foundation, to take his equipment. Without it he cannot continue his work," Marieanna says.

"How could he continue his work, if he quits the University?" I ask.

"Doc tells me the State of Alaska is planning to create a new Environmental Department to include all aspects of oceanography," Marieanna replies. "He anticipates approval to take his equipment to the new Environmental facilities being set up in Juneau. The fact that most inhabited areas lie along the extensive Alaskan coastline, along with major economic and defense interests, makes oceanographic concerns of vital importance to both the State and Federal agencies."

"For now, he wants all his equipment discretely packed without telling anybody that his whole team will quit," Marieanna continues.

"No problem," I say, "we only have a new station manager with a secretary and an assistant, who is a marine biologist, to keep from getting suspicious. The biologist uses white mice to test potentially toxic red tide organisms that could affect edible clams in Southeast Alaskan waters.

We must continue to act as if everything is normal."

"Great," Marieanna says, "how do we make packing everything appear normal?"

"We do it during the day, but keep the doors closed. Doc can remove the filled boxes at night and replace them with empty ones. Nobody will notice if boxes in the cabinets are filled or empty," I say.

On September 28, I am called to a conference with Doc.

"Your termination may be abrupt, but I don't want to set any dates," he says. "There may be a possibility for temporary employment with the State but it will be difficult since you are not a US citizen."

September 30 is payday. Next day the white mice get loose.

"Help!" Jane, the new secretary who replaced Julie, screams as she jumps up on a chair when I come in.

"What did I do to scare you so badly," I ask laughingly, because it looks so funny. I never saw anyone in real life jump up on a chair in fright because of a little white mouse.

"One of David's mouse cages next door is open," Marieanna says. "Mice seem to be everywhere, and I cannot get hold of Dave."

"Will we be terminated today?" Marieanna and I wonder.

"Until we know, we better catch mice." We catch seven dirty white mice in our lab that day. We carry them by the tails, one in each hand. As Jane meets our procession in the hallway, she screams again and rushes back to her office.

"You are scaring the mice away by screaming," I tell Jane.

"Maybe that's just as well," Marieanna says to me. "With the mice loose Jane won't dare enter our lab. We don't have to worry about her catching us packing." Four days later, on Tuesday, all mice are accounted for and the hole in the wall between our and Dave's lab has been closed.

Thursday morning October 7, my phone rings as I am eating breakfast. It is Doc. "I have sprained my leg and can barely walk," Doc tells me. "I want you and Marieanna to come to my house."

Cardboard boxes line the hall as we enter Doc's house.

"I will probably terminate you October 15," Doc tells us. "I plan to make an official announcement next week. If asked, you may say you will be terminated, but you are not to volunteer any information before the announcement," are Doc's instructions.

October 14, Marieanna and I get the final word that we are terminated effective October 15. We are also thanked for a "tremendous" packing job.

During afternoon coffee break Marieanna and I announce the news. No one can believe it! They think we are joking about being terminated tomorrow. No one noticed we packed 141 boxes. Some are upset over our secrecy. We are sad it had to be done in this sneaky fashion. Was it really necessary? We don't know. Doc feared IMS would have sealed his labs with contents, had they known of his coming termination. Our loyalty was to our boss, although we never understood what was the reason for the problems between him and the IMS.

Our last day, October 15, Doc invites Marieanna, Bob and me to a farewell lunch at the Breakwater Inn. Lobster is not on the menu this time. As we return to the lab, cherry pie is waiting as a final farewell.

Douglas Marine Station closes and the operations move to Seward. Our research team is dissolved. Dr. Nayudu becomes the director for Alaska's new Department of Environmental Conservation and Marieanna goes with him. Sally moves to a US Geological Survey lab in California, Bob Rice retires and I get a new job with IMS in Fairbanks.

8

Prisoner of Clouds

"My research grant is almost exhausted. You better take a vacation but don't waste any money," Dr. Nayudu tells me before leaving for a conference.

What can I do for fun without spending money, I wonder as I consider my options.

I offer my services to Dr. Maynard Miller's group in glacier research on the Juneau Icefield by slipping notes under their hotel room door in Juneau. No one ever answers the phone. The communications between the half dozen field stations on "Dr. Miller's Ice Field," which covers 1,500 square miles, are dubious. After some time the question is no longer *if* I may come but *when*?

One early morning in the middle of August 1971, I start hiking from "The Road" in the company of Chris Smith, a guide from Juneau. I had been advised to bring everything from a bikini to a down parka but in particular, good hiking boots. After thorough consideration, I feel satisfied with my selection of 30 pounds for a 2-week stay in a glacier camp. I carry more for a day of downhill skiing in Douglas on days when the snow cat is broken.

After three hours of climbing through dense tall spruce forest, we reach a ridge above timberline. We have ascended 3,000 feet in a mile. We have four more miles to go. It is raining and foggy. After lunch we barely see a thing.

"I've never seen that lake before," Chris exclaims with surprise, "and I've come here for many years. We better turn around."

I am disappointed since we have climbed the hardest part.

Four days later I get a second chance. The weather is broken clouds but we hope to squeeze in to Camp-17 (C-17). A seven-passenger Alouette III, the largest helicopter of Livingston Copters, is loaded with provisions, building material and me. I add skis and rubber boots to my gear, which turns out to be a wise choice.

This is my first trip by helicopter. Except for the noise it feels like riding one of those glass elevators some hotels use as incentive to visit their rooftop bars. The low-lying clouds enhance the fantastic view from my co-pilot seat in the glass cupola. I get a glimpse of Juneau between the feet of the pilot. We fly along a glacier. Its upper part disappears in the clouds that cover the ridge with C-17. That's where I was going, but a helicopter doesn't fly blindly in the clouds. We continue towards the southeast along the coast of Gastineau Channel until it meets Taku Inlet where we turn north along Taku glacier, one of the largest on the Icefield.

After half an hour of flying we land on the Taku glacier by the main camp, C-10, on a 4,000 feet high nunatak. This is the Eskimo name for an island of rock in an ocean of ice.

Our cargo is rapidly exchanged for four waiting men with their packs. We don't have enough fuel for another attempt to reach C-17.

"What an interesting hour," I say enthusiastically to the pilot after landing in Douglas.

"I don't think so," he replies.

Next morning we successfully reach C-17 in thinning clouds. Camp 17, consisting of six shacks and two outhouses doesn't look like much. The buildings appear to be rapidly erected from surplus lumber and covered by tarpaper and corrugated metal. They are anchored to bedrock by steel wires and surrounded by piles of rocks.

Helicopter landing at Camp17 August 1971

The helicopter ascends from the 3,800-foot-high mountain ridge after a flash exchange of crew. Three men leave camp with the following departure advice to us:

"Take a good look at the Lemon Creek and Ptarmigan glaciers, chances are you'll never see them again. This is the first time we see them since we came here a week ago."

At the moment I am, however, more interested in forming an opinion of my companion, Richard Warren, a gigantic man who looks like a gold miner from the turn of the century. His wide-brimmed hat covers shoulder length hair and gentle eyes in a red- bearded face. His red-checkered wool shirt is torn, the heavy wool pants, connected to the red suspenders with a mixture of rope and electrical cord, are too short, and the soles of the boots are ajar. A toothbrush in a leather holster hangs from a rope around his waist.

Later I find out he got the clothing from the Salvation Army. The pants cost 25 cents — and he found 10 cents in the pocket.

Who is he and what are we supposed to do here, I wonder?

Suddenly I see us with the eyes of a spectator: a ragged gold miner and me with blond pigtails dressed in yellow Helly Hansen fishing gear. We are surrounded with skis, ice axes, big backpacks, and piles of cardboard boxes with food and oil drums on a desolate mountain ridge between two glaciers. We proceed to the cook shack to figure out how the radio, our only contact with the outside world, works.

The cook shack with the radio station and the generator shack have small towers with poles and doors on the roofs. In the beginning of the season, in June, the whole ridge is snow covered. Only the poles with attached shovels are visible. The first arrivals have to dig down to the attic doors and dig tunnels between the buildings. Now the snow has melted on the ridge. The annual layer on the glacier can at times reach a depth of 100 feet.

The generator shack has an oil barrel on the roof and a ladder leaning against the wall. That's the shower! C-17 has many modern conveniences if you know how to use them. To shower you just have to boil water on the gas stove, climb on the roof and pour the water in the barrel. There is running water in the kitchen — when it rains. A plastic hose from the roof enters the kitchen through a hole in the wall, together with the radio antenna.

The outhouses are specially constructed, based on bitter experience. The Lemon Tree stands as its name indicates, firmly anchored with wires on the edge of the Lemon Creek glacier. A bridge with wire rails leads to the second story that is used when the snow is deep. At high wind speeds the first floor with a panorama window is used. For safety, there is an optional use of a safety belt, handhold, and automatic buttons for special needs such as anchor, prayer, and parachute. The doors face in different directions to provide choices when it is windy. The idea is good since there is a problem with doors and outhouses that tend to blow away.

After a while all clouds are gone and the sun is shining. Dick Warren, the "gold miner," who transferred from C-10, studies geology and is a university assistant in mathematics.

"Take all the pictures you plan now," he says, "it might be your only chance."

We climb the closest peak, the 4,500-foot-high Vesper, to get a view of our desolate ice world. Pointed, barren nunataks and ice as far as we can see in every direction except to the west. There we can see the Juneau airport five miles away with inlets and forest covered mountains beyond.

Dick is taciturn but I manage to figure out we are to do weather observations every third hour and maintain radio communications with the other field stations and Douglas.

The radio informs us we will get company. Marshall Calvert has just started out from C-26 on the Canadian side, thirty miles from here. After this joyful message Dick lights his pipe and gets lost in a book.

The sun is still shining so I step into my mountain touring skis for an August glide on the Lemon. The suncups make the lemon peel rough. The snow is wet from the 41- degree summer heat. Carefully I ski to one end of the glacier. From there I can look down on the Salmon Creek reservoir 3,000 feet below. There is no danger of skiing unaware into the city of Juneau drinking water as I almost did in Douglas. I am very careful to cross perpendicular to all crevasses; although they are so small I cannot even look down into them. So far I have nothing with which to compare them.

Marshall Calvert arrives the next morning by helicopter before our flying weather is gone. I go out to welcome him while Dick attends to the aeronautical radio. One more bearded guy, but this one can talk. He shakes hands with me and energetically heads for the orange colored Ptarmigan Terrace.

"The Ptarmigan is already occupied," I interrupt. "I established myself there since it is the smallest building."

"In that case you get to be the camp manager since you took the camp manager's lodging," Marshall says. "I was camp manager at C-17 for two weeks while the Summer Institute was here. I have had enough of the honor."

"What is the Summer Institute?" I ask.

"The Institute is the field program in glaciology of the Michigan State University. This year there was a foreign researcher from Finland. Under the guidance of Dr. Miller they learn theory, field research and expedition technique. Unofficially, they are also exposed to character building, learn to improvise, survive, and take responsibility."

"Did Dr. Miller know you from before?" I ask.

"My last summer trip here was a prize in a Boy Scout competition. Always prepared I dug out the old program and everything went well. Now, at the end of the season, the main responsibility of the camp manager is to keep a journal and make the 7 a.m. weather (MET) observation since the Ptarmigan Terrace is also the meteorological station."

At 8 a.m. I have the oil heater in the kitchen fired up when Marsh appears on the scene for the first radio contact.

"The common radio operator refers to our transmissions as the ice show," he tells me.

Marsh concentrates on the radio traffic while Dick and I share the meteorologist's job. The heavy Army surplus parka labeled FGER (Foundation for Glacier and Environmental Research) fits both of us but is better tailored for Dick.

The rain pours down all day and visibility varies between whiteout and fog. We are sitting in a rain cloud and spend the day reading, talking and repairing clothing.

The next day the wind blows a steady 45 miles/hour with gusts over 65. It almost blows me off the observation hill. The wind direction indicator has blown down and the wind sock for the aid of the helicopter is gone. It doesn't matter. We are encased in clouds and only hope the wires and piles of rocks will keep our shaking cook-shack anchored to bedrock. We tie one door and nail an attic door but we have already lost one of the doors to the generator shack. It's OK; no one plans to shower anyway. Dick, who weighs the most of us, takes over the MET- observations for the day after he wakes up at noon. I write the journal and Marsh demonstrates his creative talents by baking a cake and decorating it with purple frosting and poison green spots intended to make a peace symbol.

The fourth day the wind calms to 20 miles/hour and it is almost dry between the showers. Marsh manages to start the Polaris snow machine on the Ptarmigan glacier. With joint efforts we pull it across the rocks to the Lemon.

One of the attractions at C-17 is an ice cave at Lake Linda at the end of the Lemon Creek glacier. Linda is a 700-foot-long "jøkulhaup" which is Icelandic for a lake that periodically drains and fills. Equipped with cameras, flashlights, ice axes, and crampons we set out to explore the ice cave. To our surprise, Linda is filled.

The entrance to the cave is under water. The Lemon takes a steep dive towards the surface of the lake where some icebergs float. Marsh gets an idea.

"Kristina, you have only used your ice axe as a walking stick. Now I will teach you something useful."

To my horror, Marsh throws himself on the sloping ice and starts to slide down towards the lake. Rapidly he turns around on his stomach, grabs his ice axe at the head and jams it into the surface.

"This is an ice axe arrest!" he exclaims convincingly.

I hesitate to use the same slope as Marsh, that ends in the lake and find a safer one. I slide exceptionally well in my yellow rubberized suit but to my surprise, the ice axe stops me.

"We have to resume the observations here since the lake has filled again," Marsh says.

The following two days are rainy, stormy, and foggy. In the evening Marsh decides to ski to Lake Linda for a last observation. I wax my mountain skis with klister and dress in my yellow fishing uniform. Visibility equals the distance between the trail markers so we don't have any problems until we get there.

The lake has disappeared! It shouldn't have done it this fast. The stranded icebergs extend many feet above our heads as we walk along the bottom of the lake.

The entrance to the cave is flanked by deep-blue transparent ice with dark sediment layers on one side and a moraine slope on the other. Without light we cannot go far. On the shore of the drained lake I find a 5-inch-long fish. Marsh is surprised.

"That's no lost lunch sardine." After some hesitation he puts it in his shirt pocket.

The story about this small fish spreads wide around the Icefield and creates more excitement than the filling and draining of Lake Linda out of schedule. Soon ice rumor creates a fishing village with US Coast Guard cruisers and Russian trawlers in the lake.

With the rain beating our faces we race back on our skis to return with flashlights before it gets too dark. We figure the cave must be a channel for melt- water. The floor is a mixture of ice, slick as soap, large rocks, and mud. Melt water surges from the roof but our flashlights are not strong enough for us to appreciate the fantastic formations of ice crystals.

By 11 p.m. we are back out, wet and muddy. It is pitch black and the wind has increased. One shore of the lake consists of a moraine slope in an angle of repose while the other is a steep glacier wall. The icy bottom is crowded with icebergs. A single careless step on the moraine slope can cause it to collapse. We take the shortest route across the moraine, stepping carefully in each other's footsteps, until we reach the glacier slope above the cave. Marsh cuts out steps with his ice axe. Halfway up we hear Dick's howling voice penetrate the storm. He has come out to meet us after the 10 p.m. MET-observation. The cold rain pours down, the wind gusts at 50 miles/hour and visibility is one step in the light of two flashlights. We don't find a single trail flag. Suddenly the Lemon peel slopes steeply up.

"The wind comes from the wrong direction! We are lost," Dick confirms.

"We are in the process of climbing Cairn Peak south of camp," Marsh realizes.

We change course. Tired and wet we still try to concentrate on avoiding crevasses.

What a feeling of grateful relief when we finally find the familiar shacks at C-17 with an oil-burning heater. We are excited about the privilege of experiencing the two faces of Lake Linda despite the exhaustive commute. What an evening show we had in the crystal cave; an exclusive appearance!

The predictions to get a helicopter with replacements for Dick and Marsh within a foreseeable future look slim. Optimistically both have booked seats on a flight out of Juneau for today.

"If we don't make it back to our universities on time, we will be drafted and sent to the war in Vietnam."

The day before, the guys showed me how to light Coleman lanterns, start the generator, run both short-wave radios, charge and exchange batteries for the radios and change recording paper in all meteorological instruments.

"It's unlikely you'll have to be alone for more than a day or two," Marsh says encouragingly as they prepare to walk out. "If we meet a furry bear we'll send him as company for you."

By 10 a.m. the wind has decreased. Visibility is 50 yards. We are still in the clouds. Sad and worried I watch as the fog engulfs Dick and Marsh despite their large bright backpacks. They have five miles to go but must first climb over 4,500-foot-high Cairn Peak where the gusts can be fierce.

I resume the ice show. There are a lot of static disturbances. C-10 can only hear the highest camp, C-8. I have difficulties understanding anything on the radio. The traffic from Douglas to C-10 has to be relayed through two field stations, giving me instant practice. To my relief I learn that Dick and Marsh made it down in five hours and only got lost a couple of times. It was the best message on the radio.

As I dress in rubber boots and FGER-parka for the 10 p.m. MET-observation, the Juneau KINY radio catches my attention.

"Someone by the name of Kristina is all alone among nunataks in Camp 17 on the Juneau Icefield. We'll play James Taylor's "You've got a Friend," especially for her."

Touched to tears I float out on imaginary clouds to record the real ones.

I move my sleeping bag to the kitchen bench from where I can reach the microphone for the radio. The weather at C-17 remains stable. This means rain, 35-miles/hour wind, and 100-foot visibility but the clouds never rise more than 300 feet above my head and the temperature hovers around 35°F.

Wonderful weather for a summer vacation!

A Coleman lantern I try to light flares up. It didn't do that at Marshall's demonstration. The heater is almost out of oil so I use it sparingly. When I ask for advice from C-10, the disturbances over the air decrease. Is the fishing fleet tuning in to the ice show?

After detailed instructions from C-10, I manage to light the Coleman lantern without burning down the shack but I don't manage to start the generator although I know how to do it. C-10 is concerned about the radio communication.

"You must restrict the transmissions," C-10 says. "The batteries cannot run out."

All day I give the generator a jerk. In the afternoon I have worked up enough embarrassed muscle power to pull the generator rope to a start. The Icefield cheers. At 10 p.m. I proudly announce to both C-10 and Douglas:

"I have everything under control!"

Suddenly it gets dark and silent. Officially my radio call to C-10 is

"KND 3035 portable 10 portable 17," but now I just cry out "ten seventeen!"

"Calm down, everything is OK," C-10 replies." The generator just ran out of gas. Unplug the battery charger."

Every morning I am ready for a rapid departure and every night I unpack with resignation. The third day the heater is out of oil. I dress in everything I have including my quilted pajamas and light some Coleman lanterns. The shack leaks through other holes than the water hose. I notice I have company. Mice eat the strawberry jellyroll I made.

The Juneau radio continues to play "You've Got a Friend" for a special Kristina in C-17 but it is no longer as beautifully assuring as my first night alone. The fourth day I don't even bother to pack after noticing I am still a prisoner of the clouds. Without the oil heater nothing dries and a few candles only warm my fingers.

Still I have to go outside six times just for the MET-observations.

The first snow falls but doesn't yet remain on the ground. I find some black sooty balls with grids. They must be heaters! I don't manage to light them. C-10 gives advice:

"Turn them upside down so the kerosene wets the surface and strike a match, outside of course."

I put the heater in the open space between the buildings and check all fire extinguishers. I use up two boxes of matches in the rain and wind. Cold and desperate I take the Blazo container and drench the largest catalytic ball that almost started to burn before and strike a match. Success! The flames dance wildly licking the clouds but fortunately the rain clouds protect them from outside view. Someone could have got concerned. In twenty minutes the flames have subsided and I put the glowing ball on the oil heater that is surrounded with asbestos sheets. In the afternoon the shack is finally warming up but I am getting a headache.

At 7 p.m. I once more stand on the MET hill. While I try to estimate visibility, which started out at 100 feet, the clouds suddenly disintegrate. I can see a mile across the Lemon. There is Juneau airport and Lynn Canal beyond.

I rush to the radio. Arlo Livingston himself answers my call to Douglas base.

"We'll send a chopper immediately."

Fortunately I have concentrated all operations to the cook shack so I can pack while negotiating over the radio. A fishing boat, the "Black Bear" interrupts. "Congratulations, Seventeen can finally pack her suitcases."

9

Juneau Icefield

The sun shines in Douglas on August 27, 1971, the day after my return from Camp 17. It is almost like summer. Unfortunately, the ice camp administration has nothing but me to send to the main camp. While waiting, I fluff my sleeping bag in a large dryer at the Laundromat. At work, no one has heard from the boss. I assume I still have a job and work one day.

Next day at eight I call Douglas base.

"We don't have flying weather at the moment but be ready. We'll call you."

At 10 a.m. there is a knock on my door. "The helicopter is waiting. The weather is clear!"

I am ready to go.

"It's blowing a lot harder than Camp 17 reported," the pilot shouts angrily over the engine noise.

We flash land at Camp 17 to disembark one person. My joy at seeing C-17 again is nothing compared to my relief of seeing it disappear below us, but despite the strong wind, it is really flying weather. We take the direct route across the Icefield to Camp 10 on Nunatak Chalet.

The helicopter lands in a whirlwind of blowing snow. The whole crew, led by Bob and Joan Dilts stands on the upper glacier to welcome me. Bob Dilts has been in charge of the Icefield since Dr. Miller moved to the Atlin base in Canada. Bob is well groomed with a dignified black moustache. The other people left in the main camp are two elderly meteorologists, Drs. Edward Little and Harry Thompson, and a curly blond, tousled and bearded Thiokol- or snow cat driver, Harte Bressler.

Wise from experience at Camp 17, I immediately photograph everything in view on the nunatak. Joan serves lunch, which compared to standards at Camp 17, is very formal with many courses on different plates.

It is strange to sit in Camp 10 and hear the radio call from Camp 17.

"Everything here is OK but the mice squeak with a Finnish accent."

"Have you really climbed the highest peak in North America, 20,320-foot-high Mount McKinley?" Bob Dilts asks me with curiosity.

"Who says that?" I ask with surprise.

"Icefield rumor. We thought you were a tough, strong, Arctic heroine type comparable to the Thiokol drivers on the Icefield until you started your radio quiz: How do you light a Coleman lantern, etc.? That made us worry. Dr. Miller, out of radio reach, was convinced that a person who had climbed McKinley, without problems also could handle an ice camp in the clouds alone."

"Who started this rumor?" I wonder.

"Nobody knows, but it might explain why you are here. Dr. Miller planned for you and one of the Thiokol drivers to walk out from the Icefield along a route few have tried before. It would have been a dangerous tour of 45 miles across icefalls and crevasses," Bob explains.

After lunch we haul our backpacks and fresh food to the Taku glacier 400 feet below the camp. We load them and some corrugated aluminum sheets on a couple of sleds. Harte fills up the Thiokol named Rolls with gas and we head north. Joan and Dr. Little remain in Camp 10. The weather is ideal, cloud free and sunny. I get into the Rolls because I don't yet know the advantages of sitting on a sled.

I am concerned about some big cracks on the Taku Glacier but the belted wheels cross them easily with the sleds following after a small respectful bow before each crevasse. The progress gets smoother after we turn onto Mathes Glacier. Visibility is fabulous. Harte points out all named nunataks that stick their steep tops over the ice.

"You are lucky to see tops neither I nor Bob have seen before," Dr. Thompson tells me. "We have traveled this way before but never in full sunshine."

We stop every hour to call Camp 10 with our small walkie-talkie radio.

"KND 3035 portable 10: portable Kamikaze." After a while Camp 8 and Camp 18 replace Camp

10. Al Clough meets us. He is a big bearded man with many years of Icefield experience. He is the Arctic hero-type, a tough, young Thiokol driver who forms the core of Dr. Miller's Icefield program.

Al lies down on his stomach on the last sled. Soon we proceed steeply down towards Camp 18. Al tries to brake with his toes to prevent the sleds from going faster than the Thiokol and ending up under it.

Camp 18 is located on a barren rock outcrop 1,600 feet above the Gilkey Glacier. Its crest disappears under the Vaughan-Lewis Glacier. The camp consists of one little hut covered with corrugated aluminum, a generator shack, and the outhouse "Be-gone ya II", pronounced Begonia. The outhouse is new after number one blew away. It is close to a precipice with a panorama window. To reach it I have to use both hands and feet to get down small rock ledges.

"Al and I are off to Camp 8 to deliver fuel, fresh food and aluminum sheets as soon as we have emptied the sleds," Harte announces. The sun is still shining but who knows for how long.

"Can I come along?" I ask with anticipation. "We'll be happy to take a passenger," Harte says. "You'll have a chance to visit Camp 8 later," Bob, the boss, intervenes.

"Camp 17 has taught me not to count on the chance *later*," I plead.

"I promise to bring her back by midnight," Harte says and Bob consents.

We take along our sleeping bags as a normal safety procedure in addition to our ice axes we always carry.

Al drives first in the Thiokol Dick hauling a Blazo barrel while Harte and I follow in Rolls. Without slowing down Harte stretches out through the open door to call Camp 18 and Camp 8 with the walkie- talkie and give them our positions. Al also reaches out intermittently to straighten out route markers. The main route is at an altitude of 5,700 feet until we reach the base of Mount Moore. Al in the smaller Thiokol appears to drive straight up the slope with ease and determination. We follow, happily surprised that we can. Some 500 feet below camp we stop at an eight-foot wide crevasse.

Marianne Parke and Eric Reynolds connected by a long rope come happily skipping down from Camp 8 with empty Blazo cans on their backs.

"Welcome!" they greet us enthusiastically. "Good to see other faces. We've been isolated here for a week."

Camp 8, at an altitude of 7,200 feet, is the highest station on the Icefield with a climate similar to that at the North Pole. The minimum thermometer left there over winter has sunk to 90 below.

The sun has already set behind Mt. Moore and it is blowing a little. Al piles half a dozen aluminum sheets on his pack frame. When we loaded them on the Taku glacier we carried one at a time. The sheets are eight feet long. I am surprised Al doesn't blow away with wings like these. It would not be pleasant since I am tied in a long rope between Al and Harte. It is hard to climb in the deep and wet snow although Harte has only given me a can of ham to carry while the others have their pack frames filled.

The ice is treacherous here on the slopes of Mt. Moore. We cross the large crevasse on a snow bridge but cannot see how many others are covered by snow. When someone sinks, the others tighten the rope and avoid stepping in the same tracks.

We arrive at Camp 8 and unpack our treasures. Fresh tomatoes and ground beef are luxury in the land of the tin cans. We are all starving. Marianne and I start to peel and fry 20 potatoes and a couple of onions while the guys start the generator. There are no windows at Camp 8 for practical reasons, so it is dark.

"You have to see the view from the top of Mt. Moore before the sun sets," Marianne tells me. "The guys can continue dinner preparations."

We climb the 7,300-foot-high peak. It is still light enough for us to see the highest peak on the Icefield, 8,584-foot-high Devil's Paw 12 miles to the Southeast on the border to Canada.

Dinner is ready when we return at dusk. Table manners are crude but what else can be expected when five starved field assistants, of which three are Thiokol drivers, sit down to eat. This is a longed for feast where the food is the main point. The hamburgers are delicious. We consume the entire store of tomatoes and meat. It is warm and cozy in the cabin with three catalytic heaters going. Our spirits are high. When every plate is empty, Al divides a large cake in five parts.

We sit far apart because piles of supplies unessential for eating cover the table. Al grabs half a piece of cake with mildly clean fingers and throws it onto my hamburger-onion plate. The bowl with glazing is passed around. Everyone has previously tasted it with a finger.

Eric and Marianne are slightly embarrassed. "We were afraid you wouldn't want to visit Camp 8 if you knew what our outhouse is called."

"No need to worry about that. I am happy I had an opportunity to come here. Marshall told me the name of your outhouse, of course."

The outhouse Christina is the only isolated building at Camp 8. It is stocked with emergency supplies to save the crew should there be a fire.

After an honorary visit to my namesake, Christina, named after a scandal in London, we prepare for departure.

Again, I get tied in the rope between Al and Harte before we descend the slope. We leave Dick and tie a sled behind Rolls where Al lies down to brake and enjoy the stars.

"We made it!" Harte exclaims with pride as he pulls the brakes at Camp 18 at the beat of midnight. Tom Boyce meets us with a lantern to light my path.

"Harte and Al are tough. They can manage in the dark," Tom says.

Tom, with well-dressed shoulder length hair, serves us breakfast at 7 a.m. Today we are traveling abroad to Canada.

At nine we are ready for departure. Tom is left alone in Camp 18. Harte and I sit on the sleds. The view is a lot better than from inside and it is silent out here. It is soft and comfortable on all the backpacks. The clouds are moving in. I lie down and fall asleep in the drizzle. We reach the Canadian border after five miles but it is neither marked nor guarded. Four miles further we pass the Continental divide at an altitude of 6,000 feet. The weather is clearing.

The Llewellyn Glacier slopes gently downward. Ice cracks appear. It gets scary. Some are large enough that I can peer down into them. They appear bottomless. Still, they are seldom deeper than 100 feet on this Icefield. After five hours of traveling the snow on the glacier gets watery and the crevasses too wide for the Rolls.

"We have to carry everything the final two miles to Camp 26," Bob decides and ties a couple of 2 x 4 boards to my pack frame.

"It's a light burden for a McKinley climber," he says. "Besides, the 8-foot-long boards are good insurance should you fall into a crevasse. You won't fall far."

"I appreciate your concern," I reply with hesitation.

Bob carries a large can of Blazo, Al a roll of tarpaper while Dr. Thompson and Harte, who will replace the crew in Camp 26, have their large backpacks.

Bob keeps pace with me. I am not accustomed to walks like this and stop at the first crevasse and look down with concern.

"Jump!" Bob encourages me.

At times I have to make a running start to take the jump since I dare not fail. When the crevasses are too wide to jump we look for a snow bridge or a way around.

I hear a deafening roar. An airplane, I think until I gaze down into a witch's kettle of whirling water.

"It's a "moulin" which is French for glacier mill or a drainage hole reaching the bottom of the glacier at 1,600 feet or who knows?" Bob explains.

"What a mighty top of a waterfall. We surely don't want to see the bottom of it," I reply and give it plenty of leeway.

The vanguard is already out of view. We have to find the best route ourselves. The sun is shining, making the ice in the crevasses glisten blue. Small melt water ponds cover the vast snow surface. The dark sediment at the bottom has melted through the ice, creating a delicate grid of ice crystals on the surface.

We reach Camp 26 on a nunatak after an hour. Robert Asher and Mark greet us. It was Robert with the bushy red beard and long gracefully twisted moustache that I replaced in Camp 17. It was he who urged me to photograph.

"Tell me all the details in connection with your fish find at Lake Linda," Robert urges me.

"We don't know each other so I don't have any reason to joke," I say.

"Still, I have a hard time believing it is true. Birds don't normally carry food on their glacier flights," Robert says doubtfully.

Camp 26 is the youngest station on the Icefield. It consists of an 8 x 8-foot tarpaper covered box. Inside are a table, bunk bed, stove, and radio. A giant antenna, three times as big as the house, dominates the roof. This is the prototype of all ice camps.

Bob Dilts, Harte Bressler and Kristina at Camp 26.

Expansion starts as soon as lodging for two people is accomplished. Icefield construction is an individual improvisation depending on available personnel and construction material in camp at the moment. Everything has to be brought in by air, snow cat or pack frame.

Camp 26 is the only camp on the east side of the continental divide and has the most sunshine. Camp 26 also has an ice cave.

"Let's go and look at the ice cave," Bob suggests to me as he grabs a Coleman lantern. We crawl under the edge of the Llewellyn Glacier into a dark melt-water channel that gradually slopes upwards as it gets smaller. The sandy rocky floor is wet. It feels creepy as we almost crawl, knowing we have hundreds of feet of ice above us. After a while my concern is replaced by the joy of discovery. *What will we find?*

"Time to turn around," Bob announces to my disappointment.

Al, carrying something that looks like a refrigerator on his back and Robert and Mark with their backpacks are already far away below us on the glacier. Bob and I bring up the rear as usual. It is a relief not to carry any insurance boards on my back but this cross-glacier race with crevasse jumping is still a bit scary.

The next morning I serve breakfast in Camp 18 before the big departure. Only Bob Dilts and I are left in camp. Bob is a geologist and very talkative. He explains how the Icefield program works and initiates me into Dr. Miller's unspoken plans, goals, and methods just as Marshall Calvert did in Camp 17. Before understanding things I had voiced some complaints. I have seldom had such an attentive listener.

The day is warm and sunny. Between the MET-observations we take a walk down the Cleaver, the 1,600-foot-high point where Camp 18 is located. It is hard to kick the heels of my insulated rubber boots into the wet hard granular snow. The glacier slope is some 600 feet long. I squat down and push the handle of my ice axe into the snow, holding on to the head with my left hand and pushing down on the handle with my right hand as Marshall taught me. To my surprise I can easily control the speed as I *glissade* down. This is fun but Bob, left high above me, looks mildly amused as he slowly kicks his way down. Bob hails from the wide fields of Kansas where the possibilities for snow sports are limited.

The Gilkey Glacier, looking like a striped ice river is still far below us. Concentric wave-formed dunes called ogives emanate from the Vaughan-Lewis icefall. The difference in precipitation between summer and winter creates one ogive each year. From up here they look like waves of sand at the edge of the ocean with a narrow blue band cutting through the center of them.

"It's possible to get all the way down to the ice river," Bob tells me. "The last stretch is straight down a precipice but there are ropes to hang onto."

"It doesn't sound too enticing to me, but if Dr. Miller can get all the summer students down, with my McKinley reputation I should be able to make it."

"The tour will take a full day, so we can't start today," Bob says.

The next morning we set off with provisions and spare clothing. Unfortunately, it isn't as nice as yesterday. By now I am more accustomed to my ice axe and use every opportunity to *glissade* down on the soles of my boots. We find the first rope after some searching.

"This isn't as dangerous as I thought," I tell Bob.

Kristina descending to Gilkey Glacier.

"I will kick off the loose stones for you. Wait until I reach the next rope until you continue," Bob instructs me. At the moment he considers my McKinley reputation false and carries the whole pack while we balance with the ropes. The last rope ends at a high, steep glacier edge. Bob seems to have difficulty getting on the glacier. I leave the rope earlier where the glacier appears more approachable.

"Here might be cracks close to the mountain. This is not a place to *glissade*," Bob warns me and starts to kick steps in the ice.

I have barely stepped on the glacier when I slip. With my heart in my throat I turn on my stomach and execute the ice axe arrest as Marshall taught me. I get the axe too high above my head. It doesn't stop me. Instead my feet get caught between the ice and the mountain where Bob got up on the glacier. I should have followed him.

We get safely down on the Gilkey glacier. The dark lengthwise running bands on the glacier turn out to be small eskers of gravel and rocks worn loose from the sides of the mountains. The ogive waves created by the icefalls can be 80 feet high with a wavelength of 300 feet.

We try to cross the glacier but the small blue band we saw from above going through the ice waves is a roaring river with steep blue glistening sides. Just the thought of jumping makes my legs stiff from fright. We return to the slowly moving stone esker. We still have as much ice below us but the rocks give us a vision of stability. We have to walk around some large rocks and imposing deep blue crevasses.

It starts to rain. The rain makes the glacier ocean, frozen into stormy waves, slick as ice. We eat a can of peaches to strengthen us for the return.

"The glacier slope after the last rope was steep and difficult. I think we can easily reach the lowest rope if we get up on the mountain side," Bob says.

After a while it is sheer mountain climbing. Hanging from our fingertips we ascend a steep ledge. The hope that it cannot get worse drives us upward.

"The last rope cannot be far away?" I ask hopefully.

"To turn around now could be disastrous. Don't take a step until you have a secure hold!" Bob admonishes me.

At times it is easier said than found. Sometimes we only seem to hang on the thread of hope. This "shortcut" became a lot harder than we thought. We finally find the last rope. The rope route is now easy climbing. When we reach the upper glacier slope my wet boots feel like they were filled with lead.

"Why isn't it possible to *glissade* uphill?" I say wishfully.

We don't find ours, I mean Bob's, footprints and have to kick in new ones. We stop intermittently to catch our breaths. Through telepathy we even try to persuade Eric in Camp 18 to cook dinner and send him our menu choice.

"The astronauts made a telepathic experiment with Juneau Icefield on their way to the moon," Bob says. "Eric on the top of the mountain should be a lot easier to convince than some astronauts on a moon rocket."

It is dusk when we reach camp after four hours of climbing, twice as long as the descent. Expectantly we try to discern some smells of food but Eric hasn't even started.

The next morning we rise early to winterize the camp and pack everything that might spoil. Before I am finished cleaning inside the guys nail shutters on the windows and it gets dark. After the door is nailed shut and the hammer tied to the door, Bob discovers the program for the Icefield is inside.

"Well, it will be safe there until spring! The actual unfolding of events had a hard time following the program anyway," Bob says.

We head for Camp 8. This time the snow is so wet we cannot drive up to the wide crevasse. We start climbing up the slope with a rope between us as insurance against the covered crevasses. Halfway up Eric suddenly sinks in front of me.

"Tighten the rope!" Bob shouts behind me.

Tracks that carried Eric collapse under me but we make it up.

Marianne and Tom have everything cleaned and packed for winter. We carry down some sensitive radio and meteorological equipment. Here we only have doors to nail shut. We draw circles around the nails to make the break-in easier in spring. We finally tie a shovel to a pole on the roof.

At 2 p.m. we are ready for departure from Camp 8. We are the rear and have to manage by ourselves. The outcome is not guaranteed with four heavily loaded sleds behind the Thiokol cat, Dick, with a broken shoulder. The Thiokol, Rolls, is already in Camp 10 and there is nobody left who can drive it.

Eric sits alone in the tightly packed Dick while the rest of us occupy the sleds packed high. It is a rolling ride. We must concentrate on balancing our weight to avoid turning the sleds over or falling off. These sleds have taken much punishment but finally my sled breaks down. We tie it up scantily.

"You can share my sled," Bob calls from the top of five empty oil barrels.

After getting accustomed to the worrisomely high perch, the ropes around the barrels start to give.

"You better move back to your damaged sled," Bob says.

We reach the area with crevasses. Eric crosses crack after crack while I avoid looking too deeply. It is just to hold on and trust the Thiokol will make it. The sleds follow automatically.

Suddenly my sled dips its nose deep into a wide crevasse. I loose confidence and jump off. My sled is firmly stuck. The cat digs itself in while trying to pull my sled free. We dig out the sled but the cat is more difficult to free since we have to dig under it.

The engine now quits frequently or we get stuck. Besides, one brake lever is broken. Eric has to back up before he can turn in the direction of the broken lever. Ideally we should cross the ice cracks perpendicularly and fast. We are still in blissful ignorance about their actual size so we are relatively calm. The sleds get stuck frequently so we have to help them across. The next moment it is the cat. The engine quits strategically directly above a crevasse. The cracks are dense here so we are uneager to get off the sleds. The situation inspires Eric to act fast. The cat consents after a little nudging.

We finally reach the base of Camp 10 on Nunatak Chalet 400 feet above us.

What an experience I had crossing Dr. Maynard Miller's vast Icefield and seeing it from the depths of the Gilkey Glacier to the top of Mt. Moore and doing it in good weather. This was certainly a reward for my hardships alone at Camp 17.

10

Closing the Icefield for Winter

In the morning of September 2, 1971, Bob Dilts, commander of the Icefield during the end season, gives me evidence of his attentiveness as a listener.

"Kristina, would you mind helping my wife Joan make an inventory of all the food in Camp 10?"

We bring a Coleman lantern to the low attic where we crawl around rearranging boxes and recording the contents. We "find" many exotic items that appear to have been here since the creation of the Icefield.

"Would *you* consider eating *this?*" I ask Joan with disgust.

"Let's "schrund" everything neither of us would eat and that's been here forever," Joan decides. The Icefield method to discard things is to throw them into a deep crevasse. There they will be in safe storage for hundreds of years.

"I wonder what future scientist will think about our diet if they find this discarded cache?" I say laughingly to Joan.

Meanwhile the rest of the crew has cleaned up the Taku Glacier and brought all the things lying around, such as oil barrels to the base of Nunatak Chalet. They also selected a suitable crevasse, another proof Bob remembered that conversation too. I once mentioned I considered it basic icefield education that the crew knew what the ice looked like on the inside.

A Thiokol cat tows four of us sitting on a sled to the crevasse. Visibility is poor in the misty rain but we find the chosen one without getting caught in any other. The deep fissure in the ice is partly covered by hanging snow. One vertical wall appears to be solid. Tom Boise, with the long well groomed hair, steps into a complicated system of roped loops. The end of the rope is tied to two ice axes buried to their heads on the edge. Slowly, Tom descends over the edge and rappels into the deep unknown while the rest of us wait in anticipation. In the beginning we hear some comments but they decrease in intensity. We don't hear anything — for a disturbingly long time. Finally we hear a faint call.

"I've reached bottom."

We anchor a 100-foot long rope ladder with ice axes and wiggle it down. Marianne Parke, who took me to the top of 7,300-foot-high Mt. Moore while the guys prepared dinner at Camp 8, ties a safety line around her waist. Eric Reynolds wraps the other end a few times around himself and then around the head of an anchored ice axe he sits down on.

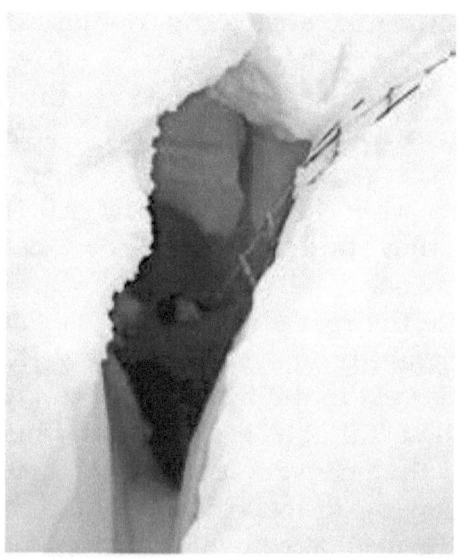

Marianne Parke inside a crevasse

Safely belayed, Marianne starts to descend the rope ladder. After a while she calls:

"I'm stuck and cannot move."

"Come on," Tom calls from the bottom of the crevasse, "you can make it."

"No, I have to wait until I slim down or the ice melts," Marianne replies.

Fortunately it doesn't take that long but Marianne runs into other obstacles. We wait for an eternity that may not have been longer than half an hour, for her to reach bottom. It takes as long until both of them are up on the ice again.

"What an unbelievable sight! The rest of you have to see it," Marianne says with conviction, "but the snow cover over most of the crevasse is disturbingly thin."

It is my turn to get the safety line around my waist while Tom belays me. Nobody intends to rappel down to encourage me, but if Marianne can make it so can I, at least some distance down.

Without further discussion I am on my way. In the beginning I feel uncertain. The rope ladder clings to the snow wall. It is difficult to scoop out enough snow to grab it. I have to kick my toes into the packed snow to descend a step. Tom tightens my lifeline, which makes me feel a little bit safer. It gets easier after I pass the packed snow and encounter ice. Now the ladder hangs some distance from the wall and I can rest my back against the opposite wall. I can see along the crevasse and understand why the others were worried. The fissure widens in one direction and is big enough to swallow the cat. The covering layer of snow is deep blue where the light filters through. *This certainly isn't the only wide, covered crevasse on the icefield. We must have crossed many of them without knowing they were wide enough to eat us.* Tom tightens the line after each step while I admire the fabulous blue fairy world in ice. *This isn't dangerous! It is a heavenly art exhibition,* I think.

Twenty feet down I seem to come to a stop. A protruding ice corner sticks through the rope ladder and blocks the crevice. *It was here Marianne got stuck!* To my left the crack widens below a deep-blue high ceiling of snow. I can see neither sky nor bottom. I jerk the line to get Tom to tighten it and try to crawl around the ice block. The ladder is twisted a couple of times below the ice block and then hangs free, too far from any ice wall from which to get support.

When I try to take a step to climb down in a spiral, the ladder moves away from me, leaving me hanging from my arms and safety line. The tight line cuts uncomfortably into my ribcage. Soon my arms are shaking from exhaustion. Knowing I am not as strong as the others who have been here all summer, I feel embarrassed. I get my feet back on the ladder. Photography gives me an excuse to rest on my unsteady platform. *I must be halfway;* I encourage myself, barely daring to gaze down into the disappearing depth. *I can't make it any further,* I realize with alarm!

I am too exhausted but also too tired to climb back up. I can no longer hear the others; they cannot hear me. *I am alone.* I stand for a long time on the same step with my shaking elbows bent around the ladder. My only chance to get a rest is to find a solid foundation for my feet. I get the idea to wrap my legs around the rope ladder from the side and to stick in one foot from the front, the other from the back. It steadies the ladder. Elated with my new invention I get a second wind and rush towards the bottom as fast as Tom can pay out line. There isn't much room on the bottom but at least I can get my feet on a narrow ledge. The crevasse continues down further away but I consider myself deep enough. It is ice- cold, literally, and the melt water pours down from the warmer layers above. The entire crevasse is a symphony in blue where each layer of ice has its own tone while icicles hanging from protruding layers constitute the notes. The sight is certainly worth my trouble.

When I get back up, Joan is no longer interested after hearing our comments.

"Take at least a few steps so you can look into the crevasse," Marianne persuades her.

"It's too late, we are cold and wet," is Joan's excuse. "We have already been here for a couple of hours."

We try to warm up in the cat while Bob takes his turn belayed by Eric on top.

Longhaired Tom, realizing we all must be tired, opens a can of sardines.

"Even Joan, without comments eats sardines from the hand of a dirty hippie," Tom muses.

We pull up the rope ladder and count the rungs.

We did climb down 75 feet.

***

The man in charge of the whole Icefield, Dr. Maynard M. Miller — called M3 — has planned to return to his headquarters in Camp 10. Apparently he left it in great haste after putting up a sign: DO NOT DISTURB ANYTHING!

It is already September. We receive a message from M3:

"Marianne and Kristina are to clean my quarters."

We survey the battlefield while making a plan of attack.

"For safety, we better start by deactivating and collecting all the rat and mouse traps," Marianne says thoughtfully.

The impressive field library of the Summer Institute consisting of more than a thousand books is situated here. We pull out all the books a little from the shelves so that air can circulate behind them, and cover them with newspaper and clear plastic. I haven't met M3 but

I feel I know him well after cleaning up after him. Under the bed I find a box surrounded by rattraps and rifles.

"Look, Marianne," I exclaim with astonishment, "this box seems to be fortified."

"Open it!" she says with curiosity. Inside we find a collection of high quality distilled liquids.

"What is the best way to handle these wares?" I wonder.

"We can't leave them unprotected, that's clear, since we have removed the rat traps and artillery," Marianne says. "We must tell Bob about our discovery."

"Let's have a surprise farewell party by the open fireplace tonight," Bob declares.

Marianne and I feel a bit guilty, but Eric, who has been here before, calms our consciences.

"It's tradition the clean-up crew consumes the stores," he says.

While Marianne and I have been busy cleaning, Eric and Tom have driven both snowcats from the Taku glacier to the upper glacier. How they managed it over all the rocks is a wonder.

"It will be a hard job to carry up everything along the 400-foot high mountain wall," Bob says, "but if we use our brains instead of our backs we might get Dick, the cat, to pull everything up."

"It's a brilliant idea!" Eric immediately accepts. "If we connect all wires and rope ends in camp we should be able to tie the front sled to Dick on the upper glacier."

Eric settles in Dick while Bob, Marianne, Tom, and I take up positions along the towrope. The slope is so steep Eric cannot see the sleds. He drives forward. The line tightens, the ropes vibrate a little but all knots hold, and the sleds slowly, start to ascend. We watch the line with excitement, ready to anchor it with an ice axe should the sleds start to slide back. The project is cumbersome in the rain and fog but our will to succeed is rock fast. The other option is exhausting work.

We made it!

The next problem is to lodge the cats for the winter in the party quarters with the open fireplace. Our most serious task is solved after hibernating the cats. Now we can think about our departure. It is already the 4th of September. My vacation is finished and so might be my job in Douglas.

"As soon as we can get a helicopter, Dr. Little and Kristina can fly out with part of the cargo," Bob decides. "Presently it is foggy so you can relax but be ready."

In the beginning of the summer a scientist from Finland built a plywood box and wrote "SATU SAUNA" (fairy tale sauna) above the door. The architecture, which I have criticized, is typical for the Icefield. Bob sees a new opportunity to show he has listened to me.

"We have to cover the box with tarpaper and give the sauna a sloping roof. Isn't it suitable that both the first and the last hammer blows are made by a Finn?"

"I can help Kristina," Marianne volunteers eagerly.

"The girls cannot handle this," Eric and Tom say skeptically.

"With me as supervisor, the girls can do anything," Bob says confidently.

***

Twelve years later, in July 1983, I participate in a permafrost conference in Fairbanks. One evening at a hamburger feed, Harold Jorgenson, invites me to a post party.

"My wife, Laura, a Minnesota Finn, wants to meet the four participants from Finland.

At the party, Matti Seppälä from the University of Helsinki, tells me:

"I was on the Juneau Icefield in 1971 and built a sauna there."

"We Finns know how to appreciate saunas, so when I was there, I finished it for you."

We stay in regular radio communication with Camp 17 and Douglas. The citizen band radio gives us problems so we also use the aeronautical band.

"An airplane has crashed!" Complete chaos erupts over the airwaves. Nobody knows anything. Rumors are flying. It appears to be close to the Taku Glacier. Our cats are out of commission but maybe we could ski to the rescue? The plane hasn't been found yet. We follow the conversation of the rescue pilots through the aeronautical radio.

One of Livingston's helicopters locates the plane on a precipitous mountain slope 20 miles outside Juneau. It is Alaska Airline's flight from Anchorage with 109 passengers. No survivors. Shaken, we hear the radio list the passengers. Many names are well known, most of them from Alaska.

All helicopters are used for the rescue. We feel ashamed to even ask for one, but Livingston has us in mind.

"I don't know when I can do anything for you, but contact us when the weather clears."

Marianne, who knew many of the victims personally, is most shaken. She chases Joan from the kitchen and starts to cook. I help Bob saw boards for the sauna roof.

The next morning there is snow on the ground. It snows all day. Marianne and I shovel snow from the flat sauna roof before covering it with tarpaper. In the afternoon Bob and I start to erect the ridge of the roof. Next day is a whiteout. No chance to get away so we calmly concentrate on our icefield projects.

Around 6 p.m. Eric comes running to the radio shack. "It's clearing up! Contact Livingston."

"Alouette III is on its way. We didn't have time to hook on the cargo racks so you can send passengers instead of freight. The helicopter will be there in half an hour," Livingston announces.

Most of the work for the closing of the Icefield is done. The Dilts can be substituted for cargo. Bob and Joan flash-pack. The flying weather is unreliable. The pilot doesn't want to lose any time. We wave goodbye to Marianne, Eric, and Tom. I heard they had to wait a week. By that time the snow cover was deep.

Part of the helicopter flight is totally on instruments but it clears when we approach the coast. Shortly past 7 p.m. we land in Douglas. Nancy and Arlo Livingston meet us and serve us a goodbye drink.

"We were so worried about you when we realized you were alone in Camp 17," Nancy Livingston tells me. "You did a good job with the weather reports," she says with appreciation.

On the morning of September 7, I walk to Douglas Marine Station. The sun is shining again and I relish the luxury of lifting my eyes towards the snow-covered peaks that had become my friends.

The boss, Dr. Nayudu, hasn't returned so no one knows if we still have a job.

11

Traveling by Train

The tourist season is over by the middle of September 1971 although the vegetation sparkles in the golden colors of autumn. The riverboats are pulled up on the banks of the Yukon River in Whitehorse as they have been for years. The decrease in tourist traffic allows 17 heavy ore cars to be connected to the train. It is the freight from the harbor town of Skagway and ore from the lead, zinc, and asbestos mines in the Yukon that finance the railroad.

The White Pass & Yukon Route narrow gauge, 110-mile long railroad between Whitehorse, Yukon, and Skagway, Alaska, is famous for its scenic beauty and historical background. Railroad construction through the difficult terrain started in May 1898 to support the Gold Rush to the Klondike. Men with muscles of steel and considerable amounts of gunpowder hacked and blasted the route in two years without access to other power than horses. Workers had to be lowered by ropes to prepare the rail bed in particularly steep places.

This morning, the little engine whistles the signal to move at 8 a.m. The large wooden armchairs with padded plastic cushions in my passenger car are lined up along both sides of the walls. The seats face each other but can be moved at will, which means towards the windows and the view. A large iron stove keeps the compartment warm.

After the lowland around Whitehorse and the rolling hills in the south of the Yukon, the rail follows the shores of Lake Bennett. An enterprising businessman in his homemade canoe raises a sign saying "Film" when the train passes. We see a dark brown wooden church on a hill on the other shore.

The train stops in Bennett. The passengers get off to eat lunch at long tables while they wait for the train from Skagway. We have to swap engines with it. I have time to go to the church.

The artistically built tower is covered with shingles. The wooden walls are gray from age. Layers of vertical boards connect aesthetically with diagonal poles. The window openings gape empty, as does the interior of the church. There was not time to finish it before the ice broke up in 1898.

The gold miners' old church is still in occasional use although it never got finished. Later I heard that the dangerous Skip, my host in Skagway, was married there.

The gold miners on their way to the goldfields built boats during the course of the winter. At break- up they launched 7,000 of their homemade contraptions and continued their perilous voyage to the Klondike. Many boats and men were unfit to survive the rapids.

Nutritionally satisfied and historically enriched, we continue our train trip behind a more powerful diesel engine. The evergreen forest thins and our speed decreases as we approach the White Pass.

The engine groans while it slows down further until it comes to a complete stop. The wheels continue to spin but we don't get anywhere. The engine backs down a distance for a fresh start but despite many attempts, it only results in well- polished rails. We are above timberline in a desolate landscape. I wonder if the men who hooked on the ore cars in Whitehorse were too greedy to realize that ore cars weigh more than passenger cars?

Speculations run wild among the passengers. No one knows what is going on. Nobody tells us anything.

After an hour and a half, the train slowly starts to creep forward. Someone had the idea to sand the rails.

White Pass, at an elevation of 2,900 feet on the border between Canada and USA, lives up to its name and greets us with fog. The White Pass Trail used by the gold miners is in the vicinity. A deep mountain crevice where 3,000 packhorses perished bears the telltale name, Dead Horse Gulch.

From here it is 19 miles to Skagway on a protected bay of the Pacific Ocean. Now the wheels roll rapidly. The narrow rail passes through a dark tunnel in a mountain and runs across a dizzying trestle that looks as if it was built from wooden matches. At times the rail skirts a precipitous mountain wall with waterfalls.

If you want to preserve your peace of mind, it is better not to gaze too deeply into the abyss if you are inclined to be disturbed by old trains lying there. They have certainly been derailed a long time ago and been forgotten. The White Pass & Yukon Route tourist information doesn't mention them.

When we arrive in Skagway, two and a half hours late, after 10 hours on the train, the ferry has left. It only waited an hour. A minibus from the Klondike Hotel is waiting, but the price, $20 for a night is more than I want to pay. It is twice as much as the inn in Whitehorse. I approach the driver who looks familiar.

"Hello. I think I have seen you on the ski slopes in Douglas. Aren't there any cheaper hotels in Skagway?"

"Hello, my name is Skip. All hotels have the same base price, but you appear to have a sleeping bag,"

Skip says eyeing my backpack. "I have a bunkhouse where you can sleep for $2. It says Klondike Safaris over the door. Just go in and select a bunk. There is probably no one else there."

Some of the other passengers charter an airplane to Juneau.

In the evening I attend a Gold Rush show from 1898. There I discover that my bunkhouse host, Skip, is the renowned "Dangerous Dan McGrew" from the ballad by Robert Service.

Amused I crawl into my sleeping bag in the empty bunkhouse. I wonder if anyone else might show up? Anyway, I feel safe trusting the hospitality of the dangerous Dan McGrew.

I want to see Skagway but all sightseeing tours have ended for the season.

"I can give you a tour of Skagway with all the old cemeteries and surroundings," one of Skip's guides offers me. I accept.

Skagway was founded in 1897 when gold was discovered in the vicinity of Dawson City in the Yukon. This port to the Yukon had 15,000 inhabitants in the beginning of the Gold Rush. Now, in 1971, Skagway is a peaceful town of 750. A book about the Gold Rush with pictures by the Swede, Eric Hegg, is displayed in the window of the city's old photo shop.

The Chilkoot Trail to the Klondike is shorter but steeper and higher than the trail over the White Pass. It starts in the abandoned town of Dyea at the mouth of the Taiya River, 9 miles outside Skagway. Dyea was torn down in 1900 when the railroad was completed and the timber re-used in Skagway.

Our mini bus gets stuck in the mud in Dyea. We are far from assistance and have to manage on our own. We collect boards we can find from the time of the Gold Rush, jack up the bus, and stick the boards under the wheels.

"This episode was not part of the tour," the driver tells me apologetically as we successfully drive off, "neither that the passenger had to help to free the vehicle."

"Don't worry. I am happy. I got to see everything that was promised. I am willing to pay for the tour."

"I am still embarrassed that we got stuck and can't accept your payment."

"OK then. Thanks for the free tour. Let's part as friends who shared a good adventure," I say and shake hands with the guide.

The ferry departs in the evening. I roll out my sleeping bag on deck on a box with life preservers where it is most peaceful, and fall asleep. The steam whistle wakes me at 2.30 a.m. My sleeping bag is damp from sea spray. We are about to dock in Juneau.

Three years later, after moving to Fairbanks, I take the blue and yellow train of the Alaska Railroad. When I arrive, half an hour before the train departure at 8.30 a.m. it stands on the tracks in Anchorage but the door from the waiting room is closed. The man at the ticket counter recognizes me despite an impressive queue of people. I was there two days ago checking and left with the final words:

"I'll take the train if I can get off where I want." The railroad announces that the train will make a flag stop anywhere. Prepared to walk home two miles from milepost MP465, I carry my luggage in my backpack.

"Talk nicely to the conductor," the ticket man advises, "maybe he will stop the train."

A few weeks earlier, on a beautiful summer day after work, I parked my car in the intersection of Sheep Creek and Miller Hill roads. I walked down to the railroad tracks to scout out the closest milepost for future needs. When I managed to find MP465, despite bloodsucking mosquito attacks, I felt well deserved to get off the train there. Unfortunately, the rules had changed. The train stops anywhere but only until Happy, ten miles from Fairbanks.

The train has five passenger cars, of which two have glass cupola roofs, and three cars for freight. The door to the tracks is opened at quarter to nine. A sign outside the waiting room directs local passengers forward and passengers to McKinley and the end destination, Fairbanks, towards the cupola covered cars. Only two doors to the train are open. The conductor stands welcoming at the second car from the end where you have to step on a silver stool to reach the door. I carry my backpack.

"Sorry, all luggage must be checked," the conductor stops me.

Exactly at nine o'clock the train starts to move discreetly. Slowly, ever so slowly we glide out of Anchorage. It is cloudy but the sun seriously attempts to break through the clouds. We reach Elmendorf A.F.B. after fifteen minutes at seemingly walking speed. Now, finally, the train dares to increase the speed. The cupola car sways a little from side to side but otherwise everything is surprisingly silent. I don't hear the characteristic jerky joints between the rails. It feels as if the train moved on rubber wheels but it is rather the rails that have swollen in the heat.

Anchorage is Milepost 114. The count starts in Seward. The construction of the railroad started in 1915 to connect this ice free port in the south of Alaska with the navigable rivers, coal fields and farming in the interior of the Territory. The railroad construction was completed in 1923 in Nenana. From there it was possible to continue by riverboat to Fairbanks and later by train as the track was continued.

Both Anchorage and Nenana owe their existence to the railroad. Fairbanks was founded earlier, in 1901, where a riverboat with goods went aground.

The forest with birch, aspen, willow, and spruce stands lusciously green on both sides of the track. Fireweed gleam in reddish purple in the middle of July. Some passengers from the "smaller states" or "Lower 48" as the inhabitants in the 49th state call other Americans, get wildly exited when they see a moose through the window.

We arrive at the first station, the small airport of Birchwood with an old prop-plane and some thirty small private airplanes. The conductor arrives.

"Where are you going?"

"Milepost 465. Is there any chance that we can stop?"

"The next conductor comes on duty at 7 p.m. I suggest you go forward in the train and talk to him. If the train stays on schedule it is possible he will let you off. If not, you must choose between Fairbanks and Happy."

Mountains rise in the east with clouds hanging around the tops. In the west we pass a lake and occasionally rivers. A few raindrops sprinkle against the windshield of the cupola. The sun has given up the battle at the moment. We arrive at a road 36 miles from Anchorage after an hour and 25 minutes.

The train moves at a scenic speed of 26 miles per hour. Seventy miles north of Anchorage we get our first glimpse of the highest mountain in North America, Mount McKinley. The view of the impressive snow covered 20,320-foot tall mountain improves, as we get closer. After 170 miles, the train passes over the 918-foot long bridge above the dizzying Hurricane Gulch. We get a rapid glimpse of a little river 296 feet below. A few miles later, at 3 p.m., we meet the train from Fairbanks, still 180 miles away. The train doesn't have any problems with the 2,363- foot pass through the Continental Divide in the Alaska Range. Several passengers get off in Denali National Park at the entrance to the six-million-acre park. There is a crew change in the coal-mining town of Healy. We can see wide black coal bands in the mountains to the east. The new conductor comes through the train in Nenana.

"Can I get off at Milepost 465?" I ask.

"I don't think I want to stop the train only five miles from Fairbanks, but let me think about it."

We rush past Ann's Greenhouse in Happy and approach the last railroad crossing at Sheep Creek road. The train makes no indications of slowing down. Disappointed I watch MP465 and the University of Alaska experimental farm swish by. I brace myself for a long walk or an outrageous taxi fare.

The conductor arrives. "I'll drive you home in my car," he consoles me. "It's easier than to stop the train. It has to stop a few minutes later anyway. Before I drive you home I have to reset a few switches."

The 356-mile long track from Anchorage ends in Fairbanks. The trip has taken 11-1/2 hours.

The extra conductor loads my orange backpack into his red Porsche and drives me home to my trailer in the outskirts of Fairbanks by the way of the switches in the train yard. I didn't expect this kind of personal service from the Alaska Railroad. This was a lot better than letting me off in the woods at MP465.

12

Moving to Fairbanks

On a dark night in November 1971, I go to the movies to stay awake until the Alaska State ferry leaves Juneau at 2 a.m. Normally, I don't go to this type of late night show. The movie is in Danish with English subtitles. Discreetly, I sit down on the last row, not to be seen in case somebody would recognize me. However, the movie is so funny I cannot keep from laughing out loud. The moviegoers, who don't understand Danish, turn around to gaze at me. The point, in the translation, comes later or not at all.

Clear awake I drive aboard the ferry and sadly wave good-by to Juneau and Douglas. A new chapter in my life is about to start.

The next morning we dock in Haines that has a road connection to the outside world. On the dock I am surprised to see Olle Eriksson, who used to live in Douglas. I hadn't told him I was coming.

"It's nice that you came to the Purple Bubble ball," Olle greets me. "I am here to welcome Sven Bertil Anderson, conductor of the Swedish dance band."

"I am not prepared to attend a ball," I reply. "I am just passing through, continuing directly to Fairbanks."

"You don't have a chance in your small Volkswagen. The safety control will stop you. There is blowing snow above timberline in the St.Elias Mountains. Only high-clearance, four-wheel drive cars can get through. Come and have breakfast with me and Anderson," Olle says.

"I remember you playing in Sitka last summer," I tell Anderson.

"That was a good party with the Governor singing," he replies.

When Olle and I arrive at the ball, the band is playing loud modern American music, followed by a schottische. After the schottische, Anderson announces:

"A Swedish waltz for Olle and Kristina."

Olle and I continue dancing while the rest of the dancers vacate the floor. That's the consequence of inviting the band home for Aquavit and Swedish records before the ball. Olle is an excellent dancer so I don't mind being the only couple on the dance floor. My flaming red dress is beautiful, but the thick furry wool fabric in a style with a high neckline and long sleeves wasn't made for the High-Society ball in Haines. However, it is the only dress I have in my luggage.

"Kristina, may I have an American waltz?" Anderson asks.

Proudly I accept and enjoy the dance, feeling special among all the other ladies in their fashionable ballroom gowns, who didn't get a dance with the bandleader.

Southeast Alaska is disconnected from the rest of Alaska. The only connecting road, the Alaska Highway, passes through Canada.

In the morning the weather is good. I carry two pairs of skis, mountain, and downhill, on my Volkswagen and make a good impression on the American road safety control at the beginning of the 152-mile long road across the 3,500-foot high Chilkat pass. They let me pass without embarrassing questions. I don't have the required chains for instance — because I don't know how to use them.

The Canadian Customs, however, isn't fooled by looks and quizzes me.

"Do you have extra food, warm clothing, and something to warm yourself with such as candles, a lantern or a camping stove?"

"I have a down comforter, thermos bottle, and turkey sandwiches," my landlady in Douglas sent along.

Driving to Fairbanks in my Volkswagen bug
in November 1971

The first three Canadian safety stations check me through without incident. The road is plowed and I don't have any problems driving across the rolling hills above timberline in the mountains. On the other side of the pass visibility is poor. Everything is a white haze. I have a hard time distinguishing the road when it gets dusk. The eateries I remember from my two summer trips are closed. I start to think about lodging and apply my brakes to read a poster sign. The road is slick. I have little experience in winter driving and helplessly slide off the road.

Traffic is very sparse. It is not a ferry day. I did pass one parked pickup in the mountains. The hope that it will eventually come my way keeps me calm. To pass the time and to stay warm I start to dig out my car with a small spade that I have as the required shovel. If I had the required chains, they wouldn't have done me any good. After half an hour I hear the welcome sound of a car. It pulls me from the ditch. Carefully I continue driving, scared of another mishap, knowing I am the only car on the road. It is dark when I arrive at the last safety control outside Haines Junction.

"We got worried about you. It has taken you three hours to drive the last 60 miles. A pickup driver said you were on your way."

I was lucky. I heard the driver of another car that slid into the ditch burnt two new tires to stay warm through the night. The man at the safety control had fallen asleep.

There are no more road controls after Haines Junction. I have only to follow the Alaska Highway for 500 miles directly to Fairbanks. The place where I had planned to have lunch is off the road. Concerned about getting stuck again I continue, assuming I will find another place to eat. I do so after driving 75 miles. That's why the Canadian Customs asked how much food I had! I stop now and then to munch on my provisions but seldom turn off my motor. It is -13 F and my car isn't winterized.

"You can have your car winterized in Fairbanks," the mechanic in Juneau told me. "The only thing we can do here is to install heaters for your battery and oil pan and a gasoline burning heater that will blow on your steering wheel. In Fairbanks they can put thinner oil in the engine and steering wheel and repack your front wheels."

The gasoline heater kept the car warm in Juneau but here I barely notice it. My toes are freezing in the sealskin boots although I have squeezed my feet into down socks. The only way to keep my feet warm while driving is to take off one boot at a time and stick my toes into the outlet of the heater by the steering wheel. It takes some acrobatics. I also take turns sticking my hands and tape player batteries into the heater pipe. For short moments I can listen to lively accordion music until my batteries get too cold again.

This road is desolate. Traffic is sparse. Once I have to stop and honk my horn until a porcupine moves off the road. A gray wolf runs in front of my car but soon disappears into the forest. I wish it had given me more time to watch it. I see many white snowshoe hares.

The third morning it is -31F. My car with thick Juneau oil doesn't start. The tow truck at the service station in Northway is frozen. My host puts a large blow heater under my car. He then tows me until the engine starts. This delays my departure for four hours despite my plans for an early start. It is 260 miles left to Fairbanks. When I come to Delta the road makes a sharp bend. It takes all my muscle power to turn the wheel that must have frozen. I didn't turn it for at least 35 miles on the straight road. I stop for dinner but don't dare to turn off the engine.

I arrive in Fairbanks around 8 p.m. on November 30 after driving for seven and a half hours. It is dark with an icy fog that makes visibility almost nonexistent. Fairbanks is in a valley surrounded by mountains. When it is cold and calm, the cold air gets trapped in the valley and the exhaust from cars freezes to ice fog. The street signs and most of my windows are covered by ice, which doesn't improve the situation. I drive around the main streets a few times looking for a motel with a plug-in I can back up to, because the cord to the oil pan heater is very short.

I was in Fairbanks a month ago in the end of October when it was 23F. Dr. Hood, director of the Institute of Marine Research (IMS), had invited Sally Wienke and me for job interviews after we lost our employment in Douglas. Our previous boss, Dr. Nayudu, could only offer us temporary work without benefits. Dr. Sharma, another marine geologist from India, wanted to hire me at IMS. I talked to the Geophysical Institute, my first choice for employment, but no one there had any money.

The Volkswagen garage can see me tomorrow. I leave the car idling on Tanana Loop below the Duckering Building at the University while I go to see Dr. Sharma. He is tall with short black hair and a tanned complexion.

"The first thing we need to do is find you an apartment," Sharma says to my surprise. I expected him to start by telling me about the job.

"I prefer to live close to the University so I can walk to work," I say. Sharma, who will pay my salary, knows what I can afford. Kindly he drives me from place to place. I seriously imagine myself living in the apartments we visit, but one is worse than the other. Sharma encourages me.

"You don't need to feel obliged to choose anything you don't like. My Swiss wife wouldn't even have set foot into some of the places we saw. Dr. Hood lets you stay in a motel for one more night."

I move into a hotel with an accessible plug-in close to the Volkswagen garage. I feel embarrassed about all the time I have wasted for the boss. I study the rental ads in the Fairbanks Daily News-Miner and call several. Sprucewood Manor, a three-story house in a forest below the University has a one bedroom furnished apartment on the third floor for

$200. I find the place in the dark. Unfortunately, it is rather dark inside as well. *This should have warned me.* Several light bulbs are broken but the apartment appears to be cozy and the location is peaceful. This is the best I have seen. I hate to inconvenience the boss any more. I rent the apartment, pay a cleaning deposit of $100, and feel proud having found my own housing. When I return to the hotel it is -40. I plug in the car.

To my delight the car starts the next morning but it is so frozen it barely moves. I get it in first gear and creep to the garage. They winterize the car with thinner oils. An extension cord makes future plug- ins easier.

Shocked I see my new apartment in daylight. Mildly speaking, it is not clean, it is absolutely filthy. The landlady lends me a vacuum cleaner and deducts $7 for moving in on December 2. I clean and scrub for three days until I feel at ease.

It doesn't take me long to empty the Volkswagen. I don't have much to do at home on my spare time while waiting for the rest of my belongings, 12 boxes, and two summer tires that I sent as freight. In the evenings I visit the local folkdance clubs.

The first Sunday I drive to a downhill ski area at Clearly Summit. It is -38F in Fairbanks but in the mountains it is only -8F. Still, my feet get cold and it is already dark when I drive home at 3 p.m. I am not yet sure if I want to join the ski patrol as I did in Douglas. Another Sunday I explore the cross-country ski trails behind the University. I wear my fashionable tight ski pants from Finland but my legs get cold at -4F. When it starts to get dark I am not quite sure where I am and take my Suunto compass from my backpack. It has frozen! To my relief I see another skier.

"In what direction is the University?" I ask. Fortunately it is close because I am cold.

On December 6 I rent a box at the post office in College, four miles outside Fairbanks. I get number 383. On December 22, my household goods arrive. "Our regulations only permit us to carry it eight steps," the movers announce.

"Fine, I live on the third floor. Can you fit 1,300 pounds on the eighth step?"

Everything is inside my apartment after an hour. As thanks I serve the movers beer and coffee and offer them a bill as tips but they don't take it.

New Year's Eve is a holiday I intend to trade for a working day. The Duckering building is locked and dark. I drive my frozen car into the empty garage to thaw the gas and gearshift pedals. When I go to the car to get my lunch I am surprised to find a parking ticket for $2 on the windshield. I thought I was the only one in the building but the police are alert. Too busy with work to remove the ticket I continue working until evening. By then the car has thawed and works irreproachably. A mechanic would have charged more than a parking ticket to "repair" the problem.

When I take it in for an oil change I am told: "You have gasoline in the oil. It is dangerous, the car might explode. You have to change your oil more often. This car is not made for winters in Fairbanks.

Every time you start the car in extreme cold a little gasoline leaks into the oil."

This is depressing news to me. I should have bought the used Volvo instead when I was shopping for cars. Strangely enough, it is not customary here to lodge your means of transportation in a garage. It is left outside to freeze. The car has to be plugged in to start at all. With my Volkswagen, only the engine oil and the battery get heated. The rest of the air- cooled engine is colder than ice. It is difficult to start the car in the morning. The wheels don't roll because they have frozen flat at the bottom. It feels as if they are square. Some mornings one tire is flat. The first time it happens I confidently jack up the car, change to the spare tire, congratulate myself on a job well done, and release the jack. To my disappointment, the thankless creature flops down on the spare that also is flat. When I have the tires repaired, they aren't broken just out of air.

Black smoke and exhaust gases spew from my gasoline-burning car heater after the oil change. I take my car on the highway and drive around for two hours hoping to burn out the accumulated soot. Outside town there is sunshine but in Fairbanks the ice fog is so thick I have to guess the color of the traffic lights. It is -50F. Since I installed Canadian frost shields on all car windows including the windshield, they stay ice-free. The shields leave an air layer next to the windows that prevent icing.

Soon I start to walk to work. It only takes 20 minutes and is easier than all the car problems. I often see moose on the way through the forest. I am now well equipped for the outdoors in padded Navy pants and a big army winter coat with a fur-trimmed hood from the army surplus store.

In the middle of February I see my first Northern Lights in Alaska. Their magnificent airy beauty impresses me. It is light enough to go out with my skis and camera. Part of the sky is light greenish in many shades with a mixture of light yellow. The colors move in wavelike bands that appear to float and flutter like sea grass on the bottom of the ocean or like a curtain in an open window.

Meanwhile, at work I make pipette analyses of marine sediments in suspension. Later I learn how to measure trace metals with an atomic absorption spectrophotometer. Dr. Sharma knows how to do these things and teaches me so I don't have to figure anything out on my own as in Douglas. The relationship with my fellow workers is good. My companions are two helpful students, David Burbank and Ed Szafran. I don't have a telephone. When I am sick for two days both independently come to check on me.

I need a bookcase in my apartment and buy boards but don't manage to get the screws into the wall. I invite Dave and Ed for dinner. Dave looks at the screwdriver for my sewing machine.

"I thought you had tools. No wonder you cannot get a screw in."

The temperature rises to 23 F at the end of January. The ceiling starts to leak above the bookcase, couch, and wardrobe. Upset I run to the landlady and give an ultimatum.

"If you don't fix this leak immediately I will move away from this cheaply built house with a flat roof."

"It's only condensation," she calms me. "It will stop when it gets colder."

I start to investigate the rental market. In the middle of April, when the water again starts to drip, not only above the bathtub but also above the bed, I hastily rent half of a doublewide duplex-trailer without water spots in the ceiling, across from the musk ox farm. The rent is the same but here I can have a garden. I move out in the end of April. The landlady compliments me

"I am happy to return your $100 deposit. The place is really well cleaned."

13

Whaling Celebration in Barrow

Patsy Aamodt's uncle in Barrow caught a whale in the spring of 1972. Among the Eskimos it is a venture that gives the whaling captain the reputation of a hero. Relatives from close and far come to visit and celebrate. Patsy Aamodt puts an advertisement in the *Fairbanks Daily News-Miner*, asking for enough travel companions to charter an airplane.

Our chartered C-46, a cargo plane transformed to carry 40 passengers, lands in Barrow, the world's largest Eskimo village and the northernmost city in USA, on a sunny day in June, three hours after our departure from Fairbanks.

Some curious Eskimo children dressed in colorful parka dresses or kuspuks with fur ruffs meet us but no airline personnel are on hand. We are prepared with a ladder to get down from the plane.

The city of Barrow with 2,000 inhabitants appears desolate although it is close to noon. The midsummer wind blows cold from the frozen Arctic Ocean and stirs up dust. There is no vegetation in the village on the tundra except for a wind-blown palm tree with black-fringed leaves of baleen plucked from the mouth of a whale. The ground never thaws during the short summer, except for the top few inches. The lack of greenery makes the whole village look dusty.

Thin pipes, some distance above the mud, connect the small, generally unpainted houses. They are insulated water pipes that cannot be buried. Boardwalks lead to some of the houses and laundry flutters between them. Snow machines and dog sleds stand around where the snow happened to melt. Black seal meat hangs on poles to dry above some rooftops where the dogs cannot get to it. The Eskimos themselves, in their beautiful kuspuks often made from fabric with big flowers over a lining of fur and slacks, are the only color spots. Everyone smiles and greets us. Occasionally someone passes on a motorized three-wheeler with large balloon tires that can go over snow as well as gravel.

We spread out over the width of the road and set course on the church tower. The Presbyterian Church has offered us lodging. We leave our sleeping bags and food there and walk down to the beach where the whaling celebration is taking place.

The small children are jumping on a walrus skin. It is a special entertainment for the Eskimos. The stretched skin, with an edge of rope like that around a lifeboat, is mounted five feet above ground in the middle of the feast place. The most interested Eskimos stand closely around holding on to the ropes. Rhythmically they follow the spring of the jumper. After a few preliminary low jumps, they give the skin an extra tug sending the jumper tramping air high into the sky. Many fall after the first preliminary spring. Few land on their feet. It is not easy.

Blanket toss at whaling festival in Barrow June 1972.

The young adults jump later in the day. They are experienced and make it look easy. Many young ladies are very graceful but the sport has its risks. Some young men become reckless and land hard outside the skin. The surrounding people are skillful in catching trespassers by bumping them back onto the skin. Occasionally someone lands on the ground or on a spectator and both of them have to be carried away on a stretcher. Barrow's blue, 4-wheel drive ambulance is attentively parked close at hand. A small tent with a sign urging people to donate blood is nearby. I see no immediate connection between the two events.

This spring of 1972 the whalers in Barrow caught 15 whales. Every hunting party that caught one or more whales has its victory flag proudly flying above the place of the festivities. Boats on edge surround the venue with tarps between for protection against the icy ocean wind.

The stretch of open water along the beach is narrow. The ice is still strong. An occasional seal hunter on the ice roars by on a snow machine towing a sled with seals. Parts of the whale harvest, meat, blubber and a few pieces of baleen, up to 10 feet long, are spread out on the ice. It is difficult to imagine that a large whale can be over 60 feet long and have its mouth surrounded by more than 500 pieces of baleen.

The non-jumping Eskimos sit on the ground along the windbreaks following the children's play. Most of the villagers sit on the beach waiting to be fed. Large containers of all kinds are filled with food. A white-haired priest in an orange kuspuk says grace in the ring around the food that is then passed around. The food consists of caribou stew, fist-size sooty pieces of moose, and wild goose soup. Muktuk is the delicacy of the feast. The Eskimo women skillfully cut the inch-thick black shiny whale skin with attached blubber into rectangular pieces with their "ulus" which are pie shaped pieces of circular saw blades with handles of caribou horn. The muktuk is raw as is the blood marinated whale meat that looks like oily rags. I taste a piece of muktuk. The taste improves while I chew on the skin but the blubber just gets tougher and appears to grow in my mouth while its consistency turns into soft plastic. People must have watched me. Since I dared try the muktuk they serve me dried fruit soup, elongated Eskimo donuts, pilot bread and tea. The fruit soup is good.

Whaling festival feeding on beach in Barrow June 1972

Everyone has brought his own plate in addition to bowls and cardboard boxes to take food home in.

The food is passed out in proportion to the size of the family. Everyone is calm and relaxed. Even the children are silently waiting. Despite the ample supply of food I am happy I had the wits to eat a couple of sandwiches in advance.

Among the Eskimos I suddenly see Ann Lillian Shell in a kuspuk with Hawaiian flowers.

"Hello, Ann, do you remember me?" I ask. "I was here two years ago with my colleague Sally Wienke from Douglas."

"Hi, Kristina. Sure I remember you. The US Naval Research Lab put you up in a Quonset hut with a honey bucket because you arrived without an invitation from the director."

"We had written in advance but the director never replied. But you and your husband invited us for the best steak dinner I ever had."

Ann has lived in Barrow for a couple of years and cuts me a piece of good black muktuk with her ulu.

"When we saw you last, you carried Sarah on your back inside your parka as an Eskimo child. How is she doing?"

"Sarah loves muktuk and the Naval Lab's wolves and polar bear cubs."

Ann works on a project to utilize quiviut, the under wool of the musk oxen. Quiviut is supposedly the warmest and lightest wool in the world. Ann teaches the Eskimo women to knit warm, lacy scarves and neck/head warmers they can sell. Every village that is part of the program has its own unique lace pattern.

When everyone is well fed and tired of jumping it is time to dance. Unfortunately the fog rolls in from the ocean so the dance will be indoors. The sun rose six weeks ago and will not set for another six weeks but this night it is shining with its absence.

A skin, sewn together from several walrus hides, is spread out on the middle of the floor. The orchestra, consisting of half a dozen men with drums covered by walrus stomachs, sits along one side of the skin. The crowd sits on the floor all around. It is crowded. A few manage only to stick their heads through the open windows. The congregation is mainly kuspuk dressed Eskimos with a few scientists from the Arctic Lab in olive green down parkas with wolf ruffs. This dance is an expression of joy and cultural traditions. I find it difficult to understand. Most of the audience is too involved following the dance to answer my questions. The young know only that it is tradition and the old don't speak English.

The drummers beat rhythmically on their tight walrus stomachs while they in monotone and elongately hum some calls. One group of dancers replaces another. At times a proud Eskimo squeezes to the front while looking searchingly through the crowd. People all around rise as on a silent command and make their way to the dance skin. It was a whaling captain in a handsome kuspuk with a wolverine ruff looking for his crew. Every whaling crew dances as a group. Sometimes it seems to be a competition between different groups. A handsome Eskimo on the walrus skin is soon surrounded by women of various ages.

The crews seem to describe their hunting in the dance. It is less clear to me what the other groups are trying to show except the plain joy of life. Everyone dances in his outdoor clothing, most in kuspuks, and all have gloves on their hands or a pair is thrown to them. I later learned that it shows lack of respect for the spirits to dance with uncovered hands. People dance more with their hands and arms than with their feet.

Compared to the Eskimo dance in Nome, this is really lively. In Nome it was a small sample performance for tourists. Here in Barrow the dance is still living tradition for celebration.

The dance ends at midnight but it is still light outside. After resting for a few hours in our sleeping bags on the floor of the Presbyterian Church we walk out to the airport where our pilot and mate are waiting. We load our luggage and help each other up the ladder to the plane that is freezing cold. The heater has frozen. It doesn't really matter because I am still dressed in my midsummer clothing consisting of an army surplus parka with a fur ruff over a couple of wool sweaters.

14

Winter Chores in the Interior

The vast surroundings of Fairbanks, far away from the influence of the ocean winds, are called the Interior. Fairbanks is in many ways, not the least historically, considered the Golden Heart of the Interior.

Winter here lasts from the time of harvest to sowing when the events in this story take place in the early to mid 1970's. Based on Fairbanks average temperatures between 1917 and 1992, the daily minimum temperature creeps below freezing on August 15 to re-emerge on June 1. The mean annual temperature for Fairbanks is 26°F, the maximum 96°F and minimum -62°F. Since the 1980's, there has, however, been a general warming in Alaska, especially in the spring and winter. The mean annual temperature for Fairbanks rose to 27.5°F from 1971 to 2000.

Spring and fall are short explosive parentheses when you almost can tell the time of day when the birch leaves burst out or the color display of fall starts. Winter is long as the below freezing annual mean temperature shows but it is generally wind- free. The air is very dry, so the cold doesn't feel worse than a corresponding dry sauna heat, if you are suitably dressed versus undressed.

The zero mark on the thermometer seems to have a considerable psychological effect. When the temperature creeps above zero for the first time from maybe -50°F in winter to only 0°F, the difference feels like a heat wave.

People open their fur ruffed parkas and some health nut might sprints by in shorts.

After a few years in the Interior, people gradually become "sourdoughs" and consider everything above zero springtime. It is a way to shorten winter. People get accustomed to the climate changes or turn sour with time. A negative Alaskan saying states that a sourdough is a person who has turned sour on Alaska and has no dough to leave.

Taking care of garbage outside the city limits of Fairbanks is a chore that is easier in winter. I want a burn barrel. A colleague takes me on a tour along the beginning of the planning stages of the road to the oil fields in Prudhoe Bay. We find an empty barrel in a ditch. It needs ventilation holes but that is easily taken care of when we stop for a picnic lunch along the road. My friend wants to demonstrate his handguns and the barrel is the perfect target. I prefer his 9 mm Luger pistol.

It is more difficult to open one end of the barrel. I ask Ed Szafran at work. "I refuse to contribute to your pollution of the air," Ed replies to my surprise. I haven't yet become aware of air pollution as an issue.

Free dinner persuades Dave Burbank to do the job.

In the beginning I burn all paper and save the rest of the garbage for a few months until my paths take me to the vicinity of the dump south of Fairbanks. It is a smelly trip, particularly in summertime, even when my windows are rolled down. In the winter everything is frozen and less smelly. Then, the damage is less if a roaming dog gets into the garbage and spreads everything out, usually the day before I plan to drive to the dump.

Despite all my efforts to acquire the burn barrel I am less delighted with the burning sparks in the middle of the dry spruce forest. Often I smuggle my garbage to work in small installments.

The normal daily chores in Fairbanks are naturally affected by winter. Car problems are some of the most common topics of conversation. The car is a direct necessity for most people, an indirect one for the hitchhikers. The only bus route goes directly from town to the University.

People who need to leave their cars standing for a while without access to electricity remove the battery and place it on a piece of wood in a heated room. Concrete floors are known to discharge batteries. Most homes and places of work have an electrical outlet for the car. At this time I don't know anybody who has a heated garage. To save electricity, modern homes have a timer that can be set to turn on a few hours before you need the car. In other cases you have to get warmly dressed and go out to plug in your car, especially if electricity is not included in the rent. As a rule of thumb, you plug in the car for one hour for every ten degrees below zero. At the University you have to pay for parking but yet there is not enough outlets. This is a good incentive to arrive early. Still it might happen that the car doesn't start although you managed to conquer an outlet. The reason could be a blown fuse in the outlet or someone stumbling over the cord and pulling the plug.

Once the police in their meanness pulled my plug. I had got the bright idea to use my 50 foot long electrical cord to share an outlet with another car further away in the crowded parking lot. Normally an outlet can only handle one big car but my Volkswagen only has a battery blanket and an oil pan heater to plug in. Fuses are often burned out in the parking areas. I soon learn to carry spare fuses and to check them before plugging in.

If something has happened and the car doesn't start, most people are prepared with a jumper cable to attach to a good battery. In real emergencies, without access to another battery, you may have to build a fire under your car to warm its vital parts. It is then possible to start it, unless something of value explodes. Some sourdoughs with old sensitive cars manage to start them with kicks, blows, a sip of medicine, sweet talk, a fire, or a large wrench. If not, they use a dog team.

Three car plug-in posts at the Geophysical Institute.

My little Volkswagen that now, in 1973, is six years old, has behaved rather well except for a few minor mishaps. Our problems have generally been caused by a lack of understanding. According to the laws of physics, air pressure in the tires sinks with temperature during the night. Last winter I didn't understand the problem and went to a gas station to fill the tires when they got empty. To prevent freezing, the garages keep their air hoses indoors behind a wall with a small exit hole. Despite the attention to my tires, one could still be flat in the morning. Wise from bad experience, I now measure the pressure in my spare tire before changing wheels.

I encountered my worst experience one morning at forty below; three flat tires. I had nothing to change. After intensive pumping with my hand pump I could drive to the closest gas station three miles away. Soon I am getting really good at changing wheels in the dark in

20 minutes at -40 with two pairs of wool mittens inside leather mittens. It feels like a task from a Girl Scout competition back in Finland. The tire problem gradually disappears by installing natural rubber inner tubes and the approach of spring.

This year it has been a mild winter so far with no less than -22°F but it is only the middle of December. I think I have solved the tire problem. Every time I add air with a warm hose from inside a garage, I get some damp air. The moisture condenses around the cold tire stem that freezes and then leaks slowly during the course of the night. This fall I over- filled my tires inside a warm garage. Since then I haven't touched them. Now, I just have to prove my theory is right. Every morning I take an inspection walk around my car and take a breath of gratitude as long as my theory is valid.

This winter the battery has attracted my attention. Some evenings I have to make many attempts to start the car after unplugged visits somewhere. Once the car just doesn't start until a helpful friend brings jumper cables.

"Do you have enough water in the battery?" he asks.

"I didn't know I have to check that. This is my first car."

"Women!..."

I drive away with grateful relief. My car should be ashamed, it is only 15°F plus. When I come home I unscrew the battery caps but cannot see any water in the light of my flashlight. The battery blanket is broken. I carefully try to squirt distilled water into the battery but it freezes in the squirt tube. Instead, I liberally pour water from the gallon container. After this, the car runs blamelessly for a week. I am proud over my newly gained mechanical skills until one evening, when I am ready to drive home from work and the car won't start. I get a jump-start. This time it is -25°F and the battery blanket is still broken.

Fortunately, my colleague from Ceylon, K.O.L.F. Jayaweera, who is a cloud physicist, has invited me for dinner. When I am ready to leave, the battery is dead again. K.O.L.F. gets a battery charger while I continue my conversation in Finnish with his wife, Irma.

"Plug in both the charger and the oil pan heater for a day when you get home," K.O.L.F. advises me.

Skeptically I make an attempt to start the car in the morning before unplugging anything. It starts! I take both the battery and the charger into the lab to keep them warm. I check the water level but to my surprise I only see ice crystals in every cell. I am proud over my car that managed to bring me to work with an ice lump as battery. The ice thaws in a couple of hours. Sulphuric acid shouldn't freeze! Maybe it was so cold when I poured in the water last week that it froze on the surface without mixing with the sulphuric acid? I check the battery at the end of the day. The reading is below death.

"A healthy battery doesn't freeze," someone at work tells me. "You should be thankful that the battery has lasted you for six years."

I borrow a battery and drive to Arctic Batteries in south Fairbanks. I have a hard time finding the place in the dark. When I arrive they have closed but a man is kindly waiting for me.

"The North Slope battery is 90 Amp, twice as strong as the one you have."

"Thank you, I'll take the strongest one that fits into my car. I also need a new battery blanket."

The next morning it is -30°F but my car starts as soon as it sees the keys.

At the same time as the battery acted up, I myself started feeling ill in the mornings. I don't normally talk about my ailments, but this time I will dwell on them for educational purposes to present the unexpected solution in the end.

I wake up with a headache and nausea a Thursday morning in the beginning of November 1973 but the symptoms disappear during the course of the day. It is snowing heavily. The snow still pours down on Saturday. I don't dare drive anywhere, afraid to get stuck on the unplowed roads. Sunday I break a ski trail to work. It takes an hour. When I return, the snow has accumulated and it takes me over an hour to ski back. Besides nausea I am exhausted and have diarrhea. After twelve days I am tired of the performance and call a doctor. No, I am not pregnant if someone should get that idea, which doesn't occur to the doctor either. He gives me a concoction for the diarrhea, but I still have a hard time eating anything in the morning. I force myself to eat breakfast until I discover worms in my granola. I bought 12 pounds at the end of August when the shelves started to get empty in the stores. No wonder I felt bad and lost my appetite after sprinkling the worm mixture on my home made yogurt. I throw out the worms but still feel listless.

It is getting dusk already by 2 p.m. this Sunday but I decide to go for a short ski tour to clean up my trail. It is totally snowed-in again. Spruce branches weighted down by snow and small trees bent over the trail disrupt my progression. I have to break and saw my way through the willow and alder brush. I am the only one who uses the first half of the trail except for some dogs, snowshoe hares, foxes, and moose. After three hours I can no longer see what I am sawing. Monday morning I feel unusually energized after forcing myself to get up early and ski to work. The morning after I feel ill again and call the doctor.

"The tests show you have a tropical stomach disease," the doctor tells me. "I will give you a new recipe."

"But I haven't been in the tropics for 9 months, if the South Pacific counts."

My nausea in the morning gets worse. The doctor prescribes a concoction over the phone to enhance my appetite. I have my murky, rusty tap water tested that I no longer use for drinking or cooking. My colleague, David Burbank, has become my new neighbor in the duplex trailer. We use the same well. He comes over.

"It smells strangely shut-in at your place but it is probably something you have eaten that gives you problems," David says.

David is a student in marine geology with a scientific analytical mind. When he comes over the next evening it smells the same at my place.

"I have thought about your symptoms," David says. "Head ache, tiredness and nausea might indicate carbon monoxide poisoning. When did you start to feel ill?"

"About three weeks ago."

"That's when our heavy snowfall started. I will take a look at your chimney."

To get up on the flat roof without a ladder, I had previously put large spikes in a corner post to the porch to get to my frozen fish. Using my spikes David gets up on the roof.

"The chimney for the oil heater is partly snow covered," David notices. "I will shovel the snow away. Sleep with your window ajar tonight."

It is only -15°F. My Norwegian down comforter should be able to stand some fresh air. I wake up the next morning without nausea, to my big and happy surprise. Maybe I should have poured the doctor's concoction down the chimney?

My alarm clock always goes off far before the winter morning has the good sense to be light. Reluctantly I dig myself out from the warming cocoon of my down comforter. The 35-degree bedroom air makes me shiver as I put my feet on a black bear skin. The double windows of the trailer are totally frost covered although they have an insulating layer of heavy visqueen plastic, between them. The window towards the road is covered with a turquoise "lava lava" cloth with pictures of outrigger canoes from the South Pacific, frozen against it until spring. A thick layer of snow and ice tightly seals the back door in the bedroom. A blanket in front of it keeps the draft away. I haven't checked how cold it is in the corners. Maybe I should put up a shelf close to the ceiling for the potatoes that I now store on the floor by the door? A root cellar for potatoes should probably be a few degrees warmer. The temperature in my living room, that is better insulated, is 50°F. Still I turn up the thermostat from the night setting of 60°F. Soon I can feel luxurious warm air blowing from the oil furnace until the room is 68°F. After scraping the ice from my porch window I can see the thermometer showing -18°F. Winter is on its way. The November snow is a third of an oil barrel deep outside my trailer in the woods.

Getting drinking water is a task made more difficult by winter. The soil around Fairbanks is very rich in iron. Most people outside the city water net have murky brown water or no water at all. It is common in this outpost of the University with a gold mining history not to have running water. I am comfortably conventional, rent the luxury, and keep a full time job to pay for it. The tap water looks good as long as it is running, but it turns black in contact with coffee, tea, and other select liquids. The first time I cooked macaroni, I thought I had inadvertently poured ketchup into the boiling water. Taking a shower makes my hair red, toenails orange, and all my tiles rusty. My new job at the Geophysical Institute has access to a shower. I use this fringe benefit to wash my hair. For my laundry I use one of the coin gulping Laundromats in town. Plugged in heat tapes keep the water pipes working. When they froze last winter I flushed the toilet with melted snow but it was a procedure that tried my patience.

Soon I learn about the Water Hole. It is a natural spring in Fox, ten miles north of Fairbanks. That water is crystal clear and good and runs perpetually. I normally go to Fox once a month to fill my two five gallon containers. During weekends there is often a line. Despite the demand, there are times when the water has built up so much ice that it is difficult to fit a jug under the pipe. Most people carry an ice axe in their car for occasions like these. Naturally, I don't waste water. For cooking I sometimes add University water to the Fox water. If the water appears clean after using it I save it.

Kristina in her sealskin parka fetching water at Fox Springs in December 1980

People with outhouses have other problems, especially if a roof doesn't cover the "privy". In such homes you might see the toilet seat hanging on a hook inside the door to stay warm. Wintertime the capacity of the outhouse might easily be exceeded when everything freezes and builds up. My folkdance friend, Bob Peltz, efficiently blew the frozen heap apart with a gunshot.

Bob is less conventional and does what he wants, as do many others in Alaska. Bob has a couple of academic degrees but too many leisure time interests to let him be tied down by a regular job. He lives without paying rent in a yurt he built himself in the forest. He normally eats what he shoots or catches. He knows how to survive during any condition and has tools and imagination to repair or make what he needs. Bob's girlfriend completed her master's degree in biology in the yurt. She works half time while Bob takes care of the household and all the dogs. Bob has an ice axe outside the door.

My neighbor David and I have our ice axes inside our doors. The duplex trailer is poorly insulated. Moisture in the warm air indoors condenses and freezes between the windows. It is not too bad as long as it is below zero. Then everything remains frozen. In springtime it is a misery when some snow and ice melts long before it is above freezing.

The trailer has double doors. The outer one of glass can be exchanged for mosquito netting in summertime. Ice normally collects between the doors. It is not too bad on my side. Until now I have been able to get out in less than 20 minutes with a rock chisel and hammer without breaking the outside glass door. It is frustrating in the morning if I am late and the door happens to be frozen. On David's side it can be worse. Sometimes he has had a whole icefall between his doors to conquer before being able to get out. The reason for this uneven distribution of nuisance ice is the kindness of David. He repaired the roof before the onset of fall. Fortunately he started on my side but must have gotten tired when he finally reached his side.

The owner lives in Douglas. His two brothers in Fairbanks don't do much to support the rental unit. When I complained about the roof leaking they actually came out with a bucket of tar. I have no idea what they did with the contents. The only evidence of the visit was some dried up tar brushes and a lot of beer cans

117

thrown around the trailer. The rain continued as usual through the roof.

I go to Finland for Christmas in 1973 and return to Fairbanks in the middle of January. The clean fluffy snow and -22°F cold feel refreshing after the fog and slush in Europe. I really have a strong need for something refreshing and uplifting after 20 hours in the air. It has been a long day.

Before the emergency landing in Anchorage and subsequent waiting for two and a half hours for the repair of the landing gear, we were treated to a 20-minute circling of the city. I thought it was strange, but nothing was said so I just thought they needed to burn up some gas before landing and decided to take it as bonus sightseeing. The landing was a bit rough but nobody was hurt.

When we finally land in Fairbanks, my folkdance friend, Bob Sullivan, has got tired of waiting. He took my car to the airport, left the keys with the airport police, and requested they call me over the loudspeakers the minute the plane lands. The police hand me the keys and a map showing where the car is parked. Bob has thoughtfully left my "new spring coat" in the Volkswagen. That's what I call the huge Army surplus parka with a fur ruff that I bought one spring. I have repaired the acid holes with new patches and added new buttons to close the parka tighter.

At home the trailer is empty. David has moved back to the University student housing where he really has more time to study. Bob Sullivan and Ed Szafran have skied by to check-up on things. A list on the table records their observations. I smile as I see their personalities reflected in their remarks, Bob accurate and responsible, Ed silly with his head in space.

1973.12.26 — Everything in order. Spigots to plastic jugs for drinking water OK, light and heat OK. Drank some apple juice. - Ed

12.26 — Minimum temperature -15°F, day temperature 2°F. Sewer pipe frozen. Asked neighbors in log cabin to call the landlord. - Bob

1974.1.4 — Minimum temperature -15°F, day temperature 10°F. Everything OK. Borrowed 5 eggs. Ice in the apple juice. - Bob

1.6 — Right, ice in the apple juice. (Comet in the oven) - Ed

1.12 — Oil heater OK, sewer OK. Water pipes frozen! Told neighbors. Minimum temperature -25°F, day temperature -20°F. – Bob

The landlord, or really his brother, hasn't done anything, naturally, and the pipes are still frozen. I am too tired to face the problem. Without a telephone I cannot get too extensive repairs done.

I am glad Bob recorded the temperature, because I had been worried about the safety of my 30 pounds of whitefish I have in a dog-proof box outside the door. Earlier I kept the fish on the roof but it was too much trouble to get up there using the spikes in the corner post. Fortunately it hasn't been above freezing so the main course of dinner is safe for an extended future.

My first work day of the year, January 16, 1974 I call the landlord's brother in Fairbanks and complain about the frozen pipes. As usual, he promises to come and look at them. I miss David who could fix what he wanted.

After work Bob S. has invited me for a welcome home dinner. He has bought a whole 90-pound bag of frozen fish. The fish come from the Colville River that drains into the Arctic Ocean. It is intended to feed sled dogs so the price is consumer friendly. I am not in too big a suspense concerning what Bob will serve me. Anyway, it is a relief not to be concerned with the cleaning and cooking. The fish are frozen whole, uncleaned.

My fashionable work clothing, a wool skirt in tweed, wool sweater, and wool stockings are insufficient for this unexpected dinner invitation. Bob lives in a small trailer that can be pulled behind a car. It is more poorly insulated than mine. The temperature is 55°F at table level, 20°F below the table where I keep my feet. Outside it is -40.

"Put on my padded flight pants and felt socks," Bob offers.

"Thank you. Appropriately dressed I can now fully appreciate the fish dinner without freezing my legs."

When I return to my trailer, at a higher elevation, it is only -20°F, but my pipes are still frozen. I turn up the thermostat to 80°F and cover the warm air duct that is connected with the cold space below the trailer, hoping to heat the pipes. I crawl under the trailer that is skirted from the outside world. It is difficult to wiggle between the mess of pipes and electrical wires. The worst thing is that I don't understand anything of this. The heat tapes appear to work but something in the pump assembly is frozen. Something with frozen plastic tubing and two large gas tanks ticks.

I feel full of energy despite the late hour. It is the first day after my trip and the hours of my day are switched. It feels like morning to me. I shovel a trail into the forest to be used for anticipated future calls of nature. The snow I took in this morning has melted but it takes a whole bucket to flush the toilet just once.

The thermostat stays at 80°F all night and the following day. I feel a bit guilty in these times of energy crisis when President Nixon has switched to summer time to save electricity and has asked people to turn down their thermostats by three degrees to save oil. When I come home from work my pipes have thawed! I can flush my toilet and turn down the thermostat to 70°F. During the process my oil furnace has got an unpleasant scraping squeaking sound and the fan is burning hot. Scared that something might catch fire I turn the thermostat down to 55°F. The next morning the pipes are frozen again. I call my landlord from work and try to scare his wife hoping for some action. When I return from my job everything works! There is a note on the table.

"*Do not* turn down the thermostat. It has to be at 70°F even at night."

I am probably the only one in the USA who has got this kind of instructions in these times of crisis. The heat is included in the rent so I don't mind. The apartment next door is still empty so little water is used in the house. That's why it has time to freeze in the pipes. Closing the door to my living room at night, the bedroom temperature drops to 45°F, which is comfortable with my down comforter.

January 27 the night temperature drops to - 44°F. In the morning it is -42°F and the pipes are frozen again. On the flats in South Fairbanks it is - 60°F. I don't want to complain about the pipes again when the owner himself, Ed, plans to move in next door in February. Instead I try the warm air method but without results. February 1 I call his brother, Don.

"Does Ed really plan to move in next to me? My pipes have been frozen for five days."

"No, Ed doesn't plan to move until March or April but I will come and look at the pipes tomorrow," Don says.

I check the oil in my car and notice with panic I have a third of gasoline in my oil. It has never been this bad although this is a typical Volkswagen problem in the winter. To calm my fear I go skiing.

When I return, I see sand on my bathroom rug and the thermostat is turned down. Don has probably looked at the pipes but the water is still frozen. Thinking Ed was going to move here I haven't mailed my rent and now feel poorly motivated to do so until I get water.

On Sunday I have invited company for Swiss cheese fondue. I never imagined I wouldn't have water by then.

Bob Sullivan has managed to start his truck and brings extra chairs. Previously I used to borrow chairs from David's side. Bob has an outhouse and wants to use my toilet.

"OK, but you cannot flush. I will do it when everyone has left. I only have one bucket of melted snow water."

"What, don't you have water yet?"

Bob loosens the toilet paper roll and looks around for matches. We learned the environmentally sound trick of burning the toilet paper last summer when we visited a friend homesteading on a rocky ridge above timberline outside Denali National Park.

Bob Peltz and Fran have skied from their yurt 2.5 miles away. They turn off their headlamps and spread out their damp clothing around the heat ducts under the couch and table. After this procedure Bob P. wants to use my indoor plumbing but prefers the woods when he cannot flush. The trail I previously dug is put to good use. None of my guests has running water — nor frozen pipes. I am thankful they were so thoughtful when I get sick in the night.

After throwing up I can flush the toilet with the snow I had melted. Oh horror, I get diarrhea also and flush down my entire supply of water. Is it food poisoning? My conscience bothers me in addition to my stomach cramps. What have I done? Did my guests get sick?

None of us has telephones at home. Before the fondue I served Chinese noodle soup with steamed whitefish. It was a new way to serve whitefish that my fish eating friends appreciated. We are the gang that survives on sled dog food. To my knowledge, no one has got sick from it before.

After a while I have to throw up again. It is -20°F. I cannot, nor do I want to, run far in my nightgown nor do I want to pollute the snow for my water supply outside the door. In a flash attack I throw up in a paper bag. It is neat and hygienic. The contents freeze rapidly outside.

The next day I am too tired to eat or ski but the day after, I eat the rest of the dog soup. I must know if it caused my illness. To my delight I don't get sick. To my relief, I later found out none of my dinner guests got sick so it was not the food.

It bothers my esthetic mind to have my frozen vomits on a table outside the door. My backpack has strings to tie on crampons. The strings work well for my frozen bags when I ski to work. This may sound gross but, unfortunately, it is true. I write my landlord in Douglas.

"I have been without water for ten days and don't intend to pay my rent until I get water — or an outhouse."

This letter should cause some action. Bob and Fran offer to rent me their supply tent if I am evicted. The next morning I over-sleep. Carbon monoxide poisoning is my first thought, but it hasn't snowed for a while. I climb up on the roof. My chimney appears to be more subsided than David's. I manage to lift it a little. The smoke appears to exit without obstructions. I call Don again. He promises to look at the chimney also. By now he has looked at the water pipes for five days without any other results than cigarette ashes and gravel on my rug.

"I cannot do any more," Don tells me. "I will ask a professional tomorrow."

The tomorrow for the professional doesn't dawn until a week later. Meanwhile February 12 dawns, which is the 16th day since my water froze. It only seems to get colder. My thermometer shows -40 but it is -65°F in South Fairbanks. It is no idea to even try to start the car. I could get it started but the danger to set the motor on fire is too big with gasoline as lubrication. Eventually it will warm up.

Spring is on its way. The sun shines into my bedroom and wakes me. It feels warm outside my down comforter. It must be 50°F. Outside it is already 15°F on Sunday March 17, 1974. I must consume my frozen food supply before the temperature gets above freezing. We can have cold for two more months but it can also warm up in a couple of weeks. I have already given most of my frozen whitefish to my old square dance friend, Walt Peirce, who has promised to smoke it.

I luxuriate in bed for a while but I have a lot a chores waiting, that I didn't get to during the week. After morning coffee with my last yogurt – I must make more today, I dress in my insulated white Bunny boots. I then lurch between the spruces in the forest along my shoveled trail to conduct my morning outing. I use white toilet paper in the winter although I burn as much as I can. I have a good view of the Yankovich road but the neighbor's log cabin is hidden. Suddenly a blue truck drives in towards the house while I am crouching. It is Don, the brother of the landlord. Shovel in hand I balance back through the snow along the deep and narrow trail.

"Have you come to repair my toilet?" I wonder slightly irritated.

"Didn't he come?" Don asks surprised. "He said he would come right away. I have to call him again. It happened yesterday, didn't it?"

"It froze Wednesday, four days ago!" "Tomorrow they will pull the well."

By now I have been without running water for two months. I no longer believe in promises until I see results.

Don's "tomorrow" is a rather stretchable concept. I am tempted to use some power words but redirect my frustration into chopping snow blocks. I shovel the hard blocks into a large steel pan I originally bought to drain motor oil into. I break them with a spade and pour half a gallon of water over them to start the melting. Some I put into a large trashcan of plastic where they rapidly melt since the container is already half filled with water.

I haven't had time to wash my dishes for several days but I haven't used more than necessary. I boil the water for dishes. It is spiced with birch seeds and spruce needles. I get my yogurt going on a special hot plate. It costs four times more to buy it than to make it.

In preparation for dinner I bring in some of my last frozen whitefish. Boiling water melts the skin of the fish so I can pull it off while the rest of the fish is still frozen. The knife cuts easily through the lightly frozen fish so I can clean it neatly before it thaws. At -40 it was almost impossible to stick even a sharp Finnish puukko knife into the fish.

I have stored my potatoes un-cleaned to make them last as long as possible. The soil comes off easily when I rub them in the snow in the steel pan in my bathtub. I give the carrots the same treatment before grating them and cleaning the grater in the snow. This makes the snow dirty but it will thaw quicker. The water will be used to flush the toilet, if the sewer pipes ever thaw or the professional, that Don has called, comes and pumps them open. At - 22°F the sewer pipes kept working. The temperature variations between day and night in spring and maybe, too conservative flushing, have frozen or clogged up the pipes.

"Pour yeast into the septic tank," a colleague advises.

I don't know where the septic tank is but I pour a dosage into the toilet. With my wide mountain skis on my feet I explore the area behind the trailer. Summertime there is a marsh with a slight odor. Two wooden pipes with thick hats of snow stick up above the snow. I don't detect any smell from the pipes. The snow crystals inside are clean. A dosage of yeast in each shouldn't harm? It doesn't do any good either.

Two days later the situation is unchanged. Last night I tried with a can of Heet, intended to prevent the gas line in the car from freezing. "Fumes dangerous," it says on the can. The toilet doesn't even react with a cluck, but instead the fumes spread into the room, although I closed the bathroom door. I rapidly escape into the bedroom, where I normally keep the door closed. The ventilation there is very good and the temperature stays 15-35 degrees colder than in the rest of the house. I still think it smells dangerously and pour my last melted snow into the toilet. It doesn't flush but the worst smell disappears and this morning I used the woods.

Still I have electricity and heat to be thankful for, but as things develop, I wonder for how long? I have a couple of Coleman lanterns and candles on stand- by. As extra insurance I order a new expedition rated down sleeping bag good to -40. When the sleeping bag arrives in March it is -30°F at midnight. I dress for the night in padded pants and reindeer skin slippers and crawl into the sleeping bag in the snow pile outside the door. It is uncomfortable to breathe with the wolf ruff parka hood tightly pulled around my face, because the hairs froze together. The ground pad is insufficient so I turn often in the sleeping bag, which is an action of skill with all my clothing. It is actually difficult to sleep. By 4:30 a.m. I realize I can continue to lie here grilling myself and being uncomfortable until morning. It is too cold to fall asleep but I can survive in my sleeping bag. I go inside. With this night clothing, the 32°F bedroom temperature feels warm. Clem at Clem's Backpacking confirms my discovery.

"A -40 sleeping bag is not intended to keep you warm at -40, just alive."

March 22 a professional company thaws my pipes. The owner and his wife move in next door in the beginning of April and have a new pump installed in the well. After 67 days I finally have running water again.

"We hope you will stay," Ed's wife tells me. "We will plow the whole meadow behind the log cabin. You can have as big a garden as you want."

15

Harvest Dinner

The darkness of fall already looms behind the corner. The few mosquitoes left are too tired to cause trouble. The yellow birch leaves tremble and the rhubarb leaves are in the process of turning red. Mushrooms and rose hips are drying. The blueberry leaves have already dried to a brownish red. The last rays of the summer sun warm a little as the days shorten. The time is the middle of September 1973. My rented half-trailer is at the edge of a forest six miles Northwest of Fairbanks.

A busy day that started with the cooking of lingonberry jam has ended. My legs are sore from the unusual task of bending over a hoe in my potato patch. I have worked very carefully to find every one and not damage too many of the few spuds. The tops froze some time ago. This cultivation together with peas, a little dill, spinach, and beets, that didn't grow up, lies in a forest glen outside the neighbor's log cabin a hundred yards back in the forest. I haven't had much time for this plot because I have concentrated my efforts on the garden outside my trailer.

There I dug up a small patch to have my kitchen garden close to the house. The fight against roots, horsetail, and fireweeds is tough. Maybe the soil needs fertilizing? Karl Neuman farms in a sunny old horse pasture. His success is a lot better than mine. Karl is born in Russia, lived in Germany and is married to Ritva from Finland,

"You can probably get musk ox manure from the farm next door," Karl suggests.

I try to call the University musk ox farm from work, where I have access to a phone, but the lines are disconnected due to a phone strike. Instead, I muster my courage and drive past the sign, "Unauthorized entry forbidden." After some hundred yards, I come to a gate in the tall fence. The road continues through a pasture with half-wild beasts. I can see the farm in the distance on the other side of the fence. The gate is, however, locked and the fence impossible to squeeze through. After some thinking, I write a note to the director of the farm and sign it, "Your neighbor to the south" and weave the note into the netting of the gate.

Early next morning a big truck drives up to my trailer. It is the musk ox director, Mr. Dee McConnel. "If it suits you tomorrow, I will leave the gate unlocked so you can drive in with your car."

Sunday morning dawns with pouring rain, but I have an important appointment. Dressed in rubber boots and rain gear I drive past the unauthorized sign. The combination padlock hangs noticeably to one side. It is just to lift the wire ring holding the gate and step in to the musk oxen. Despite that, the entry gate remains closed for me until McConnell comes to the rescue.

"The ring is too tight to lift," I complain.

"That's why the birch stick hangs here in a wire. You use it for leverage to lift the ring," McConnell explains. He takes a look at the cardboard boxes in my Volkswagen.

"Don't you think you need a little more?"

"I have no idea how much I need. My kitchen garden is only 5x20 feet but I have a farm patch by the log cabin and some flower beds."

"We better take the truck," McConnell says and purposefully backs it to a tall pile with old musk ox manure. We both shovel dung in the rain, McConnell with a large barn shovel and I with the small spade I keep in my car for unforeseen events such as keeping warm when I slide off the road. I get the whole load dumped in front of my trailer. Despite thorough fertilizing half of the pile is still left.

After the manure intermezzo, I plant four tomato plants and three cucumbers in the glory. Despite the musk ox dung, the soil looks poor. I sprinkle Canadian peat in the rows before sowing lettuce, radishes, dill, and parsley.

The first frost warning comes on August 15, before the tomatoes have turned red and while the cucumbers are still in bloom. Perhaps I could protect the plants against the night frost if I cover them with visqueen, the name Alaskans use for plastic sheeting. The nights are still reasonably light but I have to stop the construction of my green house at midnight when I no longer can distinguish a nail head from my finger. The next day I finish covering my creation with visqueen, something I should have done already at the beginning of the summer. Fortunately, the first frost warning was just a threat, at least in my forest, but the vegetables perk up below the plastic.

Last year I bought ten pounds of seed potatoes and got a good harvest. I saved some — or so I thought. When sowing time comes, the weekend around June 1, I open my bag with seed potatoes and count six! Potatoes are cheap to buy but I pine for the new potatoes. They are not sold here in the USA. Guess it isn't economical. Later I inherit leftover seed potatoes from Karl. They are small, dried up and lack sprouts. The variety is called Swedish Butter with two inches long banana shaped yellow potatoes. It can't hurt to throw everything into the ground I think, especially since I have more soil dug up than I need.

Since I don't expect to harvest much today I am very careful. To my surprise I get more than two buckets full. Many of the dried ones have rotted but surprisingly many have sprouted and even produced larger potatoes than I can eat in one meal. Some though, could have grown a bit more.

The spinach is sufficient for two makings of thin pancakes and the beets, well, they barely emerged. The peas are still in bloom in red and purple. Two and a half to three frost-free months are not long enough if you have to start by breaking new ground in a spruce forest.

For my harvest dinner, I boil 85 of my smallest just harvested potatoes. Some are not larger than peas, so I plan to eat them all. I pick lots of dill that reminds me of my native Finland. For the salad I pick five curly leaves of two different kinds of lettuce and mix them with tomatoes, cucumber and dill. I thought I was only going to get one, half-foot-long cucumber but it looks like there will be one more. Most of the tomatoes are still green. Only a half dozen have had the good sense to blush. That's a bad payout on the tomatoes. No wonder they cost a dollar per pound in the store. The radishes are gone a long time ago.

I open a can of Danish mackerel filet in tomato sauce to enhance the enjoyment of the main course, the 85 boiled new potatoes. I bought the can three weeks ago in Whitehorse in the Yukon Territory, 625 miles Southeast of Fairbanks. The drink to accompany these delicacies is also freshly harvested. It is wild chamomile. The pineapple smelling yellow buds of this weed makes a tasty tea.

For dessert I enjoy the last blueberry pie for the season, filled out with some crowberries. I picked the berries last week on top of 2,364-foot high Ester Dome outside Fairbanks. The last pie for the summer is topped with my last bag of vanilla sauce imported from Finland.

A large bouquet of sweet peas on the table, a bouquet of cornflowers, violets, and white sweet peas on a packing crate covered by a tablecloth and a bouquet of nasturtiums on another crate soothes my aesthetic eye and enhances the atmosphere of the harvest dinner. All these flowers finally bloom around my trailer these last days of warmth when snow might fall any day. Last year the snow came in September to stay.

The lettuce perks up under the visqueen after David, my trailer neighbor, lends me a heat lamp I can plug in with the extension cords from my car. Although it is snowing on the visqueen I can still pick flowers below it. On October 6 I harvest my last lettuce and parsley and unplug the heat lamp in my temporary green house.

The next day I change to winter tires on all four wheels. The only thing I cannot manage myself is to get the wheel hub covers back in place but David manages this with a few well-positioned kicks. Again I learn a new mechanic trick. Studded tires are forbidden between May 15 and September 15 because they damage the roads. The timing appears liberal considering all of the USA, but May 15, 1972, my first spring in Fairbanks, I still had an icy driveway.

A week later, October 14, I make my first ski trip under good conditions. This shows how fast the transition is in Fairbanks from harvesting to skiing.

16
Trading by Radio

Radio communication is important in Alaska, the largest state in the Union. The population is spread out and many live beyond the roads-well-traveled or actually without road access to the outside world. Many don't have telephones, newspapers or daily mail delivery. For them the radio becomes an important friend.

When I first arrived in the capital of Juneau in 1969, some of the radio programs surprised me. One was the Problem Corner. Another was the Bulletin Board of the Air. First it might sound like a listing of information. The announcer talks about events of the day and the coming week such as the movie theater showings, sales, change to summer time, advice for the Christmas dinner and how to lose weight after it, and the Police blotter. Those who don't have access to a telephone have written letters that are read. Others call in and talk over the air, if they manage to get through.

A staff member of the radio needs an apartment. Someone wants a recipe for an impressive dish to serve at a surprise dinner.

The librarian calls: "Many customers haven't returned their books. You don't need to feel embarrassed for keeping them so long. You don't even need to come in. Just put your books in the box outside the door."

The harbormaster urges people to have their boats inspected. "No problems will be reported."

Real estate and travel agencies and non-profit groups call regularly. The announcer questions them according to his whims. At times it turns into plain gossip. In between, the program consists of the job market and lost and founds.

The most popular calls concern buying, selling or trading of used items, especially cars.

I came to Alaska with my thick canvas rucksack I had used at numerous Girl Scout camps and ski trips to Lapland. It was wide and shallow to keep the point of gravity low, for balance while skiing. In Alaska people use tall narrow backpacks of nylon with a frame. They are more comfortable and weigh less. I call Problem Corner. A man calls and buys my rucksack.

A woman will move to the Pioneer's Home and no longer needs her kitchen supplies. She sells her hand held electrical mixer to me for a dollar — and I still use it.

The radio comforted me when I was left alone on the Juneau Icefield. After my companions made it down safely, they sent me the song: "You've got a friend," by James Taylor. The radio continued to play this song especially for me for many weeks.

After moving to Fairbanks I listen to different radio stations but the trading and information activity continue.

KIAK sends its "Pipeline of the North," at 6:45 a.m. and p.m. every day. Except for announcements about lost horses, I have heard the following:

"If no one is there to meet you in Fairbanks, do not charter a plane but take the regular scheduled flight."

"You have an appointment with the dentist."

"To Walter at Circle Hot Springs: Your air fare to Fairbanks is paid. I'll meet you at the airport."

Galena: "I'll need beaver meat for a dog race. Call Anchorage. I'll pay."

Minto: "I'll visit new Minto to discuss the organization of a community fishing advisory."

Alaska Range: "The truck works again. I expected you to come to town. I'll send a plane for you at 2 p.m."

Wood River: "The weather report was bad for today. I'll come when the weather improves. Don't worry that the cabin will burn down. The wood stove is safe. "

Colville River (Monday): "I'm planning a C-46 flight on Thursday. I'll need a rear ski. Call when the landing strip is secure. I have 20 empty oil barrels. Greetings, Mom and Dad."

Rampart: "I plan to visit Rampart May 7. If I don't get a letter by Saturday, I'll assume it's OK. Kaarina Abel, health educator in Fairbanks."

The KIAK radio station runs a big advertising campaign sponsored by several local businesses at Easter time in 1974. They have hidden an Easter egg somewhere in the Fairbanks North Star Borough. Many of the businesses are located in College, so I think it would be logical to hide the egg in this area. The radio gives a lead every day as the value of the egg decreases with $100. The radio lists the first leads:

"The egg is plastic but has the same shape and size as a chicken egg."

"The egg is hidden on land accessible to the public, not on private land."

I think about hiding places I could check out. The area around the musk ox farm sounds logical, but I don't do anything. Next lead:

"Don't look further north than Goldstream Road, further east than Steese Hwy, nor further west than Chena Ridge."

This is an area of roughly 50 square miles. When I remember the egg, I am either at work or it is dark. A beautiful sunny Saturday it enters my mind again.

With determination I walk to the viewing platform by the musk ox fence. There are visitors and I feel a bit embarrassed. Well, they have come to look at the musk oxen and not me. Searching, as if I lost something, I climb the platform. If I have come this far for a stupid egg, at least I will be thorough. I crawl under the platform but don't see anything I like to talk about until — I come to the lowest point where I must crawl. Am I dreaming? A yellow egg lies on the inner side of a support pole. I barely believe my eyes. I am looking for a white egg — I think. The egg is heavy. There is something inside. Trembling, I put it in my pocket. Nonchalantly I try to walk home, aware that I might have $800 in my pocket. I hope nobody saw me find it. At home I cut the egg open and find a battery and a note:

"Congratulations, you have found the KIAK Easter egg. Bring it to the station."

Still shaken I drive to the radio station.

"Where did you find the egg? The note appears to be written with our typewriter, but we must check it."

I don't find $800 every day so I plan to buy something luxurious, maybe a fur coat? In Anchorage I find a hair seal parka I like immediately. The hood, hem, and sleeves are trimmed with silver fox. A row of Alaskan animals, in black calfskin, sewn into a strip of white calfskin, run along the hem of the parka. The inside of the zipper is lined with soft beaver. I look at the fur coat with admiration.

"Try it on," the salesman says.

"The sleeves are too short. I would like to have a hood with a wolf ruff with an inner strip of wolverine that doesn't get frosty in the cold."

"I am the furrier. I can do anything you want. I will lengthen the sleeves with a strip of wolf fur. The parka will be ready tomorrow. Can you pay me now?"

"My money is at a bank in Fairbanks."

"That bank has an office in the vicinity. Come, I'll walk you to the bank."

Money paid, the decision is made and I am the proud owner of a warm fur coat.

After a while I start to understand the full impact of the radio on Alaska's isolated population. Cities have their problem corners most people call while radio stations covering outlying areas give their listeners a connection to the outside world. People organize their activities so they can listen to at least one broadcast a day. Everyone knows who gets visitors or needs something. Everyone generally knows everything about everybody.

The radio announcer becomes a well-rounded and knowledgeable person people respect. For many, it has been a path to political influence and elected office.

17

Fur Seals on the Pribilof Islands

Remote areas, the more difficult to get to the better, have a special lure for me. When an opportunity arises for a tour to the Pribilof Islands in the Bering Sea, my explorer's soul cannot resist the temptation.

From Wien Air's, Fairbanks to Anchorage flight I see how the clear waters of the Chena River transit into the glacier-fed milky Tanana River, before the clouds cover the rest of the scenery. Captain Jim Binkley of the stern-wheeler Discovery, used to call the dancing, whirling eddies at the intersection of the two water masses, "the wedding of the rivers."

We land in a hazy Anchorage in July 1974, after a flight of 45 minutes for a ticket price of $46. I must overnight in Anchorage. I check in at the Sourdough section of the Anchorage Westward Hotel where I get a beautiful corner room on the fourth floor with a view over the Cook Inlet for $16.

At 6:30 a.m. I am the first to check in at Reeve Aleutian Airways. I am eager to get a good window seat. The plane is to leave at 7:45 a.m. I am delighted over the sunny morning that promises an exciting view.

"Fog has rolled in over St. Paul. Departure will be postponed for an hour," I hear a disappointing announcement.

My seat does have the best view on the fully booked 56-seat airplane. The plane obviously has old traditions.

The window is so scratched I can only see out at one angle with the rays of the sunbeams reflecting in the scratches. The location of the life preserver is written in French.

The plane ascends smoothly over Cook Inlet. At low tide a wide area of mud transected by streams surrounds the shoreline. I watch carefully, trying to interpret what I saw on satellite pictures last winter. The dark, lengthwise running bands on the pictures must have been caused by the mud, I figure. Cook Inlet has the second largest tide range in North America. The maximum can reach 38.9 feet.

My seat companion is a university lecturer. She is the leader of a group of 30 bird watchers. All have refined photographic equipment and field glasses around their necks. I am alone on a six-day tour and hope my future roommate will be as sensible.

We pass a majestic snow-covered 10,000-foot peak of a volcano. It is Mount Spurr, Redoubt, or Iliamna. They are all close together. The characteristic peak of St. Augustine volcano shows at the horizon. Iliamna, the largest lake in Alaska, is partly covered by low clouds or fog. It looks like ice from above, but I have already seen on our satellite pictures that it is ice-free. This flight shows me how easy it is to misinterpret satellite imagery without access to ground truth.

After passing King Salmon and Dillingham, we fly out over Bristol Bay before reaching the open cloud-covered Bering Sea. What happened to our cloud-free day?

The mystery-enshrouded seal islands emerge after three hours of flying. Sea voyagers in the mid 1700's had seen herds of awesome furred animals swim northward between the islands in the Aleutian Chain. No one knew where they were headed; they just dissolved into the fog of the sta. The Russian explorer, Gerasim Pribylov "discovered" the islands after a three-year search in the fog. Aleuts that had been driven off course by storms and fog while on hunting trips in their kayaks knew about the islands.

The Pribilof Islands represent the same to the million and a quarter of the fur seals as the Sargasso Sea to the eels; a mysterious distant goal where they are annually beckoned to ensure the survival of their kind. The fur seals annually swim 5,000 miles from Southern California. The Pribilof Islands, situated

350 miles west of the continental Alaska and 250 miles north of the Aleutian Chain, consist of two small islands, St. Paul and St. George. The islands were uninhabited until the Russians forced Aleutians to settle there and assist with seal harvesting.

From the misty air, St. Paul looks like a lush lawn with a handful of conical hills left by extinct volcanoes. The airport is a wide road, covered by rusty-red lava gravel with a windsock at the edge. A new white and blue bus, just unloaded from the boat and painted with the sign "Pribilof Tours" drives up to the airplane. The boat, presently anchored off shore, comes three times a year with provisions and cargo. I stand on the field running my Super-8 movie camera until everyone else has boarded the bus. Doing so puts me at the front of the bus as we drive to a gray-green, board-paneled, three-story house with a sign "St. Paul Island Hotel." As one of the first I write my name in the hotel ledger.

"Your name is not on any of our lists," the hotel clerk says to my concern, but continues, before I have time to panic. "You can have room number one." To my delight I get to share it with Kristina. I don't ask any unnecessary questions and quickly disappear up the steep narrow stairs to the second floor. Again, I get a nice corner room on the same floor as the shower equipped ladies' room. This is *the* Hotel, the largest, the best, the only one. Half of the group has to climb to the third floor.

There is not enough room for the last two visitors. They are eventually lodged in the seal hunters' quarters.

After lunch we, fifteen official package tour participants, get the new white-blue bus with the Aleutian driver guide, Andrey. There are at least a dozen fur seal rookeries on the island, but only one of them is open to visitors. On the way we disturb an Arctic blue fox family that withdraws into its den.

It drizzles as we leave the bus and walk down a grassy slope. In the distance we can hear a loud symphony of something in between bleatings and belchings. The sound emanates from a seemingly empty, steep, rocky beach below us. As I study the light brown rocks further, they appear to be transected by dark brown waves. I have to gaze closer to notice that the whole beach is covered by hundreds of fur seals in different shades of brown. What a surprising and impressive sight! Most of the seals rock and wave their dark tail flipper. Soon I discern a certain order in the congregation.

Fur seal beach master guarding his harem
on the Pribilof Island.

A few large dark seals, the beach masters, are spread out at suitable distances from each other. They had arrived in May and staked their territories that they aggressively defend. What counts here is raw force. The males can weigh 600 pounds and are up to five times larger than the females. The giant red-brown fur seal males expose their sharp fangs, surrounded by a long drooping light moustache below the small eyes, when they open their mouth to roar or yawn.

The fertile females, between four and 20 years in age, start to arrive in the end of June, just before they are ready to give birth to their annual pup. They are a lot lighter in color than the males. The females may look for a good home site rather than a handsome groom.

The males have recently started to collect their harems. They no longer dare to leave their spots to feed or drink. They live off their blubber with very little sleep. A few beachmasters by the ocean are surrounded by apparently admiring females, who sit with their short moustache endowed noses in the air looking adoringly and dreamingly submissively up at their master or sheik while gracefully fanning their tail flippers. At times they get a kiss on the nose from their sheik. A few females quarrel with each other. Now and then they voice belching bleats.

It is strange to see a male with a harem of twenty in front of him while his neighbor, fifteen feet away, doesn't have a single one. He has to wait until the stronger male has filled his harem. Some use the occasion to rest. The sheiks sit with their bent front flippers as paws in front of them guarding their females. Sometimes they make a threatening bluff charge towards their neighbor to strengthen their authority. They can move surprisingly fast over the rocks on their powerful tail flipper while using the arm flippers as levers or legs. When they consider one of us too intrusive, they bleat threateningly. At the height of the breeding season, a bull can have a harem of 75-100 cows, but 30-40 is more common.

After a cow has joined a harem, she is jealously guarded by her sheik. If she tries to escape, she is brutally grabbed by her neck skin and returned to the harem. If, however, she has serious intentions to leave, the male cannot prevent her. In this case she is claimed by another male. The performance, with its accompanying background sounds and sensations of smell is fascinating. The atmosphere is erotically loaded as we watch seals mating and giving birth.

Several seal cows already have a small black pup that they suckle. The mother grabs the gleaming black pup with her mouth as soon as it is born, places it in front of her, and licks it clean. When the young have grown a little, they gather in groups while their mothers swim out for 250 miles or so to feed. Returning from the long fishing trip, each mother finds her own pup. If she doesn't return, the pup starves. A cow will not suckle a strange pup.

Some gleaming black young seals play on the rocks by the water's edge. Only strong males, at least seven years old, have a chance to mate. The idle bachelors surround the rookery. They are the ones who lose their coats when furs are harvested. In the beginning of 1900, the fur seals were close to extinction due to indiscriminate slaughter. Thanks to international agreements concerning controlled harvest, the fur seal stock has recovered.

From the seal rookery we drive to the bird nesting grounds, six miles northwest of town. We pass many closed side roads to fur seal rookeries.

The marine biology lab on the island conducts research at some rookeries. Controlled harvest is done at others. We even pass a sign: "Watch out, seal crossing." We see many Arctic blue foxes, some with white tail tips. Often they sit very close to the road until the bus approaches, when they run away.

The treeless, tundra-covered island has precipitous rocky beaches where over 180 species of birds are known to nest in 1974. I find a spot where I can lie on the lupine-decorated, lush blue-green carpet and stretch over the edge to gaze down on a thick-billed murre hatching a turquoise colored pear- shaped egg on a dangerously narrow cliff ledge. Space is limited. The black, white-chested murres sit close together. From my vantage point above, I only see the heads of some of them. The adorable white- chested black puffins look like toys with their yellow bills and large red webbed feet. The sun penetrates the fog to illuminate the red tip of the thick yellow- orange beak. Long-necked large black cormorants, with green-blue metallic gleaming backs, sit closer to the water. Small mottled black parakeet auklets, with short broad red bills and a white plume extending back from the eye, congregate in groups or pairs. White kittiwakes with black-tipped wings, some of them red-legged but most black-legged, fly over the whole slope.

Broken turquoise colored eggshells show that the fox has been around. It is a riddle how the fox can navigate the precipitous slopes. As evidence, a well- fed blue fox, the bandit, lies curled up on a low cliff shelf. To my surprise, the gulls don't disturb its sleep.

Driving back, the fog rolls in over the island. Despite the dense fog, our driver, Andrey, spots the island's reindeer herd. The animals look like unreal, stately horned ghosts, speeding towards the hills. *Did we really see them?* My movie must bear witness of that later in the sober light of the projector.

We return to the hotel with little time to spare before the dinner gong sounds. Our group is becoming accustomed to the family style meals at long tables. No one hesitates to ask his neighbor to pass spices and plates with meatloaf and mashed potatoes. The kitchen girls waste little time to pass out individual, identical bills, $6.18 for dinner or $2.58 for lunch, to be paid at the exit.

During a half an hour vesper in St. Paul's Russian-Orthodox church, a pale yellow-colored, wooden temple from 1906, women stand to the left and men to the right with the youngest in front. Worship consists mainly of singing in English, Aleutian, and Slavic. The ceremonies are numerous. Many candles are burning. The priest swings a big hanging pot with incense towards colorful icons and the congregation, blessing them. The assisting priest guides with an occasional cough. The occasion is solemnly serene.

The sun is still high at 8 p.m. when I go for a walk with the bird observers around the village peninsula. St. Paul, Alaska's largest Aleutian village, with a population of 450 in 1974, stretches up a hillside. The small houses in white and grey are neat, some apparently of an older date. The water supply in three cisterns is on top of the hill, with tanks for heating oil and gasoline further down. The evening sun illuminates the village and its two cemetery squares on the green grassy hill. An arc of light above, almost like a rainbow, adds drama to the scenery. Unfortunately, I didn't bring my camera because it was foggy when we left. I am not accustomed to the rapid changes in the weather.

The ship is still being unloaded. I heard the beer has not yet reached land. A small motorboat tows an old "oomiak" or skin-boat, nowadays covered with impregnated canvas. A man steers it with a long oar from the stern.

Every day we make tours to the breeding grounds of the fur seals and birds. The group leaves on the fourth day and a new group of twelve tourists flies in. I stay for two extra days but don't keep much company with the new group. After watching the seals for 15 minutes they are cold and return to the warm bus. Andrey lends me his big field glasses and leaves me alone with the seals. I notice that six are almost ready to give birth, but nothing happens before it is time for me to hike the two miles back to the hotel. Another day the bus leaves me by myself on the red-brown lava road. I want to climb the island's mountain, 590-foot high Bogoslof Hill.

"If I see you when I return, I'll give you a ride," Andrey promises.

"If not, I am prepared to hike back," I reply.

"If you haven't returned by dinner, I'll come and look for you."

The next day I am well prepared with clothing in my backpack for any change in weather when I am let off the tour bus. I walk to a seal-free sandy beach hoping to find some Japanese glass floats. Instead I see a blue fox running between the rocks at the water's edge. The sun is shining and the sea is as calm as a mirror. Long swells form close to shore and slowly wash up on the sand.

Suddenly fog creeps up towards a red plastic box with the sign "Sapporo" and a large rusty sphere with a handle, maybe a buoy? Soon I don't see where I am going.

The sandy beach becomes rocky. I start to hear strange sounds and see poles with numbers. I realize in horror I have entered a rookery where seals are studied. Knowing how rapidly a beachmaster can move, I don't wait for a confrontation.

I feel excited I had the opportunity to visit the fog enshrouded seal islands at the height of the breeding season. It was perfect for me to start out with a serious group of bird watchers so I could learn and get my bearings. I am glad I stayed two extra days. Having the freedom to explore on my own, to sit silently above a fur seal rookery and to walk along a desolate beach gave me the time to ponder the cycles of life.

18

Encounters on the Way to Work

When conditions are favorable, it takes me half an hour to walk or ski from my trailer, through the forest, to work at the Institute of Marine Science (IMS) or the Geophysical Institute (GI). Depending on research funding, I have moved back and forth between these two institutes, located next to each other on the West Ridge of the University of Alaska.

The West Ridge was used by ancient people as a lookout. From here you can see the whole Tanana valley. The Alaska Range with the 13,000+ foot peaks of Mt. Moffit and Mt. Hayes and 12,000+ Mt. Deborah rise at the horizon, 100 miles to the south. The highest mountain in North America, 20,320-foot high Mount McKinley or Denali, the High One, as the Athabascan Indians call it, lies 150 miles to the southwest. Wintertime, temperature inversions create mirages that make the peak appear very wide as seen from Fairbanks.

When walking home, I start by going downhill towards Smith Lake. Sometimes I jog this far. In the spring I often sneak to the lake to watch the returning ducks. To refresh my duck memory, I regularly go on guided bird walks in the spring. Brina Kessel, ornithology professor at the University museum, always brings a powerful scope for the walks. On these outings I have seen: mallard, Northern pintail and shoveler, blue-winged teal, American wigeon, canvasback, ring-necked duck, greater and lesser scaup and bufflehead on the Smith Lake.

In the spring, part of the trail is covered by water, depending on what route I choose. This is a problem, but rubber boots and ski poles for balance helps. In the morning the ice is strong enough — in most places. On my way home I step through, but never above the top of my boots.

The ski track I put in myself as a shortcut, becomes invisible when snow melts and greenery takes over. I mark the trail with red surveyor flagging after getting lost a few times. I don't overdo the flagging and get lost again when I mistake a wild rose for a pink band.

Summertime I often walk for the exercise. Wintertime I ski. I have no other choice because of car problems. The University owns the forest south of my trailer. It is mainly spruce, interspersed with birch, alder, aspen, willow, and an occasional tamarack. Since way back, it is crisscrossed by ski trails established by the Norwegian professor Skarland. Large fenced-in areas support studies of veterinary medicine and forestry. One forest experiment tries to grow lodge pole pines.

Pink wild roses, lungwort bluebells, dogwood, fireweed, Labrador tea, raspberries, blueberries, and lingonberries grow along the trails. I have seen cloudberry and nagoonberry blossoms but never berries. In the fall there are shaggy manes. Once I found a meadow mushroom so large it served me for more than one meal.

My route to the University is interesting besides giving me refreshing exercise. I never know whom or what I can meet or see on the way. Wintertime it can be an Olympic skier. A famous scientist can cross my path any time.

Dr. Hannes Alfvén, Swedish Nobel prizewinner in physics 1970, gives a seminar at the GI, on the origins of the solar system. The next morning I walk to work through the forest. As I approach the Institute, I see an elderly gentleman on the trail. I greet him in Swedish:

"Good morning, Professor Alfvén. I appreciated your talk about the solar system and learned a lot."

He looks at me with utmost surprise. One day the GI intercom announces:

"Watch out when you go into the back parking lot. A black bear has been seen there."

I give the bear plenty of time to leave before I walk home that evening. To calm myself I assume it has left. I am probably right. I don't see it.

In winter when days are short, I provide my own lighting with a flashlight-operated headlamp for the dark route home. The cord from the light to the battery is long enough to keep the battery in a warm pocket, which is a necessity to keep it working. My double leather ski boots covered by large Army surplus felt liners fit into the cable bindings of my metal edged mountain skis. They feel heavy as lead compared to my fiberglass skis. When it is cold my clothing is so heavy and the skis glide so poorly it takes me an hour to ski home.

One day after work in January 1974 it is completely cloud free. I can still see the ski tracks in front of me at 5:30 p.m. but not too far ahead. The reflecting white snow and the establishment of energy saving summer time by President Nixon make it light enough to see without a flashlight. On a long straight stretch through the forest I suddenly see a red star fall from the sky in the north. Someone must be shooting fireworks, I think. It appears so close I am concerned about getting hit in the head. A few minutes later I see a thin hazy bluish cloud. Surprisingly early for Northern Lights! While I am gazing at the cloud, it thins and the moon appears through it. What a moon! It is so high up I must bend my neck. The "moon" is dark red as a giant blood orange that swells as I look at it. Suddenly it turns into a greenish yellow smoke ring, that expands while it appears to sink and fills out into a large greenish yellow disk. Suddenly the disk is gone. Only the hazy bluish cloud remains.

I blink several times and shake myself. I don't quite know what to believe. Am I hallucinating? We are between two full moons. It is impossible to see the moon now. While I am still gazing at what I think to be Northern Lights, the show repeats. It has to be real! This time, both the red moon and the green yellow smoke ring appear to descend. After a third performance I am scared that *It* might land.

My chin is cold from gazing up. It is 30 below. I can barely discern the ski tracks. I didn't bring my head light. While resuming skiing, treetops cover the cloud from my view. When I see it next time, it has dissolved into four small puffy clouds forming a bluish auroral curtain next to the Big Dipper with a bright yellowish cloud below. I ski as fast as I can in the dark with one eye towards the sky but the performance seems to be over. Despite the glorious colors the whole thing feels uncomfortably ghastly. What have I seen? Is *It* still outside? My ears are on high alert. The radio says nothing.

The next morning at work I learn that the GI, that operates the only university owned rocket range in the world, launched a four-stage barium rocket last night. Most people only saw three explosions. The red star I saw was the second stage of the rocket. Very interesting to learn after the fact. Had I known it before, I could have enjoyed the show without anguish and had a peaceful sleep.

When I can, I try to leave from work while I can still see the trail. One day at dusk I suddenly see an animal by the trail in front of me. It looks like a dog from a distance, but lose dogs are not allowed in this area. The animal sits down and waits as I approach on skis. It doesn't let me get too close. As it gets up I can see its large bushy white-tipped tail. I seldom see foxes. The fox stays well ahead of me turning its head now and then to look at me.

One winter day a young lynx sits outside the glass doors on the second floor terrace. It doesn't appear bothered by several of us watching it from the inside of the glass. While waiting for someone from Arctic Biology to arrive, some camera fans sneak out another door. The lynx doesn't wait for the biologist. Leisurely it gets up and almost floats across the terrace on its unusually long legs. It walks down the stairs and disappears into the forest behind the GI.

The route to the NOAA CDA (Command and Data Acquisition) satellite station at Gilmore, where I work every third week, provides different experiences. Our original one-year pilot project is extended by another year after we show enough inventiveness in the use of the satellite pictures. I make a gigantic poster board with pictures from all the projects we study. In addition, I post strange pictures we cannot explain. One I call the Octopus cloud. It shows smoke like clouds emanating from a central spot south of the Aleutians.

Often we have visitors and I am asked to take them to Gilmore. The project managers, Drs. Gerd Wendler, or K.O.L.F. Jayaweera come along as hosts when the guests are especially important. We use a large official car and I am the driver and guide. Visitors from government agencies in Washington D.C. arrive in thin coats and shoes, unaware that we might have snow early in the fall. I lend them my special Army surplus parka, with all the acid holes patched up. It is big enough to fit most anybody. My favorite route is Goldstream Road where we seldom see any other traffic along the 10-mile stretch of the road before reaching Steese Highway. Our guests from the capital seem concerned despite the beautiful snowy scenery.

"We haven't seen a single gas station!"

"Don't worry, I have filled the tank at the University."

Dr. Preben Gudmandsen and Lars Thrane from the Technical University of Denmark arrive in the end of November 1974. They plan to erect a satellite antenna in Greenland. Dr. Gudmandsen is excited about going to Gilmore and tells everybody:

"Kolf and Kristina are taking us on an expedition."

At Gilmore, Gudmandsen insists that I explain the satellite pictures in Swedish although there is nothing wrong with the Danes' command of English.

"But, I don't know any of the technical terms in Swedish."

"It's OK, we still want you to speak Swedish."

Driving home along Goldstream Road, I sometimes stop and pick raspberries.

In July 1975 there is road construction to prepare the road for paving. The road crew leaves a gravel ridge in the middle of the road.

As I drive to Gilmore this morning, my lane is well spread out. The opposite lane, however, is very narrow. As I round a curve, I suddenly see a car coming towards me in my lane. Fortunately, I have time to slow down and stop at the edge of the road. There is enough room for the other car to pass me. Instead, it tries to get back to its side of the road across the gravel ridge. The wheels get caught in the gravel. The car rolls once and changes direction 180 degrees in a cloud of dust and airmail, before stopping on the opposite edge of the road. Everything appears to happen in slow motion in front of me. The driver is still in the car. Scared that the car might explode, as normally happens in the movies, I run to the rescue and help the driver out of the car. She is bleeding from a head wound.

"I have a first-aid kit. I can bandage your wound," I offer, relieved that her injuries are no worse.

"I am OK. Just tell my husband I rolled the car. He works at the Post Office. There is a CB-radio in the car," she says.

The woman wanders around screaming. Mail is spread out all over. I try to use the CB-radio but don't have a clue about wavelengths and protocol. I press the microphone and urgently start calling:

"Can anyone hear me? Can anyone hear me? There has been a car accident on Goldstream Road between Ballaine Road and Steese Hwy. A woman is hurt. Send an ambulance."

No one answers. I turn the channels and try again and again. In between, I get the woman to calm down and relax on the ground so I can bandage her head.

"I want my husband," she insists with urgency.

I cannot get any help from her with the radio and try it again.

After many repeated calls for help I get a reply and ask for an ambulance.

The woman is fiercely waving her arms and tries to tear off the bandage. We sit down on the gravel by the edge of the road. I get her to rest her head in my lap while I am trying to comfort her with calming words, keep the bandage in place and chase off the mosquitoes. Suddenly she trembles, stiffens, and her face turns gray. Urgently I send off a prayer:

"Dear good God, don't let her die now but make her well again and help the ambulance find us soon."

My prayer is heard. Her shock reaction subsides and color returns to her face.

"Thank you, dear God!"

A police car arrives after half an hour.

"The ambulance is on its way," one policeman tells me. "Can the woman walk?"

I lead her to the police car, but she starts to fight the police.

"Can you come along and hold her?" the policeman asks me.

We meet the ambulance on Steese Hwy and transfer the woman.

The policeman drives me back to the scene of the accident where the second policeman collects mail along the edge of the road assisted by a passer-by.

"Maybe it was unnecessary that I ordered an ambulance?" I wonder.

"That woman was in worse shape than you can imagine," the policeman tells me. "Do you happen to have your driver's license?"

"Yes, I have it. This is the first time the police has asked to see it."

An hour and a half late I arrive at Gilmore with blood on my sweater sleeve. I feel shaken by this experience for most of the day and find it hard to concentrate on work. This is the first accident I have been involved with. Fortunately everything works out well. I call the hospital the next day. The woman is no longer there.

19

On Thunder and Ice Patrol

Slicing through thunderclouds on a Lear-jet, and flying with NASA over the Arctic Ocean, these are fieldtrips that satisfy my appetite for adventure and new experiences. I am working on a satellite picture contract at the University of Alaska with a team of seven scientists. Three of us are technical experts who assist Robin Muench in Oceanography, K.O.L.F Jayaweera in Cloud-Physics, and Bob Carlson in Hydrology; a research team under the leadership of Gerd Wendler in Meteorology. We are an international group represented by USA, Finland, Germany, Sri Lanka, and Australia. Bob Muench is my direct supervisor, but I also work on projects with Gerd and K.O.L.F. This first year pilot project is a big and exciting experiment. We let our imaginations run wild. The goal is to find uses and users for a new American satellite launched by the National Oceanic and Atmospheric Administration (NOAA), the NOAA- VHRR (Very High Resolution Radiometer) satellite.

Gerd Wendler, the chief scientist of the satellite project, wants to know how much sea ice there is in the Arctic Ocean and in which direction the leads, that are cracks of open water, are running.

"Can we see different types of ice, leads and open water?" Gerd wonders. "How often is it cloud free? The US Air force has its own satellite but in 1973 we are not permitted to mention that they have aerial pictures.

155

They call them DAPP-data. You can start by analyzing their data," Gerd tells me.

Most of the pictures are cloudy. First I don't have a clue to what I am looking at. It is very discouraging.

The NOAA CDA station at Gilmore Creek starts to routinely process pictures in February 1974. Studying the pictures taken from an altitude of 900 miles, I feel like a star looking down on the Northern Hemisphere. The station tracks satellites through a large dish antenna and records the data on magnetic tape.

Using a map I got from Scandinavian Airline's polar flight in January 1974, I gradually learn to recognize the individual Canadian and Siberian islands in the Arctic Ocean. The map is conveniently in almost the same scale as the satellite pictures, 1:9 million. With the map I locate the 1375 x 4125 mile satellite passes over the Arctic Ocean. One orbit over Alaska can go from Northern Greenland past the Aleutians. From Gilmore I get the coordinates for each orbit. To know which landmarks to look for, I make an orbit map in the same scale as the imagery, showing how each pass transects the Northern hemisphere.

Next I subdivide a quarter of the Arctic Ocean, from Northern Greenland to the West-Siberian Islands, into small areas that I can distinguish, and end up with 46 different ones. I analyze each separately. I feel like a real estate multi-millionaire with the map of the Arctic Ocean in front of me.

We can only use the IR images in the winter when it is continuously dark in the Arctic. Don Sundgren, the engineer at Gilmore, develops a computer formula to enhance the IR imagery to make selected features stand out. Eventually we can even read surface temperatures.

"How can we recognize threatening thunderstorm clouds?" K.O.L.F, the cloud physicist wonders.

Most forest fires in Alaska are started by lightning. The Bureau of Land Management (BLM) only fights fires that threaten communities and houses. Other fires are left to burn. The new growth after a fire provides good moose forage and morel fertilizer. BLM flies daily surveys to look for fires and check out areas with menacing thunderclouds that might cause forest fires.

The NOAA-VHRR satellite scans simultaneously in two wavelength bands, the visible (VIS), and the infrared (IR). The towering cumulus clouds are compact and easy to detect by their form and high reflectance, showing them very white on the VIS satellite imagery. Their tops are much colder than anything else the satellite sees, since they can reach altitudes up to 33,000 feet. The lower the temperature, the whiter it shows on the imagery. By photographically double-exposing the VIS and IR images, the whitest spots show the locations of the cumulonimbus clouds that often rapidly develop into thunderhead clouds.

Ken Meyer, the photographer at Gilmore, develops the afternoon pass of the satellite as soon as the technicians in the control room have transferred the satellite signals from the magnetic tape to a film cassette. The double-exposed picture is still wet when Ken hands it to me. Time is crucial. I highlight the bright spots with circles, locate their geographical coordinates, and fax the results to BLM so they will get it before their reconnaissance flight.

"If our satellite interpretations are accurate, BLM could save a lot of money by using satellite imagery instead of flying," K.O.L.F says.

One afternoon on July 17, 1974 I get to fly on a thunder patrol. Well perfumed with mosquito-dope, I walk to work this morning through the cool spruce forest. The day could get hot. In the interior of Alaska this means something around 85° F. Cumulus clouds form when moist warm air rises and cools. In the afternoon they can build up to cumulonimbus clouds with thunder and lightning.

The guard at Fort Wainwright army base checks our identifications and lets K.O.L.F and me drive in. A seven-passenger Lear-jet waits on the tarmac. It looks like a private plane for an oil sheik or maybe James Bond.

It is still sunny and warm when we take off at 2 p.m. Very soon we reach our cruising altitude of 41,000 feet. At 555 miles per hour, we fly faster than the big passenger jets to Anchorage. We are interested in observing the cloud development over the forests between the Brooks Range in the north and the Alaska Range in the south. First we head northwest across the Tanana, Yukon, and Koyukuk rivers.

Eagerly I survey the terrain through the window until I see them — the Great Kobuk Sand Dunes, a 25 square mile area of bright sparkling desert sand. I feel proud and content to actually see the enigmatic reason for the hot spots scientists at NOAA's headquarter in Washington D.C. had marveled over. The boss there contacted K.O.L.F. He delegated the problem to me.

"Kristina, can you figure out why there are hot spots in Alaska on some night passes." At that time we didn't know there are vast sand dunes in Alaska, but I "discovered" them when I compared the satellite images to topographic maps. The hot spots show on the IR images at night because the barren sand dunes can retain the heat of a hot day better than the surroundings.

While gazing down at Kotzebue the pilot tips the wing down giving me a better view, or so I think, but he makes an abrupt turn, almost pivoting the plane on the tip of the wing. Around Fort Yukon we see large dark shadows from clouds on the ground. The pilot's voice comes through the headphones with a slight tone of amusement:

"The Gilmore guys think they see towering cumulus clouds over Fort Yukon." His tone changes to amazement in an instance. "They are right!"

Gilmore also sees threatening clouds along the Canadian border. We fly there to check them out. Suddenly we have dark thunderstorm clouds in front of us. To my concern, we fly directly towards them. I tighten my seat belt anticipating turbulence but to my surprise we glide smoothly through the clouds.

Physically unshaken, we land at Fort Wainwright just in time to see soldiers lower the American flag and ceremoniously fold it into a small blue triangle. We all have greater confidence in our satellite images after this 1,500-mile patrol without thunder.

In the December 1974 issue of the *Journal of Forestry*, we publish our results in an article titled: "Detection of Thunderstorms from Satellite Imagery for Forest Fire Control" by Jayaweera and Ahlnäs.

Gerd Wendler travels to Germany for an extended stay. In March 1975 he sends a message.

"I have submitted an abstract about our sea ice research in the Arctic Ocean to the upcoming POAC (Port and Ocean Engineering under Arctic Conditions) conference in Fairbanks this summer. You are the first author, Kristina. You do the work and give the presentation. I will help." I am shocked and feel very inadequate. Gerd wants to push me to my limit and he is too far away to complain to.

Here I sit studying sea ice at my desk without much more practical experience than having skied and skated on it in Finland. Real sea ice researchers are on the ice at this moment, in one of many AIDJEX (Arctic Ice Dynamics Joint Experiment) camps on the sea ice in the Beaufort Sea. NASA sometimes flies reconnaissance over the camps. Steve Marvil, our new technical expert in meteorology, after Neil Streten returned to Australia, tells me that NASA will make a flight from Eielson Air Force Base in Fairbanks.

"I convinced them they need my help with the meteorological observations," Steve says.

I cannot think of any good reason why they would need me, but I call Dr. Bill Campbell, the sea ice expert in charge, who stays at Eielson between flights.

"I have gazed at satellite pictures with sea ice for over a year without having seen much sea ice with my own eyes. If there is room on the plane, my analysis of the imagery would improve if I could see what the ice really looks like from the air," I say with hopeful anticipation.

NASA's Convair 990, the Galileo II, rolls out of the hangar as Steve and I arrive at Eielson early in the morning of April 21, 1975. Imagine, I will fly with NASA! I feel proud and almost as important as an astronaut.

"A real girl!" I hear a comment as I board. I take it as a compliment and smile. The plane is filled with instruments. I get a window seat with an information monitor on the backrest of the seat in front of me.

Headphones let me follow the conversation between the flight deck and the instrument operators. We head north across Alaska's frozen, meandering rivers, the mountains of the Brooks Range and the grid of small frozen tundra lakes on the North slope, before we fly out over the pack ice of the Beaufort Sea.

The sun reflecting off a dark lead indicates that it is covered with thin ice. When the ice is thin, it is impossible to tell from satellite imagery if a lead is open or frozen. In the cold Arctic air, a lead immediately starts to freeze after opening. Freezing starts from the leeward side to where the wind has blown the ice slush. That's why some leads are striped in different shades of gray. Normally we don't see details like these on the imagery unless the leads are many miles wide. The resolution of the satellite is 0.6 miles.

In my headphones I hear something that sounds like an invitation.

"We will soon descend to an altitude of 300 feet. If somebody is interested in photographing through the periscope, please go ahead."

"Thank you, I am interested," I reply.

Nobody answers. Everybody is busy with his own observations. Nobody pays any attention to me as I get up. Looking around I find a spiral staircase to the "bilges" of the aircraft, where I assume the periscope must be. I don't see anything I would consider a periscope but there is a camera mounted through the floor. A crack around the mounting lets me look down. Am I in the right place? No one else has followed me. I lie down on my belly and stick my movie camera through the crack while the plane takes a nose dive towards the sea ice. Should I really be here, I wonder with a sense of guilt, but this is exciting. The lower we get the faster the ice flickers by. Pressure ridges, that didn't show earlier, appear whiter than the surroundings. The leads get wider. Some edges seem to have shadows, or maybe it is slush? Suddenly red boxes fly by. It must be one of the AIDJEX camps. Soon another follows.

At the end of the workday we return to Eielson Air Force base. I am overwhelmed by all impressions and experiences. I have gained a lot of new knowledge in how to interpret sea ice imagery. Three days later NASA repeats the mission. I get to fly again, which is really helpful, so I can sort out my impressions and observations.

At the third international POAC conference in Fairbanks I give my talk on "Sea Ice Conditions in the Chukchi, Beaufort, East Siberian and Northern Bering Seas During March 1973, 1974 and 1975 as seen from the NOAA-2, 3, and 4 satellites." I feel pleased that a scientist from the time I was a mess girl on the Finnish research ship attends my presentation. Dr.

Erkki Palosuo, director of the sea- ice department at the Institute of Marine Research in Finland is one of the invited speakers to the conference.

Gerd assured me I could do it and I did deliver my first talk at an international conference! My sea ice reconnaissance flights with NASA gave me a lot of confidence. This paper was published in the POAC 1975 proceedings. A formalized version by K. Ahlnäs and G. Wendler titled "Arctic Sea-Ice Conditions in Early Spring Viewed by Satellite" was published in *Arctic and Alpine Research* in 1977.

20

Power Outage

Grrrrr... grrrrr... Power outage again. I have lost track of how many times it has happened today. Everything started yesterday night, Saturday January 4, 1975 around 9 p.m.

It is 50 below outside, maybe colder? My thermometer bought in Gothenburg, Sweden has bottomed out. It is -54°F in Fairbanks where it normally is warmer than at my place. I am hungry. I haven't had dinner yet. I plan to cook a gourmet dinner to celebrate New Year, since it wasn't convenient at the time in question. This morning I took in a bag of salmon, frozen in water to preserve its flavor and prevent it from drying out. I bought the salmon last fall from an Indian with a fish wheel in the Tanana River. He charged me $3 a fish. The salmon hasn't thawed yet although it has had all day to do so.

I hear the neighbors laugh on the other side of the wall in the duplex trailer. They have company, all new arrivals connected with the building of the oil pipeline. I sigh with resignation. My plans for a gourmet dinner just froze up. Isn't it enough that the neighbor already cracked the water pipes leaving me without water since yesterday? He probably tried to fix the pipes when he exhausted the electricity, I think with annoyance. I light a candle, dig out my backpacking stove and settle for a simpler dinner. I close the door to the bedroom that keeps heat like a sieve. The double windows there are covered with thick ice on all sides. The spare door is rimmed with ice and the brass doorknob is well encased in ice.

The nail heads in the floor trim are ice covered, as are all the corners. I hear the neighbors do something outside. Frustrated I confront them assuming they caused the outage.

"What happened?" I ask.

"Power outage," the man replies.

"What did you do?" I ask.

"We didn't do anything," the wife replies with resentment. "We were just sitting around talking when everything went black. The fuses are OK."

"My fuses are also intact. It must be a problem with the power grid. Who knows when it will be repaired? They might have some difficulties at 60 below," I say with resignation.

From the road I can only see stars. The Musk Ox Farm is in darkness. No lights are visible from the neighbor in the log cabin. The whole area must be without electricity. This is serious since my oil heater is controlled by electricity. To my surprise — and relief, the power outage is fixed in 20 minutes. In this short time the room temperature has decreased by 10 degrees. After a quick meal it is time to crawl under my Norwegian down comforter.

In the morning I lie around in bed until 10 a.m. in honor of Sunday. It feels unusually cold when I finally get up. I have turned down the thermostat to 60°F as usual and slept with the door open between the bedroom and the living room so it should be warmer. The thermometer in the bedroom shows 35°F while the living room is 46°F. The Christmas crocus looks frozen. The power is out again! I light a candle and cook my morning coffee on my French camping stove. The frozen water pipes are no longer disturbed by a little power outage. I have attached candleholders to both sides of the bathroom mirror a long time ago for both necessity and pleasure. The sewer pipes still work so I can flush, if I manage to melt enough snow. There is still joy in my existence.

The temperature has been around sixty below for four days. On Friday morning it takes me almost half an hour before I manage to back my little Volkswagen Beetle out on the road. When I check the oil, it has gasoline to the edge of the dipstick. It has never been this bad before, nor has it been this cold. With this amount of gas in the oil, the motor might either explode or catch fire. Neither alternative is attractive, but I have to get to work. The car is so frozen that the gears won't stay in place. It shakes with agony when it gets under way on square frozen tires. The tires gradually resume their normal rounded shape and the ride gets smooth. Going home at night the performance is repeated. I must change the oil tonight!

Late in the evening, I drive back to work to change the oil. To my relief the garage at the Geophysical Institute is empty. Wise from experience, I always keep some cans of oil in my desk drawer to keep them warm. As I lie with my head under the car at midnight, as so many times before, I am suddenly surprised to see some pant legs. Expecting an offer of help, I look out and see a strange young man in a blue down parka.

"Excuse me," he says, "but I have to give you a parking ticket."

"What?" I exclaim with unbelief. "You are a Policeman, but still!"

"University regulations forbid private vehicles inside the walls of the university," he recites the law.

"Yes, but the Geophysical is an exception," I say with confidence.

"I am not aware of that," he replies. "I have to answer to my superior and must ticket you."

"Are you new?" I ask. "Other Policemen have accepted the fact that I work here."

"No, I am not new. You can always contest it," he says.

What an uncooperative Policeman. The garage of the Geophysical Institute is always filled with private vehicles after 5 p.m. that's why I am here at midnight. I return to my task ignoring the Policeman, who doesn't bother me any longer. When I re-emerge from below the car, he is gone, but not without a trace. A parking ticket is attached to my windshield.

When the oil is changed, I discover one of the front tires is flat. No problem here, I think, but unfortunately I don't have enough muscle power to turn on the pressurized air. I have to pump the tire by hand as usual. Tired and depressed, I finally get under way. The car is warm and cozy. The wheel, clutch, and gearshift move fluidly. Despite that, the motor starts to cough and grab when I get out on the road. Still, I have poured a can of "Heet" gasoline deicer in the gas tank to prevent the lines from freezing. The temperature shock from indoors to outside is around 100 degrees.

The weekend doesn't provide much opportunity to rest. Frequent power outages and temperature fluctuations keep me busy dressing and undressing. It is no idea to sit inside readjusting my clothing. Should I go for a walk, ski or do something useful is the question. As mentioned, it is 60 below outside. It is a good temperature to test my winter clothing. I dress in the Navy surplus padded flight pants and insulated white Bunny Boots, down parka with a wolf ruff, water free Vitalis cream from Finland on my face and a wool scarf covering my mouth and nose. The musk oxen lie motionless in the snow inside the fence on the other side of the road. They barely blink when I approach, pull the camera from inside my layers of clothing, and snap a picture.

While walking a mile I try to analyze how I feel. My toes are warm. I have three pairs of socks inside the thermos-insulated bunnies. You cannot be too picky about size at the Army surplus store. Most soldiers are bigger than me. My hands are also warm. They are imbedded in the long Army surplus padded leather mittens with a fleece pad on the outside to warm your nose in. The mittens are somewhat ungainly. For safety they are joined by a long cord I have around my neck not to lose them when I take them off. I have two wool mittens as liners on one hand. One is of Norwegian, the other of Icelandic wool. On the other hand, I only have one Icelandic mitt-liner. Both hands are warm, but it is easier with one liner when I occasionally pull my hands out to take a picture or to blow my nose. I don't have a cold but my nose always starts to run when it is cold. Blowing it doesn't help much. My handkerchief is a piece of ice after the first blow, if I use civilized methods. I soon resort to a direct snort. I wear heavy wool slacks and wool long johns under the padded flight pants. This combination keeps my legs warm. My arms and upper body are a little cold although I have a wool sweater under the Canadian down parka. The Army surplus padded parka, my so-called "spring coat," might have been warmer. My sealskin coat with a wolf ruff would be warm, of course, but might lead to other problems — would I be considered an animal of prey?

I admire the birches and alders, gracefully bent by the weight of the snow, and the snow loaded spruce along the road. From the top of Miller Hill I can see a hazy pale red sun hanging between the treetops as an abstract Japanese watercolor painting. The snow is deep on both sides of the plowed road. It has snowed a little since the road was last plowed. My large Bunny boots leave their tracks along the edge of the road, but they are not the first. Large paws have walked ahead of me. The paw marks lie neatly in a row. Sometimes two paws have almost stepped in the same print. I see marks as drawn by a large fork with two pins an inch apart. For comparison I step into one print and notice they are as wide as my boot. I hope the prints are made by a big dog. My boots are four and a half inches wide! Would I really like to meet this dog or would it be better to meet a wolf? I wonder. The wolf would be shy at least and have a certain respect for humans. A pack of wolves is around. They have eaten some thirty tied-up dogs. The *Fairbanks Daily New-Miner* has warned parents from letting their small, especially fur-clothed children walk alone in the dark. If I walk to work it will be dark both in the morning and when I return. The walk would probably take me an hour in either direction. I don't think I would feel too well at ease in my warm fur coat with a pack of wolves in the neighborhood.

After returning from my walk, convinced that I can walk to work if I choose to, I intend to investigate the ski alternative. Ski boots don't keep my toes warm. I must use my insulated Bunny boots. With great difficulty I get them to fit the cable bindings on my mountain skis. The electricity goes out again, this time well timed, when I leave the house. The cables are slightly too short. It is an effort to squeeze the boots into them. The gigantic Army mittens and the neighbor's two puppies add to the challenge and make me warm despite sixty below. The skis are heavy as gold bars. The soles don't want to bend in the tight cables. I am ready to abandon the experiment but want to give it an honest chance first. I advance along my private snowed-in track, with the whimpering puppies on my heels, until I come to the University's six-mile trail. My thumbs are freezing from holding on to the ski poles. The effort makes me exhausted. When I stop, the puppies sit down on my skis whimpering and shivering from the cold. Since they refuse to turn around, I better do it. If I am going to ski, I must figure out a better way. I might try felt socks over my ski boots and lighter skis another time. The idea to ski with a headlight doesn't intrigue me either.

I would rather meet a wolf on the road where some car occasionally drives by than alone in the forest where my chances to see another human are slim. Besides, I have experienced that it is a lot easier to walk than to ski in severe cold.

Consequently, I have solved my transportation problem for the moment, in a way that takes the least effort. I have chosen to walk. Besides, I have passed the time while electricity periodically has been on and off. Candlelight and a Coleman lantern have lighted my existence during the off times indoors.

My salmon filet has thawed. Since a few hours, it is marinating in lemon juice, white wine, and herbs. I will steam it in wine and celebrate the return of electricity. If electricity doesn't cooperate long enough, my backpacking stove is prepared. Anyway, I will celebrate the delayed New Year and momentarily forget that I must start for work exceptionally early the next morning with an hour's walk ahead of me at maybe sixty below.

If I was a school kid I could stay home. The radio just announced that the schools are officially closed tomorrow. It is too difficult to keep the school busses running and to see something in the ice fog. If it is below -35°F, parents can decide if they want to send their children to school.

Why do I have to go to work then? I have important things to accomplish despite my seemingly primitive living conditions. First, my boss, Robin Muench, is going to Seattle to discuss future research in the Bering Sea and the Arctic Ocean. I am presently analyzing the ice conditions in the Bering Sea with the help of satellite imagery.

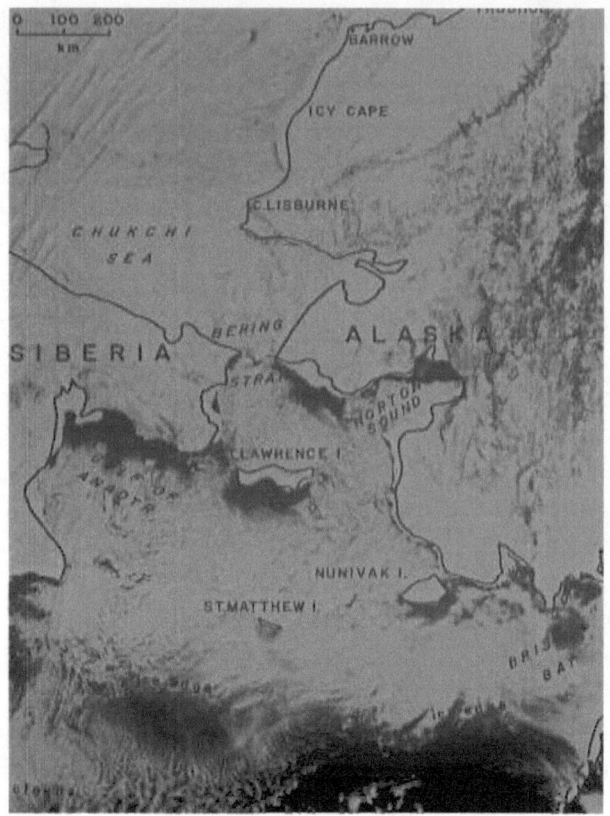

Maximum sea ice extent in Bering Sea April 30, 1975.
NOAA-4 satellite image.

"I like you to finish the work as soon as possible so we can publish the results," my boss says. "If we can refer to research we have already done, before anyone else does, our chances for support are good." In 1976 we publish: "Ice Movement and Distribution in the Bering Sea from March to June 1974" by R.D. Muench and K. Ahlnäs in the *Journal of Geophysical Research.*

I discover an error in the computer program for the newest satellite. The remotely sensed surface temperatures don't agree with those produced by the previous satellite. It is my task to figure out what is wrong.

Kristina Ahlnäs

A visiting Norwegian scientist, Kjell Henriksen, is interested in the possibilities of the NOAA-satellites to register northern lights. I am to help him. Consequently, I am needed at work. Besides, I consider my responsibilities interesting and challenging.

My salmon filet gets cooked on the stove. Long live electricity! In sheer delight, I continue to melt a pan of snow but that was over ambitious. I enjoy my salmon with melted butter and wine-cooked homegrown potatoes (cooked in the frying pan together with the fish, of course) in the romantic light of a candle. Washing dishes must wait. I can neither melt snow nor heat water. I try to make minor repairs on my down parka in the light of a lantern while the battery-powered transistor radio entertains me. I hear the worst at 10 p.m. A variety of areas including my road are listed.

"If electricity hasn't been restored to these areas, they must wait until morning. The temperature will likely drop to sixty below."

I quickly collect the most essentials from the bedroom: down sleeping bag, pillows, and alarm clock and close the door. I settle on the couch in the living room. I have previously tested the sleeping bag outside at thirty below so I am not worried. Before blowing out the lantern I check the temperature: 46°F. I hear the neighbors drive away although they have a fireplace.

In the morning it is 18°F in the room. It is 7°F in the closed bedroom I had the sense not to use. It is cold outside the protective cover of the sleeping bag. I light all candles and lanterns but don't manage with the backpacking stove. I should have taken it into the sleeping bag with me! The butane gas is so cold it won't light. I warm the gas container with my hands, after heating them over a candle, until I get my morning coffee. Despite all flames it just seems to get colder indoors. It is -54°F outside. The car has been unplugged all night so it is useless to even think about starting it.

171

I have never walked to work along the road but the shortcut through the forest isn't accessible by foot in the winter. If I walk along the road there is a good chance that some car stops and offers me a ride even if I don't try to hitch hike. In the morning, this would be a clear advantage, but in the dense evening darkness, it might be a danger to be seen walking in an expensive fur coat. The oil pipeline construction has attracted a lot of less desirable types to the area. A driver wouldn't know I found the money for the fur coat. Maybe it wouldn't make a difference. I better wear my bulky Army surplus parka and project an image of strength to any prospective predators.

With my headlight tied to a belt and the flashlight batteries in the warm padded pocket, I step outside. I feel slightly dizzy for the first steps. Three cars from Golden Valley Electric stand on the road. A cable has broken. They are trying to do something.

Gradually I get accustomed to the cold air, especially after reaching the top of the hill. My fingers in the large mittens start to ache while thawing. They got frozen already inside the house warming the camping stove.

It isn't as dark as I thought outside. I can turn off my flashlight. Miller Hill luckily slopes downhill towards the south for three quarters of a mile. It is easy to walk downhill despite my heavy clothing. I feel light and free in the dawning morning. The grey- lilac colored sky starts to turn red-orange. For now, the colors are very faint, in hues of pastel, frozen like everything else. The snow-laden spruce trees in the foreground frame the color symphony of the early morning. In places someone has crossed the road: a moose, a fox and there they emerge again from the forest, the giant steps by rounded paws with long scrapes of the claws. I wonder if it is a wolf?

The air gets cooler as I descend the hill. Here it can be -64°F or ten degrees colder than at my place that is higher up. I can feel it in my eyes, the only part of me that isn't covered up. The parka hood with the fur ruff turned in forms a tunnel around my face. The first car passes me on Sheep Creek road after I have walked for half an hour. Traffic increases slightly after two miles as I encounter the road going to Anchorage. I am the only pedestrian. I don't try to hitch a ride and nobody makes an attempt to pick me up in my large Army parka.

The Geophysical Institute on the West Ridge rises seven floors and can be seen from far away. Only a few windows are lit up although it is 9 a.m. Everybody doesn't live within an hour's walk as I. What a joy and luxury to work in a building that stays warm and light all day.

21

Side Effects of the Oil Rush

Oil leases in Prudhoe Bay on Alaska's North Slope are auctioned off for a value of 900 million dollars when I arrive in Alaska in the summer of 1969. Processes with environmental concerns and native land settlements delay the signing of the permission to build the 800-mile long oil pipeline from Prudhoe Bay to the ice-free port of Valdez until January 23, 1974.

Rumors of fabulous jobs lure hordes of prospective workers to Alaska. Some arrive early, before the end of April, when the construction of the pipeline and a parallel road along it are to start. Many don't get the jobs they expected and can only afford to live in their cars. Crime rate soars. Police advice people over the radio to lock their doors. They also lend a scriber to mark valuables. I normally lock my door but leave the key on a ledge above it. If some of my friends come by when I am gone they can always let themselves in. David, my previous neighbor in the trailer never got a key to his door.

Fairbanks is the center for construction. The population inside the narrow city limits increases from 18,000 to 27,000 during the course of the summer of 1974. Someone pastes a board saying "ENOUH!" over the population sign but it doesn't help. The population increases with 20,000 before the end of 1974. Traffic increases both in the air and on the roads. A lot of the cargo flights north appear to fly directly over my place disturbing my sleep at night. It gets difficult to find a parking place in town and difficult to make a phone call. Most private phone lines are shared by three parties.

Price increases, temporary shortages of goods, lines, and accidents accompany the influx of people. I have to wait long in line to renew my driver's license. The first thing a new arrival does is to get an Alaskan driver's license, to make an appearance of being a local on the job market. Many write bad checks. Stores start to demand two pieces of ID with photo, in addition to address and telephone number, before they accept a check. My P.O.Box is not accepted as an address. After moving to my own place in a forest without road names, I have to give a long explanation before I can pay by check. The cashiers, often new girls from the Outside, don't understand that somebody can live at a place without a street address. In desperation I call my road *Cache Lane* and have the name printed on my checks. It solves my problem. Nobody questions that the name only exists in my imagination. Pay and Pack, a big chain store selling construction supplies, demands finger prints before cashing a check. Schools run double shifts. People start to rent beds instead of rooms. My rental situation deteriorates.

In August store shelves get empty where flour, sugar and toilet paper used to be. Everyone doesn't come here to do an honest work. Second Avenue, now called Two Street, where bars crowd each other, turns into a veritable bordello. Girls with heavy make-up stand in the street corners even in the middle of the day soliciting customers. Fights are common. People without business being there are unwelcome. A couple of my women friends cruising along "Two Street" just to look, get shot at. Many of the newcomers from big cities drive a lot faster than the locals. When there is snow on the road, they often end up in collisions or in a ditch.

The road north of Fairbanks must be extended by 415 miles to get all construction material to Prudhoe Bay and the Northern parts of the pipeline. "The Haul Road", excluding the bridge across the Yukon River, gets completed in September 1974. In the winter it is no problem to drive across the river. During the height of the construction, in August 1975, 21,600 workers are spread out over 31 construction camps along the pipeline route. They work long days, every day and make good money. A truck driver gets as much a week as I get in a month at the University in 1974.

I share the first twelve miles of the narrow winding Steese Highway with long trucks every third week, when I drive to Gilmore satellite tracking station. It is impossible to pass the slow-moving trucks even when they don't carry 60-foot-long pipes with a diameter of four feet. This traffic lengthens my driving time considerably. Suddenly one day, my Volkswagen bug develops a strange noise. I am worried something serious might happen and leave me stranded on the road. The noise disappears when I slow down and shift to second gear. A big truck catches up with me and cannot pass. Every time I speed up, I hear the car protests with the disturbing noise and I slow down again.

The Volkswagen mechanic doesn't find anything wrong with the motor but suggests some part be exchanged. This part must be ordered by mail and the price is discouraging. With mixed feelings I slow down the pipeline traffic for one more day with my little car. Shamefully, I feel a malicious joy for all the times my advance has been hindered by a big truck. At the same time I am embarrassed to be a nuisance and a bit scared to accidentally be pushed off the road.

I discuss the problem with my colleagues.

"Have you done anything special to the car before you started to hear that sound?"

"No, I don't think so, except for installing a roof rack," I recall.

"Remove the roof rack! It can cause vibrations at certain speeds."

Thanks and glory to technically analyzing colleagues! No need to pay a mechanic to order a part I don't need.

The car refuses to start in February 1975 although I recently had it towed to a shop that replaced the starting motor. The oil pan heater is broken. At twenty below it is too cold to work on the car outside and inconvenient to make it to work without it. I have no other choice than to ski. On days when I am going out to Gilmore I can drive an official car from the Geophysical Institute. At times only a big truck is available. It needs a long time to warm up to start. I am uncomfortable driving it. If someone was to ask:

"How are you doing?" I am tempted to reply: "Physically pretty well, mentally — what problem

are you interested in: the car that doesn't start, the apartment where most things are out of order, the job where I am about to be evicted because of insufficient funding."

My new neighbors on the other side of the wall in the duplex trailer, a couple from Oregon, have come to work for Alyeska Pipeline. Gradually, more and more homeless job seekers gather in their apartment. I don't know how many men are there. The thin wall conveys the sound of their singing throughout the night. Neither the repertoire nor the timing is to my liking. One day when I expect company for dinner, I shovel a place for them to park outside my window. The next day a yellow Alyeska truck is parked there. I am annoyed that the neighbors waist all raw muscle power lifting beer bottles rather than shoveling their own snow. They are supposed to be able-bodied males coming to Alaska looking for work. At work I am about to lose my office at the Geophysical Institute with a view of McKinley and the sunset behind it. K.O.L.F. Jayaweera, who is now in charge of the satellite project after Gerd Wendler went to Germany, doesn't want to make a great fuss. "Your future as an oceanographer is with the

IMS. You should not sacrifice it for a window. You need to talk to your boss, Bob Muench."

When Dr. Sharma's research grant in marine geology ended, IMS didn't do anything to help, although Sharma promised to rehire me as soon as he got new money. The GI didn't have money either but their director urged me to talk to those who could use me. The result was a job with six bosses at the same time in five different fields: geochronology, geomagnetism, glaciology, meteorology, and volcanology. This job really gave me use for my degree in geophysics.

When on February 11, I return after a 40-minute walk in the forest, it is 40 degrees inside. The oil furnace has quit. Four days later, with occasional periods of below freezing temperatures – inside, the landlord looks at the furnace and leaves the door unlocked for the furnace repairman, who doesn't come. I get the idea to heat the house with the door to the baking oven open. The landlord has already increased my cost for electricity, because the new neighbors use more power and we have a common meter.

The last week in February passes with few inconveniences to speak of until the toilet backs up. It over-flows on the floor and sewage fills half of the bathtub. I shovel a trail into the forest for private sit-downs. The performance repeats next day. The landlord leaves a note:

"The septic tank is either frozen or full."

On March 3 everything is wet in the bathroom cabinet. Did the pipes break? I leave the door unlocked for the plumber, who doesn't come. The neighbors discover my trail and fill my excavation in one sitting. A week later, the toilet works again. A month later, in the middle of April, the sewer line freezes. When I return from work on April 14 both the toilet and the bathtub are filled to the rim. Pink toilet paper floats in the tub. It is not the color I use! Carefully I bail everything through the high window in the bathroom. This is the last drop in my bucket of patience!

I have read the housing rental and for sale ads in the *Fairbanks Daily News-Miner* since the three-day power outage in January, when I had seven degrees in my bedroom. I hope to find a better apartment, but don't find anything suitable to rent. During the process I discover that my housing for three years, including the log cabin further back in the forest, with the surrounding 2,5 acres of land are for sale for $86,000. Housing is scarce and there are lots of pipeline workers with huge salaries.

I take a class in log cabin construction, but will I be able to build a cabin after this? Anyway, I consider this knowledge part of my general education if I plan to continue living here. There are so many decisions to make and I feel so uncertain and indecisive. What shall I do? What should I do? What do I want to do? Meanwhile I try to glean everything I can from the log cabin class.

Hoping to see something for sale, I ski around in the area. There are a few homesteads, 160-acre areas people previously could stake for agriculture. I hope someone would sell me a small corner of their property for a reasonable price.

"How much land do you want?" one homesteader asks.

"One acre would be enough."

At the time I don't understand that I ask for too little and make an impression of not being able to afford much, not that driving my old Volkswagen would have made me look more affluent. I cannot afford good land on a south-facing slope.

On April 16 I see an ad for property to a reasonable price in an area I know from my ski tours. I drive there immediately but the road is not drivable all the way. My high rubber boots fill with snow when I walk down an unused road but there are power lines. I find a poster of Meyeres real estate agency in a corner with birch forest on a Northwest slope. Far away I can see low mountaintops. I know this is a good deal compared to what I have previously seen; 2.5 acres for $7,500. I barely take the time to empty the snow from my boots. I know it is wasted effort to find a telephone and to successfully get a call through. The fastest way to contact the real estate agency is to drive there. I throw a $100 bill on the table.

"I am interested in the property. Here is my down-payment."

"You can resume the owner's bank loan and pay $50 per month with a 6% interest." These are terms I can afford. Driving home I see the geese arrive to Creamer's Field. Spring is here.

Two days later the sale of the land is approved, the same day my office moves to IMS.

I get an A in the log cabin construction class and I am a property owner. When I signed up for the class I had no plans to actually build a log cabin. Now, I have no choice but to put the knowledge I have acquired into action.

22

Camping and Building on my Own Property

Enthusiastically I scramble over the brush pile along the edge of the narrow dirt road to reach the real estate FOR SALE sign. I reach for my Finnish puukko knife in the back pocket of my jeans and cut the protective seal around the champagne bottle. The cork shoots out with a festive bang. The foam is refreshing in the warm spring air on May 17, 1975. This time I am not celebrating the Norwegian Independence Day. The occasion in question is newborn. As every ship of class is launched with the help of a bottle of champagne, taking possession of my own piece of Alaska deserves no less. However, I feel it is not environmentally nor economically sound to break the bottle. . . A sprinkling of the bubbles on the FOR SALE sign is enough.

To prove my ownership of this piece of forested property, where I plan to build my cabin, I cut down a few trees with my new bow saw. I record everything I do with my Super-8-millimeter movie camera. While visiting my parents in Finland for Christmas I proudly show them the results.

"Are you drinking champagne from plastic mugs?" my Mother blurts out with horror.

My friend, Carol Hagglund, a third generation Finn from Minnesota, helps me celebrate. She is tall and strong with a nice but scarce smile. We met taking a wine making class a year ago at the University of Alaska.

"Where will you build your cabin?" Carol asks as she pulls some white yarn from her pocket and ties her curly brown hair into two pigtails. I keep my blond hair tied in a high bun with a red scarf around my head.

"The forest is so dense I cannot see what the land looks like. We must cut down some trees. Let's start with the alders and willows. With only the birch and spruce trees left, I should be able to see where would be the best spot for the cabin," I answer. "You can use my small saw."

The trees grow so close that I can, sometimes, cut two at once with my bow saw. Despite our enthusiasm it is tiring. After cutting trees and piling brush for two days, I can start to see through the forest. I probably have permafrost in the ground since my land is on a northwest-facing slope. Permafrost is layers or lenses of perennially frozen soil some feet below the surface. If not disturbed it stays there because the mean annual temperature in Fairbanks is below freezing. If an ice lens melts, a cavity is formed and the soil above sinks into it. The trick is to avoid building on permafrost, or if you have to, keep it frozen. It is important to choose the cabin site wisely. There is an area with large birch and two old tall spruce 130 feet from the road. The drainage must be best there and the likelihood of permafrost less I conclude.

"Why don't you get yourself a chain saw?" Carol asks the second day. "That would speed things up."

"I don't like them," I answer.

***

The most popular classes at the University of Alaska Community College this spring were log cabin construction and belly dancing. I took them both. With the final, I handed in drawings for a log cabin. I planned to build two cabins, an 8 x 8-foot cache and a 16 x 16-foot cabin, both on 8-foot poles. The normal meaning of a cache in Alaska is an elevated storage for food, out of reach of wild animals. The idea was to start with the cache, to learn the tricks of the trade, and to make my mistakes on a small scale.

Last Sunday, Axel Carlson, my log cabin construction teacher, invited me home for dinner to see if we had any common relatives, since his ancestors came from both Finland and Sweden.

"What kinds of tools do I need to build a log cabin?" I ask Axel.

"What have you told them in class, if she doesn't even know that?" his wife asks.

Axel leaves the table after dessert and returns with his hands full of drills and chisels that he piles on the dining room table. There is no chain saw.

"Do you have a chain saw?" I ask.

"Everybody has one," Axel replies and brings out a small yellow saw. We go outside.

"Can I try it out?" I ask with anticipation and apprehension. "I never used a motorized saw."

Axel pulls the cord to start the saw and hands it to me. It is noisy and vibrates a lot. My arms shake in a very unpleasant way.

"I don't want to use a tool like this," I say with disgust.

I wonder what kind of chain saw my neighbor, Jim Baldridge, is using? He is very meticulous. He is also building a log cabin and has cut down many big spruce trees. I participated in his log peeling party last month, when there was still snow on the ground. We split into groups. I work with Bob Peltz, a folk dancing friend, and Margaretha Elborg, a visiting veterinary student from Sweden, who works at the Musk Ox Farm. I met Margaretha on my way home from work one day. She stood at the edge of the road and appeared confused. I stopped and offered her a ride and wondered where her accent came from. Then we continued speaking Swedish.

We haven't heard anything from the other groups for a long time, when Margaretha cuts herself in the knee with the drawknife. The wound is deep but doesn't bleed. We figure she might need some stitches. Looking for the others, we find a note on Jim's door: GONE TO THE HOSPITAL.

"Why would they go to the hospital before I got hurt?" Margaretha says.

"That's very inconsiderate of them," Bob replies. "Can we get you in my Volkswagen bug?" I ask Margaretha.

"That will be OK, I am not hurting."

We drive to the Fairbanks Memorial Hospital. "What's a drawknife?" the girl at the check-in counter asks.

"It's a sharp steel blade, about two feet long, with two wooden handles, that you use to peel logs with," Bob explains.

Margaretha is placed in a wheel chair and given a long form to fill out.

"What does race mean?" Margaretha asks.

"Write human," Bob instructs. He is the only American among us.

"What does color mean?" Margaretha asks. "Say no," Bob replies.

"What does sex mean?" Margaretha asks.

"Say yes," Bob says. "I better help you with this form, it's too confusing for you," Margaretha finally completes the form when a nurse enters. "We have already treated the drawknife case," she says.

"No, you haven't even looked at me," Margaretha protests.

At this time a wheel chair is rolled out of the emergency room with Jim's girlfriend, Marty, in it.

"Did you also cut yourself with a drawknife?" we shout in unison.

Most of the tired log peeling gang is in the emergency room, still dressed in wet boots, jeans and wool shirts with pitch and bark all over us. We eagerly fill each other in on the latest, while waiting for Margaretha to be treated.

"You cannot wait here, this is a quiet area," a nurse informs us.

"Getting thrown out of the hospital, this is insult to injury," Jim says.

After this log peeling experience I know that Jim has an Austrian made Stihl chain saw. I try it out. To my surprise, it doesn't vibrate at all. I go to Independent Lumber and buy my own Stihl saw with a 14-inch bar. Now I have some power behind my intentions.

On May 18, Bob Sullivan, another folk dance friend and my responsible house checker when I lived in the trailer, comes for a visit.

"I'll help you build, if I have the time. I'll do it in exchange for food and transportation," Bob says to my delighted surprise. A week earlier, he said that I couldn't count on work parties, such as those Jim had, for more than once or twice.

"You have to count on doing most of the work yourself," Bob said then.

It never occurred to me to hire somebody to build my cabin because I don't have the money. I tried to get a bank loan for the down payment on good land without permafrost on a south-facing slope but was turned down. I didn't understand that my request was too modest. Had I asked for money to pay for both the land and construction, the bank might have lent it to me.

I would love to use natural round logs as Jim does but I realize they would be too heavy for me to handle.

Three-sided six-inch logs with one rounded side that needs to be peeled would be a lot easier to use.

Construction season in Alaska is short. I am eager to start on my cabin. I call Four Star Lumber and order logs on May 27. They deliver in two weeks. Now I am committed. It feels both exciting and scary. What have I got myself into?

On the 30th of May I call my landlord. "I don't want to pay rent any more. I will live off my cleaning deposit and move out on June 15," I say. No objections.

I have given the move some serious thought. I need all the money I can save for building material. I buy an 8 x 10-foot canvas wall tent and pitch it 200 feet from the road. I would only have to live in it for two weeks, before I have my practice house, the cache ready, I think optimistically.

One 70-foot tall spruce tree worries me. It leans in the direction where I want to build my cabin. It is too large for me to tackle.

"How do you cut down a huge tree?" I ask Bob Peltz, my problem-solving friend who normally has a solution for everything.

"You just cut until the tree starts to fall and step out of the way," he replies, without volunteering to come and help, as I had hoped.

I talk to Kjell Henriksen, my visiting Norwegian colleague.

"I have cut down a few trees in Norway, but nothing this big," Kjell says. "The theory should be the same. I can give it a try," he says to my delight. Kjell comes on the evening of June 5 and runs my saw out of gas twice, cutting down birch trees, before he starts to cut the spruce.

"We have to take down enough trees to give the spruce tree room to fall," Kjell explains.

That didn't occur to me with my present experience. My heart cries for the beautiful birch trees in their two-week old new green gowns.

Kjell cuts a deep wedge half way through the spruce in the direction he wants it to fall. It looks treacherous to me as I watch from a distance. Gradually he cuts another wedge from the opposite side above the first and steps back to watch. Nothing happens for a while. Then, slowly the mighty old spruce starts to fall.

A truck with tailings, coarse gravel and rocks left over by the gold dredge operations, backs up and dumps its nine yards. The tailings are for the foundation of the cache.

Pleased I stand back in the cool evening shadows after every one has left and survey my own land. The large spruce is safely down. Piles of foundation timbers and logs lay by the roadside together with the washed out rocks. The stage is set for action. I am ready to build my home.

First I need to draw the curtain on the trailer. I pack and clean my rented one bedroom trailer all night. By 5:30 a.m. on Sunday June 15, I am finally ready to move out from civilization. I crawl into the tent and fall asleep right away.

"Kristina, wake up! Are you sleeping away your first day on your new land?" Carol shouts outside my tent at noon. "It's beautiful sunshine."

"Why don't you get up, while I start peeling logs'" Carol says. She is as excited about my construction as I.

I pour boiling water from a thermos bottle that I packed from the trailer and prepare instant coffee and tang for my first meal in my tent on my own land. With my Swiss army knife I make a cheese sandwich. I feel confident to start a new life.

Carol peels logs for a few hours while I treat the four 10 x 10-inch 8-foot foundation timbers with creosote to prevent them from rotting. Bob S. warned me that it is bad stuff, so I wear my rubber gloves.

After dinner I am very tired and fall asleep. I am awakened again at 8 p.m. My Finnish friends, Kaarina Abel, a US Public Health worker for natives, and Martti and Helena Sorvoja, builders and owners of a three-story apartment house in town, pay me my first tent visit. Carol doesn't count as a visitor. She came to work.

I take Monday and Tuesday off. Despite a down comforter, my first night in the tent is cold.

I need a table. With my new chain saw, I cut two-foot-long pieces from some 2 x 4 boards and nail them together into a cube. It is sturdy enough to stand on, so I can push a ridgepole through my tent and tie it to the trees. I am very proud of my first crude construction project.

With long daylight hours, I don't realize how late it is. I am running my chain saw late into the night. By midnight a man shows up to investigate. He introduces himself as Fred Ensign, a fire fighter living a third of a mile up the hill. When I am ready to go to bed, at 1:30 a.m., my back is hurting.

I need a closet and tie a pole between two birch trees and cover it with visqueen (clear plastic) on Tuesday, June 17. Pink wild roses are in bloom everywhere.

Based on Bob's and my business agreement of transportation and food in exchange for work, I pick up Bob after work and take him to an all-you-can-eat spaghetti feed at Cripple Creek, since I am not yet organized to serve dinners to company in my tent.

Bob is tall and slim dressed in a white T-shirt and a faded blue cap covering his light brown hair. After dinner Bob spits into his palms, showing he means business. He is now empowered to shovel gold tailings and to wheelbarrow them from the pile by the road downhill to the site for the cache, 175 feet away. This is the third time he moves dirt. When I take Bob home it is raining. Living in a tent makes me very observant of weather conditions.

On my third morning on June 18 everything is damp in the tent with water in the "kitchen" corner by the door. The tent needs a canopy. I go to work to dry and warm up. In the evening I creosote more 10 x 10-inch timbers. I don't feel well when I crawl into my Army surplus mummy bag at the back wall of the tent. At 2:30 a.m. I suddenly awake feeling nauseated. I barely have time to extricate my arms and lunge myself, inside my sleeping bag, across the tent floor to throw up in my slop bucket.

After work, June 19, I feel fine again and pick up Bob. I have ordered a new kerosene burning Optimus backpacking stove from a catalog. On it I boil potatoes and warm up a Mexican casserole Kaarina brought. She is my health concerned Finnish friend. Food stays fresh in a cooler with artificial ice packs I re-freeze every day at work. With five helpers this evening, we get all 10 x 10-inch and 8 x 8-inch timbers moved from the road to the construction site.

Friday, June 20, it is raining. I stay at job until midnight to work on the plans for the foundation of the cache.

Kristina cooking in her tarp covered tent, July 1975.

On Saturday, June 21, I hang a 12 x 15-foot plastic tarp over the tent. It overhangs the tent enough to keep out the rainwater. Carol and Bob move tailings. It takes a while to move a truckload by wheelbarrow. In the evening Kaarina invites me home for dinner.

"We have to drive to Chatanika to visit Martti's hunting partner, Eugene Laitala," Kaarina says. "He is a good Finnish log cabin builder. He can give you some advice. Besides, there are lots of men out there who might come and help you," she insists.

"This sounds too good not to act on," I agree.

After about an hour's drive, we find Laitala's large log cabin and sauna. Two vicious looking dogs run out barking. We don't dare step out of the car until Laitala, a big calm Finn, restrains the dogs. No extra men are in sight, as Kaarina promised. Laitala invites us in and scrutinizes my penciled drawings of the 8 x 8-foot cache and 16 x 16-foot cabin on yellow sheets of paper, with a serious expression.

"If you can get the cache finished this summer, you can be very proud of yourself," Laitala says finally. Laitala doesn't know what he talks about, I think annoyed. I intend to build both houses this summer.

On June 24, a colleague with a truck comes to Northland Wood with me. This is a lumberyard where you load your own material. We find a pile of 3/4" tongue and groove plywood, and load five sheets on the truck. Two thinner sheets are for the floor of the tent.

Bob gives me good construction advice. "Your floor joists are very important. They have to be Douglas fir," he says.

We drive in my Volkswagen to Fairbanks Lumber, the best lumberyard in town. The yardman starts to load the 2 x 8-inch 8-foot boards on my VW. Bob intervenes. "They have to be straight. Do you mind if we select them?" We sort through the pile, carefully eyeing each plank from both directions. By the time we have the selected boards tied to the roof of my VW bug the lumberyard has closed. This evening I can serve Bob the tuna and macaroni casserole Carol brought me two days ago.

On my birthday, June 26, I take annual leave. I try to level the cache foundation that consists of an 8 x 8-foot pad of tailings. Bob has drilled two wooden pegs as handles in a four-foot long birch log with which I compact the tailings. After an hour I have blisters on my hands, but he told me I have to compact the pad well for 5 hours.

In the evening I go to pick up Bob but I have to wait until he gets home. He compliments me on my dinner of fried sausage and potatoes. This evening he starts to saw the ends of the creosoted 10 x 10-inch timbers, so they will overlap in the corners, as they are to be placed on the pad of tailings. Before I go to bed, I light a Coleman lantern to take off some of the chill in my tent.

On June 27, I give the cache foundation an hour of compacting. My belongings are packed in boxes and trunks but only two trunks fit inside the tent. I have a pile in the woods and more under a table at work. I told my boss, Bob Muench, I needed a long table on which to spread out all my satellite pictures. My belongings need to get off the ground in the forest. Since the sun barely sets at night, I work past midnight, making storage shelves from birch poles. Even the mosquitoes go to bed earlier than I.

Saturday, June 28, I compact the cache foundation for one and a half hours and remove felled trees from the site for the big cabin and the driveway. Kaarina visits with Bill Blockcolsky, who is building his own home. Carol comes by and peels 10 logs in three hours. At 6 p.m. I pick up Bob and serve him fish balls after which he sleeps until 8 p.m.

Sunday, June 29, Carol peels seven logs. I mark the corner locations for my cache and cabin. I serve Carol leftover rice and canned mackerel. In the evening I visit Bob to discuss my construction plans.

"The materials for your cache and cabin will cost about $4,000." I am shocked by what Bob tells me. Where will I get this kind of money? I wonder. The bank has already refused to lend me money for the down payment of land. That's why I ended up with this north-sloping permafrost lot.

July 2 is warm and sunny. Kaarina and her friend Herb come with all the makings for a steak barbecue. We peel three logs and spend two hours moving all the peeled logs. After that I go to the Geophysical Institute for a shower. The Institute of Marine Science, where I presently work, doesn't have showers.

A noise wakes me in the night. I hear someone breathing on the other side of the tent wall just by my head. I listen with all senses on full alert. I can see the canvas moving slightly. I don't move and barely breathe. The door on the opposite side is tightly secured to the tent pole to keep all mosquitoes out so I don't go out to investigate. In the morning I cannot find my slop bucket. It was dragged far into the trees together with my cookie sheets and other belongings with a trace of a scent.

"Sprinkle red pepper on everything," Carol's aunt and landlady, Ailie Leikas, suggests. She came to Alaska from Minnesota in 1953 to work as a cook on the Alaska railroad. She has a lot of advice on handling the wildlife in Alaska both man and beast.

Carol brings a delicious rhubarb-strawberry sauce on July 4 and stays to help me all day.

On July 5, it is 81°F in my tent as I take a midday nap. Bob Peltz and his girl friend, Fran, visit and help me move the 8-foot long creosoted 10 x 10- inch foundation timbers into a square on the compacted tailings pad. As I walk to pick up my newspaper from a box by the main road about a mile away, I meet Kaarina's friend, Bill Blockcolsky, with a load of scrap lumber. Kaarina told him to be nice to me and not to visit empty-handed. Bill is tall and muscular with thick wavy brown hair and a mustache. His stylish sideburns end in points on his cheeks.

"I can come and help you tomorrow," Bill says in a jolly tone, "if you help me with my house in return."

Before Bill and Carol arrive I chisel the final adjustments to the corners of the 10 by 10-inch timbers. We drill holes and insert 5/8" rebar rods in the corners of the foundation square. With matching holes drilled in the ends of the 8-foot long 8 x 8-inch timbers, Bill lifts the creosoted corner posts in place over the rebar.

"You are building your floor strong enough to carry a railroad engine," Bill says as I insist on attaching the 2 x 8-inch rim joists with lag bolts to the indented corner posts.

"I am using a staple gun on my 5-bedroom house and you use lag bolts for your 8 x 8 foot cache. You are over building," Bill says as he makes three pull- ups and swings like a monkey from my first floor joist to prove it is strong enough.

It is fun working with Bill. He is in a good mood and showing off for Carol and me. We make visible progress. The day is warm and sunny. Carol and I wear sleeveless tops. All of us wear blue jeans. Drenched in "Yukon cologne" the mosquitoes refrain from eating us. Before the inner rim joists go up, we attach joist hangers to them. Metal netting is stapled to the underside of the floor joists to provide for ventilation, protection from squirrels and support for the fiberglass batts, that will go between the floor joists.

July 7 is a hot day with 100°F in the sun at Plywood Supply and 85°F in my tent. With the framing for the cache floor done I must build a 16- foot ladder to reach it. I use 1 x 6-inch 16-foot boards that I double so that I can easily insert the steps. I don't have much experience but still feel I am more experienced than the yardman who wanted to cut the boards in half so they would more easily fit on the roof of my VW. How far apart should the steps be, I wonder? A foot sounds like a logical distance but it seems too close, so I make them 13-1/2". It takes me 7-1/2 hours to build the ladder. I am so proud of the results that I sign and date it.

"Who is your carpenter?" is Bob's first question when I bring him to my place and he surveys the results of the work. It is the massive eight-foot upright corner posts with attached rim joists that attract Bob's attention, not my proud ladder.

The hot weather continues on July 11. It is still 90°F in my tent at 6:30 p.m. when jolly Bill makes a surprise visit on his motorcycle.

"I lost my brakes and drove my car into the ditch on Murphy Dome," he says as he twists the tips of his moustache.

"You have hardly got anything done in a week. I am very disappointed with your progress. Snow will fly before you know it," Bill says after looking around.

"There isn't much time left over after my eight hour work day at the University," I reply. "Things take longer than I thought. I expected to be out of my tent and living in my cache a week ago."

Saturday, July 12, Carol brings log-peeling support. It is her sister, Karen Hagglund, a high school teacher. Bill comes to borrow my Volkswagen to get to his ditched car. He returns in the afternoon. "My car should be fixed. Can you come and help

me get it out of the ditch?" Bill asks. He shows his appreciation for my help with five frozen moose steaks I label "samples," and put in a lab freezer.

July 16, Karl Neuman, my German potato friend, helps me to finish the insulation in the floor and attach visqueen over it as a vapor barrier. We have difficulties joining the tongue and groove plywood sheets.

"Herman Roelleke, my previous landlord, is a professional builder. People call him Herman the German. He could do this in no time," Karl says as he retreats to his car by the road, where I have given him permission to live for a week. I send a lunch invitation to Herman.

July 18 I go home from work for lunch to meet Herman. He climbs my ladder.

"I see you built the ladder yourself!" Herman exclaims. I take it as praise and wonder how he knew. We all climb the ladder. Herman points at me.

"Kristina, you stand on this corner of the plywood and you, Karl, on the opposite," Herman directs us as he slams the plywood sheet we stand on with a big sledgehammer. The tongue and groove plywood sheet easily slides into the groove of its neighbor.

"Thank you, Herman, it's obvious you are a professional," I comment as I serve him lunch.

"Karl can drive my truck so you can get your roofing materials home from Plywood Supply," Herman reciprocates.

There is no time to build an outhouse. I just dig a small hole and lean two sheets of plywood against each other. Between two trips to my private ditch I notice the red currants in the forest have ripened. I work to midnight.

The 10-foot high floor for my cache consists of three sheets of plywood. Since I planned to build both the cache and the cabin this summer I have ordered materials for both. Saturday, July 19, is productive. Jolly Bill brings a colleague, Don, and a gasoline powered generator. Bill and Don stack the cabin foundation timbers at the edge of the cache making a staging platform to hand up materials to the cache landing. It is reached by the 16-foot ladder.

Bill rolls out six-inch wide, one-inch thick fiberglass sill seal insulation along the edges of the two sheets of plywood that will be the floor area. The insulation is stapled to the plywood. A 12-foot long three-sided six-inch log is placed along the North edge of the plywood with the rounded side out. Three eight-foot plus logs are butted against each other to form the foundation square for the log walls. The inside area is seven by seven feet. The ends of the logs extend slightly beyond the decking. The first log course is anchored to the upright 8 x 8-inch corner posts with rebar.

Sill seal is stapled between each log course. The second round consists of three 8-foot plus logs and two shorter ones on each side of the door. The logs cross over each other in the corners making a solid attachment. With access to electricity it is easy to drill holes in the logs for the 5/8-inch 10-inch long rebar that peg the logs together. The generator, however, doesn't last very long.

"Drilling 11-inch deep holes by hand is very slow. It is difficult to drive the drill through," Don says with concern, since he is the only one who works for money.

Carol and Karen peel logs, Kaarina checks the progress, and I am very pleased.

"We got four courses of logs in place today. It already starts to look like a house," I say with delight. Bill is less impressed by my emerging 49- square foot abode, with the floor 10 feet above the ground.

"This would fit as a closet in my house," he says.

Only Carol comes on July 20. Karl still lives in his car on my property. While Carol peels logs, Karl helps me to drill and pound in rebar in the top of a log course. It starts to rain.

Construction hasn't gone as fast as I expected but it is still summer. I am confident I have time to take a break for two weeks to hike the Chilkoot trail. On July 25 I tie a double square knot on my tent and leave.

23

Hiking the Chilkoot Trail

The 33-mile long Chilkoot Trail is shrouded in the alluring mystery of history. This is the way thousands of hopeful gold miners entered the Klondike.

"We should hike it while we still can," my friend Carol Hagglund says one day as she adjusts a yarn around one of her brown pigtails.

"How long would that take us?" I ask.

"I don't know," Carol replies "but my friend Adele Miller knows a park ranger on the Canadian side. She can get the information we need."

We fly to Juneau in July 1975. I spend most of the night talking to Marieanna Lowe, my old colleague from the Douglas Marine Station. From Juneau we take the ferry to Skagway. I cannot stay awake. Some passengers with cabins disembark in Haines. I cannot resist the temptation.

"That cabin will probably not get cleaned before we reach Skagway," I conclude. "It has four bunks. Who wants a comfortable sleep?"

Carol and Adele join me. We lock the door, turn out the light and stretch out. A knock on the door wakes me after an hour. We are silent hoping the visitor will pass but soon hear the rattle of keys. Anxious we see the door open and the light turned on. The cabin steward sees only me. The other bunks are hidden behind the opened door.

"Hi, Chum, do you really belong here?" he asks me.

From that time on Carol calls me Chum.

My old friend from my last stop in Skagway, the Dangerous Skip, meets the ferry.

"My bunkhouse has burnt down," he says.

We are prepared for camping, of course, but Kaarina Abel, my Finnish friend, doesn't want to do it yet. She is a woman of action with short blond hair and a benevolent smile.

"I want to sleep in comfort at a hotel the last night before the hike," she says.

Kaarina finds a single room for the exorbitant price of $35 at the elegant Golden North with decor from the time of the Gold Rush. The rest of us plan to stay at the campground. Kaarina is always generous.

"For this price we can all share the room, but the hotel doesn't need to know."

Discreetly we tip toe past the reception desk with our 40-pound backpacks. We never walk more than two at a time hoping the concierge will not notice that we are five who plan to share the single room for the night.

"We'll cast lots for the double bed," Kaarina insists rather than claiming it as rightfully hers. Kaarina ends up on the floor. There is barely room to close the door. It has no lock. When I wake up in the morning, the door is open. Kaarina is missing. We find her under a table in a corridor turret.

"The air got too stuffy in the room," Kaarina says. In the morning we all walk down together carrying our backpacks and ask for a taxi to Dyea, where the Chilkoot Trail starts. It was in Dyea where Skip's guide got me stuck in the mud last time, when my train missed the ferry.

At the trailhead we have to fill out a form. Number in group? Five women: Carol, Kristina, Virginia, Adele, and Kaarina. We didn't intend this to be a women's lib movement, we just couldn't find any men willing to come along.

Carol, Kristina, Virginia, Adele, and Kaarina ready to
start hiking the Chilkoot Trail, July, 1975

Age? +/- 30. Kaarina who is older than the rest of us, smiles with approval.

On July 29, 1975 at 9 a.m. we throw our heavy packs on our backs. Well rested and energetic we start out walking briskly. The trail follows the east side of the Taiya River. It is flooded after three miles so we change our hiking boots for old tennis shoes we brought along for river crossings. The glacier fed water is ice cold — of course. The trail is slick and muddy, sucking our feet down. I have to tighten my laces not to lose my shoes.

"This will continue for three miles and the water will reach our knees," somebody told us yesterday. Fortunately, the water has receded and we get through it after a mile. A footbridge with boards covering two logs crosses a river. It is handy to sit down on. While washing our feet and changing to dry hiking boots a large group passes, probably in their wet boots.

We take our time to admire the beautiful scenery. It is typical Southeast Alaskan rainforest with large Sitka spruce and Western hemlock with soft bright green moss on the ground. The water in the Taiya River is milky white from glacier flour. High in a valley between the mountains we see one of the beautiful sources, the shimmering blue Irene Glacier framed by trees on a lower level. We meet two groups coming from the opposite direction. We walk rather slowly, we think, until we pass the group that sprinted past us by the footbridge.

We stop for lunch at Canyon City at 2:30 p.m. Carol and Adele are eager to try their new camping stove. It is the same make as mine and works fine for boiling water for a freeze-dried meal and a hot drink. I have bought new sturdy hiking boots from a mail order firm. I tried them out the first time hiking the ski trail in Douglas. They were very comfortable until they got wet and the seams in the heels swelled. Now they are dry and fine again. We have hiked 8 miles of 33 and don't know how long this hike will take nor even if we will make it. Adele's Canadian ranger friend, Shirley, sent a four-page handwritten description of the trail with advice. In it she claims that a hiker should average two mph with a 50- pound pack. We have taken longer than that.

We bought train tickets from Bennett at the end of the trail and must be there in three and a half days. If we could make it to Sheep Camp at mile 13 tonight, we would be on the safe side. Some feet feel tender already and the backpacks don't feel any lighter after lunch. My pack with tent, camping stove, movie camera etc. weighs 42 pounds. It is too much but I don't know what I could have left out. Still, the weight is nothing compared to what the gold miners were carrying. The big group catches up with us and settles in the Canyon City shelter cabin for the night.

The ruins of Canyon City from the gold stampede in 1897-98 are on the other side of the Taiya River. It will be an additional mile but it would be a lost opportunity not to see them. We leave our packs neatly stacked around a tree and proceed across a suspension bridge one by one.

This is fun, Adele and I think as we cross the river happily skipping and running.

"The bridge moves too much. It is unstable. This is dangerous and frightening," Kaarina says as she carefully and slowly crosses the bridge firmly moving her hands along the wire rails.

We find a rusty cup, a frying pan an enamelware coffee pot and decaying log cabins. Carol opens the door to an iron cook stove and puts the cup in the oven.

"How did they ever get these things here?" Kaarina asks as we gaze at a large steam boiler and a long metal pipe. I crawl through the pipe. We are in a spunky mood.

At 4:30 p.m. we reunite with our backpacks. The trail ascends steeply. At times we must use our hands to lift our feet high enough to plant them on a steady rock. It is hard to raise your feet with a heavy pack that works against the move. A couple we met a few days earlier in Juneau doesn't have any difficulties and passes us. We catch up with them at Pleasant Camp where they stop for the night. Two blue tents are already pitched there. It is getting dark under the large trees but it is only three more miles to Sheep Camp.

Kaarina starts to sing, maybe to announce our arrival to any prospective bears. She does it very well. I join in when she picks a familiar song. I am too tired to care how I sound or who listens. Singing gives me new energy and makes me forget the weight of my pack and my sore feet. I gather strength from some hidden source to increase my pace and take the lead. The smooth trail goes through darkening forest that reminds me of Finland. We hike two miles in record time, maybe an hour, and reach Sheep Camp at 9 p.m. The shelter cabin with its eight bunks is over-filled. We pitch our tents in a rush as it starts to rain. In ten minutes it is pouring. We are proud over our first day, 14 miles in 12 hours including the stop in Canyon City.

The rain continues next morning. The weight of the food eaten is more than offset by the added weight of our wet tents. The Sheep Camp ranger station is housed in two large warm tents on wooden platforms with wood burning heaters. We contact the Canadian rangers at Lake Lindeman by radio. Shirley promises to meet us on the Summit at 2 p.m. Some heels get a new protective layer of moleskin before the start at 10 a.m. Some blisters have already formed and some legs are awfully stiff but the inconveniences are soon forgotten. The trail slowly ascends towards the tree line, sometimes following a roaring white river. The water tastes refreshing. We don't carry any water. The trail gets difficult to follow. At times it wanders past huge boulders. Carol is ahead of me, and Virginia behind taking pictures of flowers. I try to catch up with Carol when I suddenly hear a call far behind me.

Carol was lost between the boulders when I passed without seeing her in the rain and fog.

"This was frightening. We better stay close together," I say.

Adele, who is young and slender, walks fast so at least one of us will be on time for the meeting with the Canadians on the summit. To our surprise, Kaarina has the strength to tag behind Adele. She has a heavy pack and lightweight shoes but she has a tremendous willpower and determination that is true Finnish "sisu". She will make it!

We reach the first snowfield after the large rocks and pull our wool caps over our ears. The snow appears dirty and rotten. Small flowers decorate the grass and moss patches along the edge. The valley narrows in front of us with steep cliff sides.

"Where are the Golden Stairs?" Virginia asks.

Everything is hazy in tones of gray. The summit of the Chilkoot Pass with surrounding mountains is cloud covered.

"How far must we go and where?" Carol asks.

Sometimes we catch a glimpse of a gigantic ghostlike tripod and pilings through the clouds and fog. They are remains of the tramway that the affluent used to transport their supplies to the summit. Before the tramway it was more expensive. Indians would pack 100 pounds for a dollar. I would gladly give an Indian a dollar to carry my pack.

Carol, Virginia, and I reach the Golden Stairs at 2:30 p.m. That is the name the gold miners gave the stairs they cut out in the snow. Earlier we saw Adele and Kaarina waive through a hole in the clouds somewhere high up. We try to follow the tramway cable that lies on the ground since we cannot see anything in the fog. The ground is covered with large boulders. We have to decide which ones we can climb up on and which to find a way around. It is a step at a time. Finding a rod that marks the trail doesn't make the going any easier. An encouraging sign states that we experience the climb in normal weather, that is in rain and fog, and should take the shortest route straight up.

When the gold miners struggled their way up these 1,500 or so golden steps to the 3,680-foot high summit of the Chilkoot Pass, the boulders were covered by snow. A heavy snowstorm could dump ten feet of snow on the pass. The traffic was so heavy between storms that climbers stepped directly into each other's steps. If someone had to stop to rest it could take hours before he could squeeze into the tight queue again. With a ton of required supplies the gold miners had to climb the steps more than a few times. This climb was made famous through the Swede E.A. Hegg's photographs that inspired Charlie Chaplin's classical movie about the Gold Rush.

Carol approaching the summit of Chilkoot Pass

My gloves are wet and dirty. Wiping my glasses with them doesn't improve my visibility. I no longer see anyone else. Tired, wet, and almost blind I struggle on. When everything starts to feel hopeless a strange man appears. Where did he come from? Am I hallucinating? Is he an angel?

"I can take your backpack and show you the way to the top," he offers.

I am too tired — and surprised to protest. Without a pack I still have difficulties following the man who jumps from boulder to boulder with my 42- pound pack. It is far to the top although I feel like I have climbed for an eternity. The rest of the group increased by two Canadian rangers, Shirley and Gordon, wait at the summit of the pass. This is where the Canadian Royal Mounted Police sat in 1898 to levy duty on goods and to establish the border between USA and Canada. To enter Canada the stampeders were required to have supplies for a year, which could amount to a ton including food, clothing, and necessities for gold mining, boat building etc.

My saving angel is Roy from the Sheep Camp ranger station. Gratefully I give him my mixture of nuts and raisins that he thoughtfully declines. I want to give him something he cannot refuse and quickly give him a thank you kiss.

"Is this the way you cash in your reward?" Gordon mumbles.

"Where's Virginia, she was ahead of me?" "Don't worry, she's just behind us," Roy says.

The summit is totally enshrouded in clouds. We cannot see a thing. I wonder how far we will continue today? It is 3:30 p.m. We have hiked, climbed, and crawled for six hours although we have only covered three miles. I am hungry. We haven't had lunch yet.

Maybe the others ate while waiting for Virginia and me?

The trail continues over seemingly stable snowfields. The advance party leaves a trail that can be seen for a while. Carol, Virginia, and I bring up the rear. At times the trail is visibly marked with orange triangles on poles. The last goes up a hill, but where does it continue? Small creeks that we must cross, traverse the bare ground between the snowfields. There is no longer a chance to keep our feet dry. We are in an unreal world among and above the clouds. We see a glimpse of an ice blue fairy lake. Does it really exist or am I dreaming? It must be Crater Lake a mile from the pass.

"I want to camp here and wait until the sun comes out," I shout.

Nobody hears me. I am too far behind. When the trail gets difficult to see, I notice two distant shadows waiting for a moment. Carol and Virginia are too cold and wet to wait long enough for me to catch up with them. My feet are too sore and I am too tired to walk any faster. My poncho, that is supposed to keep both me and my pack dry, flutters around my neck in the wind.

The conditions for hypothermia couldn't be better. I am concerned. We should stop and cook something warm.

Finally, at 8 p.m. I catch up with Shirley, Gordon, Carol, and Virginia. I cannot see Kaarina and Adele. They must have continued. Adele is in the best shape of us and Kaarina has "sisu".

"We are at Happy Camp at the end of Long Lake," Shirley informs us. A few small pines provide some protection. We have already hiked four miles on Canadian soil or seven miles since this morning.

"I want to camp here," I announce.

"This is worse than last night when everything got wet," Carol says.

"There is an empty ranger cabin at Lake Lindeman with floor space for all of you," Shirley says.

"I plan to change to dry clothing," I announce loudly, hoping the others would follow my example and Gordon have the decency to turn his back. Nobody reacts when I pull off my drenched corduroy jeans and put them in a plastic bag in my pack. Dry long johns and rain pants improve my life.

"Now I feel as if I could continue a bit further," I say. I am concerned nobody else takes any initiative.

"I am OK," Carol says after Shirley lends her a raincoat.

I boil water and offer everybody hot Jell-O before it jellies.

"From here you can easily follow the trail," Shirley says and goes ahead with Gordon. They have walked 10 miles from Lake Lindeman to meet us at the summit. They must be tired too.

The shore of Long Lake seems to go on forever.

"I would really like to see this scenery," I say "but who knows how often it is clear?"

We reach a footbridge between Long Lake and Deep Lake at 9 p.m. It is getting dark. The hope to be dry again pushes us forward. I wonder how much further?

The trail ascends a bit, the trees get big and flowers show up along the edge before the bushes thicken. Carol, who is leading, suddenly stops.

"I think I saw something move ahead of me." "This looks like bear country," I confirm.

I take the lead with the heart in my throat singing as loud as I can between breaths. The added rush of adrenalin powers some hidden reservoir of energy I thought I had already exhausted. I wave my arm over a fresh pile of bear droppings but the others don't notice. We make good progress while I go through and repeat the limited repertoire of songs I can remember.

Lake Lindeman welcomes us in the valley. Tired we walk around looking for the ranger cabin. Some people sit on a picnic table. It is too dark to recognize Shirley. I can barely move my feet any longer. My whole body is sore. I fall behind again. A man follows me. When the trail divides and I don't know where to go I hear a voice:

"Continue straight ahead, I am also a ranger."

Warm food waits us in the cook tent. I am only half conscious and automatically eat what is put in front of me. It is 11 p.m. We have hiked 13 miles in 13 hours with scarcely anything to eat or drink, at least not us in the rear.

The ranger women's tent is filled with lines of drying clothing but there is room for us on the floor. My sleeping bag in multiple plastic bags is the only dry thing I have. I could have camped by the glacier waiting for sunshine.

We have arrived a day earlier than planned in Lindeman. The sun is shining. In 1898 this was a tent town of 10,000. This is where the first gold miners spent the winter and built boats while waiting for spring. Those who came later, when there were no more trees for boats, continued to Lake Bennett.

"I want to go back along the trail and photograph flowers," Virginia says.

"I love to see some glaciers in the sunshine."

Nobody else is interested. I wear my tennis shoes that don't irritate my blistered heels. The stiffness in my legs from yesterday has gone away. It is easy to walk without packs until I step on something. A sudden pain stings like a sword through me and I bend like a pocketknife.

"This was strange. I have never encountered anything similar. Did I step on a nail?"

"Do you have a hole in your sole?" Virginia wonders.

I examine my sole and the ground but don't find anything. "Was this a nerve reaction?"

"This was an interesting and leisurely five-mile walk in five hours," I say with appreciation.

"Yes," Virginia replies, "we saw flowers, discarded cooking utensils, the remains of a sled, and a boat."

In the evening we invite the Canadian rangers to our four-bunk cabin. They have baked two pies. The first one is delicious. The other one, baked by Shirley and Manfred, is passed around but remains untouched. It is a moose pie. Under the golden crust it is filled with — moose droppings and unripe lingon berries.

The rangers have a motorized canoe.

"We can go by boat to the end of Lake Lindeman.

There is room for some of you."

"Thank you, I love to go by boat," I say. "Historically this is the right thing to do although we didn't build it ourselves. What a crush there must have been when the gold miners launched 7,000 boats in the spring of 1898!"

It is windy on Lake Lindeman making the waters choppy. The canoe is narrow. Those who don't have blisters on their feet prefer to walk. I wave them off and try to get reacquainted with my boots. The seams in the heels have swollen thick. They press on my blisters despite moleskin and socks. The stiffness in my legs doesn't go away today. I am very slow. I can barely move but I must make it to the train from Bennett seven miles from here.

We launch the canoe three hours after the hikers left and go ashore where they wait for us. Manfred takes my pack. Without a pack I limp along in the rear. I must use my whole body to move my legs. It might look funny but it is exhausting. We can see Bennett from the gold miners' unfinished church. The train hasn't arrived yet.

We have time for a thank you ceremony on the railroad tracks. I pull out the shyly smiling but embarrassed Manfred on the tracks and hand him a bouquet of rapidly assembled weeds and a gift in a trash bag. His joy is hesitant but surprise genuine when he unwraps the well-preserved moose pie from yesterday.

"We made the Chilkoot Trail!" This experience gave us a better understanding of the gold miners' hardships.

We take the train to Whitehorse and the bus from there, arriving in Fairbanks past midnight. At this time I am not inclined to encounter any prospective problems at my tent that has been uninhabited for ten days. We walk to Carol's home.

In the morning I am brave enough to meet the world and drive home. The double square knot on my tent door is untouched. After this R&R, I am energized to continue my cache construction.

24

Building My Cache

"When will you invite us home?" Mrs. Maini Palosuo asks me one day at the POAC 1975 conference where her husband is one of the invited speakers. I am surprised, since I haven't met her before. In Finland it isn't customary to invite your bosses and especially not if you live in a tent.

August 14, I pick up Professor and Mrs. Palosuo at the University in my white VW bug. They sit down on the floor in my tent while I serve them fresh coffee, boiled from grounds in my potato pot, and store-bought cheese cake.

"Would you do me a great favor?" Erkki Palosuo asks.

"Sure," I reply, assuming he wants a ride to some attraction.

"Would you let me come and help you one day?" he asks to my astonishment.

The next morning we arrive at my construction site and climb the 16-foot ladder to the floor of the cache. It is a beautiful sunny day. Erkki is tall and athletic with short black hair with gray streaks. His sideburns end in a distinct triangle on his cheeks.

"Tell me what you don't want to do yourself," Erkki says.

"Drilling 11- inch long holes through two logs with a 5/8-inch hand drill is the most difficult thing for me," I reply.

"I can do that," my helper says eagerly. "I have a lot of practice drilling ice cores."

I have finished five log courses. The eight-foot long walls are presently two and a half feet high, since I use 3-sided 6-inch logs.

"It would be wise to nail some long 2 x 4 boards to the walls to keep them vertical," Erkki suggests.

"A good idea, I agree." I explain to Erkki how to continue. "First we roll out the large roll of sill seal over the log course and attach it with staples. The one inch thick fiberglass insulation is the same width as the 6-inch logs. Then we lift a log on the fiberglass. The square end buts against the next log, that sticks out about a foot in the corner.

"Where do we drill?" Erkki asks, prepared with my foot-long hand drill.

"We drill about a foot from the corners so we can peg each log to the one below it with a 10-inch long piece of rebar."

"Do you want something to drink?" I ask my hard working colleague, who is toiling with the drill and pounding in rebar with a large sledgehammer.

"Not yet. Not until we have accomplished something," he replies.

The mosquitoes cannot stand the 86-degree heat so we have peace in the air. It is hot. After lunch Erkki takes off his shirt. He kneels on the log wall pushing down on the top handle of the drill with his chin. His muscles bulge as he wrestles the drilling ratchet, but he never complains about anything. After working 10 hours, we finish the seventh log course.

"Is Maini starting to worry about you?" I ask. "She is busy with a ladies' program that includes dinner."

"In that case, I serve you dinner. Canned Norwegian fish balls are one of my staples. The salad is fresh from my garden," I explain as I rinse it with water from a spray bottle.

Our dinner conversation, about old memories from five summers on board the Finnish research vessel Aranda, switches back and forth between Finnish and Swedish. Both of us try to be polite, so we address each other in that person's native language, which is Finnish for Erkki and Swedish for me. When my potato neighbor, Karl Neuman, from a mile down the road, drops in, we switch to English, with a few expressions in German.

Suddenly the sky rumbles and lightning pierces the air. A thunderstorm empties its cache in torrents. The water beats against the tarp over the wall tent but we are well protected. We admire the show through the mosquito-screen covered tent opening. No one is in a rush to go anywhere. My thoughts go back in time.

"My first summer on the Aranda I was a mess girl, since they didn't yet know they wanted to have girls in the scientific party," I explain to Karl. "In August 1959 there was a storm that over-turned the waters in the Gulf of Bothnia. The waves were so big that the cold, high salinity bottom waters were mixed with the warm surface waters. I thought the ship had turned into the Flying Dutchman, that could never come ashore, as we were going up and down the Gulf."

"I was the chief scientist on that cruise," Erkki says. "It was one of the worst storms in memory. We were trying to assist a ship in distress, but we couldn't find it. That's why we appeared to be going back and forth," Erkki explains a 16-year old enigma in my mind.

"You wouldn't believe the shock I got as I came to the bridge of the Aranda one afternoon," Erkki tells Karl. "There, at the huge wheel, steering the whole ship, was this little girl."

"I didn't take the job as a mess girl just to wash dishes. I wanted to learn all I could on the ship," I say.

"Would you please call my parents when you return?" I ask. "They are worried about me. Nothing I say seems to calm them. You are the only one from Finland who has visited me since I started building.

August 16, the sun is shining again when my Finnish friend Kaarina Abel arrives with a rutabaga-liver casserole.

"I had dinner with Maini Palosuo yesterday while her husband was here," Kaarina says. "I came to see the results."

After inspecting the two log courses we finished, Kaarina leaves me to do course eight. The logs are heavy to lift alone, but I can manage by lifting one end at a time. By 10 p.m. I have the course finished. It really feels like progress to get log course eight up, since it frames the door. With a 7x7-foot house, it feels like an unnecessary waste to allocate a whole wall for a door. I can bend a little to come in. After some thought, I have the perfect solution. I will enter under the bed. Putting the bed high will make it warmer, since hot air rises. The bed will be high enough, so my clothing can hang under it. Four feet or eight log courses should be the right height for the most efficient use of space.

August 17, Karl is outside my tent at 8 a.m.

"I came to see if you need any logs lifted?" Karl asks.

"Thank you, Karl, I have four logs ready, peeled and cut. If you can help me get them up to the sun deck, I can handle them alone from there," I say.

"Your four foot wide deck outside the cache door is handy," Karl says.

After getting the logs up, I go to work for a shower. When I return at noon it is raining, but eight new logs have been peeled. That's the kind of tracks my best friend Carol Hagglund leaves behind.

"I don't need to spend money going to a spa, when I can come here and peel logs for free," is Carol's philosophy.

I get course nine in place alone but it is almost impossible to drill the holes for the rebar that peg the logs together. I only get three holes drilled and some only big enough for a 10-inch spike.

Tuesday, August 19, I have seven notes on my desk at work. My physical oceanography boss, Robin Muench, wants to make sure I have something to do while he is abroad for two weeks.

"I prefer that you check in regularly, rather than take extended annual leave," he says. For practical purposes this means that I come to work when it rains or at nights, when I need a shower. It is already getting dark at 9:30 p.m.

I harvest my first new potatoes. It takes three plants to provide dinner.

August 20, it is 48-degrees in my tent and it is raining, so I go to work. During the POAC Conference, a volcano on the Kamchatka Peninsula in Siberia erupted, shortly before, I took some scientists on a tour of the Gilmore Satellite Station. The Russian scientists were impressed to see satellite pictures of an eruption they didn't know about. Now I have a chance to study those pictures more thoroughly.

At 6 p.m. Carol comes by with a visitor. "This is Erkki Kotelainen, a carpenter from Finland, who plans to move here," Carol introduces. Like many Finns, Erkki doesn't say much, but he looks around. "Yesterday, I could only drill two holes in my logs," I tell Erkki. "Drilling is becoming more and more difficult."

"This drill bit has the wrong angle," Erkki says after examining my 5/8-inch bit. "Do you have a file, so I can reshape it?"

"Try it now," Erkki says as he hands me the drill. Effortlessly it almost pulls its way through the logs while I crank the handle with two fingers. I am very pleasantly surprised as I easily drill the last holes in course 9.

Saturday, August 23, I sleep until 10 a.m. It is raining but I still work ten hours. I can no longer afford the luxury to choose my weather. I drill course 10 and pound in the rebar. With my chain saw I cut a 7 x 12-inch window in the eastern log wall. I fill my Coleman lanterns with Blazo, adjust my stored belongings and gaze dreamingly at *My* property.

Carol, Karen and Erkki, who all live with Carol and Karen's aunt Ailie Leikas, come by. They provide strong Finn-power. Erkki drills courses 11 and 12 while Carol re-peels the ridge beam that got dirty since Kjell Henriksen cut down the large spruce. Together we get the ridge beam and the gable logs up to the sun deck.

August 26 I wake at 7 a.m. to 50-degrees and rain. The gusty wind has spread all my stacked aluminum roofing around. I drive to the satellite station. It is cold there too. I feel lonely and depressed in the rain and stay at Gilmore until 8 p.m. writing a letter to a friend in Finland.

On the way back to town I drop in at Kaarina's. She serves me cake. After some talking, she follows up with dinner and insists I spend the night on her living room couch.

August 27 I am early at work after breakfast with Kaarina and Herb. In the evening I saw the logs I previously measured and marked for one side of the cache gable. The logs have to be cut diagonally to fit the pitch of the roof. It is a bit tricky. To get them in place, I need something to stand on.

I have an oil barrel with a lot of bullet holes I previously used for a garbage burn barrel. With block and tackle I get it up. It is just right to stand on to drill the first gable log.

August 29, 37°F. Cold! My backpacking stove runs out of butane and I cannot remove the empty canister. I take it to Gilmore, where one of the guys replaces the tank. In the evening I continue to work on the gable and finish it the next day.

Sunday, August 31, 47°F, pouring rain. I go to work for a shower and write my parents in Finland. A note from Kaarina waits for me in the tent:

"Come to Sorvojas' for evening coffee," it says. I drive to town.

"Let's go to Laitala, the log cabin builder," Kaarina suggests. "He probably has his sauna heated for a Sunday night."

Soaking up the heat in the sauna feels good. It warms me to the bones after 2-1/2 months in my tent. I haven't seen Laitala since he looked at my cabin drawings.

"You were right," I tell Laitala. "If I can get the roof on my cache before the snow falls, I will be very happy. I have come to the ridge pole, and I don't know how to get it up."

Labor day, September 1, Laitala comes for an unexpected but welcome visit together with his large chain saw.

"We need to measure and mark the logs for the other gable end," I tell him.

"No, we stack them and peg them together on the wall first. Then we snap a chalk line and cut the wall to shape," Laitala says.

"This is not the way I did the first gable," I say "but I trust your expertise."

"Let's try that small chain saw of yours," Laitala says. I start my saw with a 14-inch bar and hand it to him, where he sits straddling the wall as a rider on the top log.

"I couldn't sit like that and cut without falling down," I tell Laitala.

"Maybe not," he says with a slight smile, while calmly working the saw diagonally along the gable logs. He goes over the same logs cutting a little bit more every time so he can fine-adjust his cut rather than cutting through the whole log at once as I do.

"The ridge pole is on the cache landing, but how do we get it up on the logs?" I ask Laitala.

"We just lift it," he says. "It doesn't weigh that much."

"Guess you don't have a scriber," Laitala correctly assumes, "but I can make you one." He picks up a wood sliver and cuts a groove in it with his pocketknife. With a pencil in the groove he scribes the wall to fit the shape of the ridgepole and scoops it out with the chain saw and an ax. I watch intently trying to remember it all.

"The trick is to scoop a little extra in the middle of the log to make room for extra fiberglass, so you get a tight fit," Laitala says.

When the job is done, after 6 hours, I serve Laitala a tomato sandwich with beer.

My neighbor Karl's friend, Dan St. John, has asked me to visit. It is 9 p.m. before I have the time to go. My Volkswagen bug dies on a dirt road through the forest. I call Dan from a house in the vicinity. He comes to help me.

"Your oil bath is dirty, but you can drive without it," Dan says and removes it. "I'll follow you home. I want to see your cache."

It is dark now close to midnight so I use a Coleman lantern to show off my construction.

"Do you know how to nail 2 x 6-inch tongue and groove (T&G) ceiling?" Dan asks. I think I do, but reply:

"Why don't you tell me?" Good I did, because Dan's reply is different from my idea to just nail straight through the board. Nailing through the tongue is a lot more refined and doesn't show.

During the rest of the week I call around town trying to find a metalbestos chimney. Every store is out of chimney parts. I have already bought a sheet metal stove. It is supposed to burn both wood and gasoline, which sounds like a practical idea. I read instruction books and ask people for advice on how to build my roof and install the chimney and stove.

September 6, I start to nail T&G for the ceiling of my cache. The ridgepole is a lot longer than the top logs in the wall to make the roof pointed in the ends, because I like the look. I must cut the outside 2 x 6- inch boards diagonally. It is hard and slow with a hand saw. The next day I continue pounding T&G- planking for seven hours. Carol and Karen come to watch.

"I will not have the time to come by and help you much more," Carol says. "I will go back to school to get my degree in business administration. Besides, you won't get me up on that roof!"

"Thank you, Carol and Karen, for all the peeling. I won't need any more logs peeled until I start the big cabin."

September 9, I wake up to frost, fog, and a thick layer of ice on my car. The tops of the potatoes have frozen. It feels very cold. I stay home and work on my roof until 8 p.m. and get the northern half covered. The gable walls are slightly too high for the ceiling planks. I chisel and ax them down and get a tight fit with sill seal in between. When the sun sets at 8:30 p.m. it gets cold immediately. With two Coleman lanterns I can heat the tent to 50 degrees. I have new potatoes and fish balls for dinner.

September 10, I have a surprise package from Finland at the post office. My Mother sends me a sourdough rye bread. It has the equivalent of $2 in postage, which is eight times the value of the bread in Finland. That's the best bread I ever ate in my tent. The rain and cold make it taste even better than normal.

September 13, the sun is shining again after three days of rain. It is 39 degrees in my tent. The T&G ceiling in the cache is finished. The last board I have covers the gable wall. How lucky can you get? Half of the overhang on the porch is missing. It is convenient so I can get down from the roof. Plywood Supply, and everybody else in town, is out of T&G- boards and

6-inch metalbestos chimney pipe. It must be the influx of people in connection with the pipeline construction that is using up all the supplies. Carol arrives in the evening and climbs my ladder to the cache. We can see a lot of golden birch trees from up here.

The coals in the BBQ on the deck are hot.

"Now we'll celebrate," I tell Carol. "We'll have barbecued salmon and corn on the cob."

"Cheers to your new home," Carol says as she lifts her champagne mug for a toast. "Last time we toasted in champagne was May 17 when you took possession of your new land" Carol reminisces.

I move into the cache after dinner. I have anxiously waited and dreamt about this for a long time. It is a balmy 56-degrees inside. The boards above the door I have been standing on while working become my bed.

September 14, it is 45-degrees in the cache when I wake up and it is dry. What a luxury! The cold outside tells me I better get the roof insulated and covered quickly. First I cover the 2 x 6-inch ceiling boards with a sheet of visqueen for a vapor barrier to prevent warm, moist inside air from leaking into the insulation. My next step is to nail rafters, which make the compartments for insulation. It is difficult to keep the 2 x 10-inch rafters on the slippery surface until I saw the boards at suitable angles and attach the pairs at the top. At 11 p.m. I can feel the effect of the plastic. It is 63-degrees in the cache.

September 22, I have single-handedly got all the rafters in place on two-foot centers. Now I have something to hold on to so I won't slide off the slick roof. Bob Sullivan, who helped me with the cache foundation in exchange for food, reappears to check my progress. He helps me with the long 2 x 4-inch nailers that we attach perpendicularly over the rafters. Later I will cover them with ribbed aluminum roofing sheets. Bob cuts two of the sheets diagonally for the pointed end of the roof. Afterwards, for a change, he serves me dinner consisting of rice and tuna with cheese and zucchini.

The next day metalbestos chimney pipe finally arrives at Plywood Supply. Bill Blockcolsky, who knows I used creosote preservative for my ground timbers, comes by with a 4 x 4-inch pole he wants me to creosote.

"This is perfect timing," I tell him. "Now you can tell me how to install the chimney."

September 24, I get my three-foot chimney in place. Two weeks ago I neatly cut the chimney hole with a keyhole saw. Yesterday Bill told me that two inches of air space around the chimney is not enough. I need three inches as a safeguard against fire. I no longer have the time to be perfect. I just trim the additional inch with my chain saw. With the light from my Coleman lantern and a temperature of 50-degrees in the cache, I can work until 2 a.m. I build a log foundation for my wood stove with room for firewood under it. For safety, the stove will stand on a sheet-metal tray with sand in it.

September 25, I put 10-inch thick fiberglass bats between my roof rafters and loosely cover everything with aluminum roofing. It gets dark at 7:30 p.m. A lot of noise on the roof disturbs my sleep. When I wake up at 6 a.m. it is 50-degrees at the four-foot height of my bed and 31 degrees in Fairbanks. Most of my aluminum panels have blown down.

September 27, it is 46-degrees by my bed and 17-degrees outside. I continue to nail aluminum over the fiberglass.

My chimney must be tightened with tar, but once I get the can of tar on the roof, the tar is too cold to spread. I must heat it. Hot water! I take my Optimus camping stove, that is my kitchen stove, up onto the roof and warm a pot of water. Then I put the can of tar in the pot. The only problem is keeping the stove on the sloping roof, but I get the job finished.

Kaarina, Herb and Carol come to visit.

"Welcome up my ladder," I greet them. "I will light my first fire just for you." As the temperature rises to 90-degrees, the cache fills with thick smoke.

"What did I do wrong?" I cry alarmed.

"Don't worry," Kaarina says comforting. "This is just steam. Your walls and floor are soaked with moisture from all the abundant rain."

October 19, I can buy more T&G-boards. They all have to be diagonally cut. I mark them, load them on my shoulder and walk up to my neighbor Jim Baldridge who has a table saw. Why didn't I think about this earlier? I cover the northern half of the porch over-hang. There is a special chill in the air with 22-degrees. Snow can fall any time. My long grace period may be up. I better nail down the last aluminum roofing. I am very careful as I crouch at the edge of the roof. I don't have the time to be afraid of falling off. The job is too urgent. My headlight for skiing, with the flashlight battery in my pocket, makes it possible to finish the job in the dark. With a sense of relief for my accomplishment I go to Carol for dinner and stay over-night. It snows that night.

October 21, it continues to snow. I barely make it up the hill with my car. The snow is about a foot deep. I am the only one living down this hill, so the road will be snowed in. Without electricity to plug in my car, it is no sense to have the road plowed.

"You can park by my house for the winter," Fred Ensign, who lives a quarter-mile up on top of the hill, tells me. "I have electricity so you can plug in for a dollar a day, when necessary to make your car start." October 27, it is 27-degrees in the cache when I come home from work at 8:30 p.m. My water jugs are frozen.

October 31, I go to a theater performance. As I climb my ladder at 1 a.m., I can smell brewery fumes in the dark fresh 10-degree night air. Two gallon- bottles of red wine have cracked and the frozen wine is on the floor. I salvage most of it with a shovel. When I tell my colleagues about the mishap, Gerd and K.O.L.F say:

"We better bring our own booze when we go and visit Kristina."

I have known for a while that a blanket is not sufficient as a door covering. By November 1, I have finally figured out how to make a door. A frame of 2 x 6-inch boards on end, filled with fiberglass and covered by plywood makes the door as thick as my walls. When the two-and-a-half-foot square door is ready, it is too dark and cold at 20 below to attach hinges. I just lift it in place and climb up in bed. In the morning it is 30 degrees indoor and 18 degrees outside. The door works well to keep the cold out but, when I try to open it, I cannot. It is frozen in place from the escaping moist air and doesn't have a handle. Despite the favorable temperature difference it feels like a waterless cold shower. I am trapped! I better calm down and think. I don't want to push the door out and have it fall down to the ground. With a large screwdriver I can pry it open.

November 9, Walter Pierce, a folk dance friend and wise old time Alaskan sourdough, comes to see if I need some help. Walt is sinewy with big strong hands, thinning black hair and thick glasses.

"Your door hinges are too small," Walt says. "Somebody told me that the hinges I planned to use are gate hinges."

"They are just right. Let me exchange them for you," Walt offers. "I can also chisel a groove in a log so we can attach a clasp, if you want to put a padlock on your door."

"Do you think some evil person would dare climb my 16-foot ladder?" I ask.

"It may not be a bad idea to lock your door if you go traveling," Walt says.

He looks around inside my cache with a concerned look. "You don't have any ventilation, now when your door is in place," he says. "You may wake up dead one morning."

"I do have two ventilation holes, one in the lower wall by the stove and one below the ceiling by my bed." I point out.

"They are too small," Walt says.

"Here is my chain saw," I say as I hand it to Walt. "Do what is necessary."

November 17, I replace the visqueen with one pane of window glass in my 6 x 36 - inch picture window. At twenty below, the construction cement for the window frame hardens too fast and the pane frosts over immediately. With a door and a window I can heat the place to 105 degrees but it still feels damp. Five days later I install the inner windowpane. My six-inch thick window gradually clears.

Now I am finally set for the winter in my own nest without some of the worries other people have. I have a five-gallon can of Blazo for my lanterns, two old trees lying on the ground for firewood and an 80- lb sack of coal.

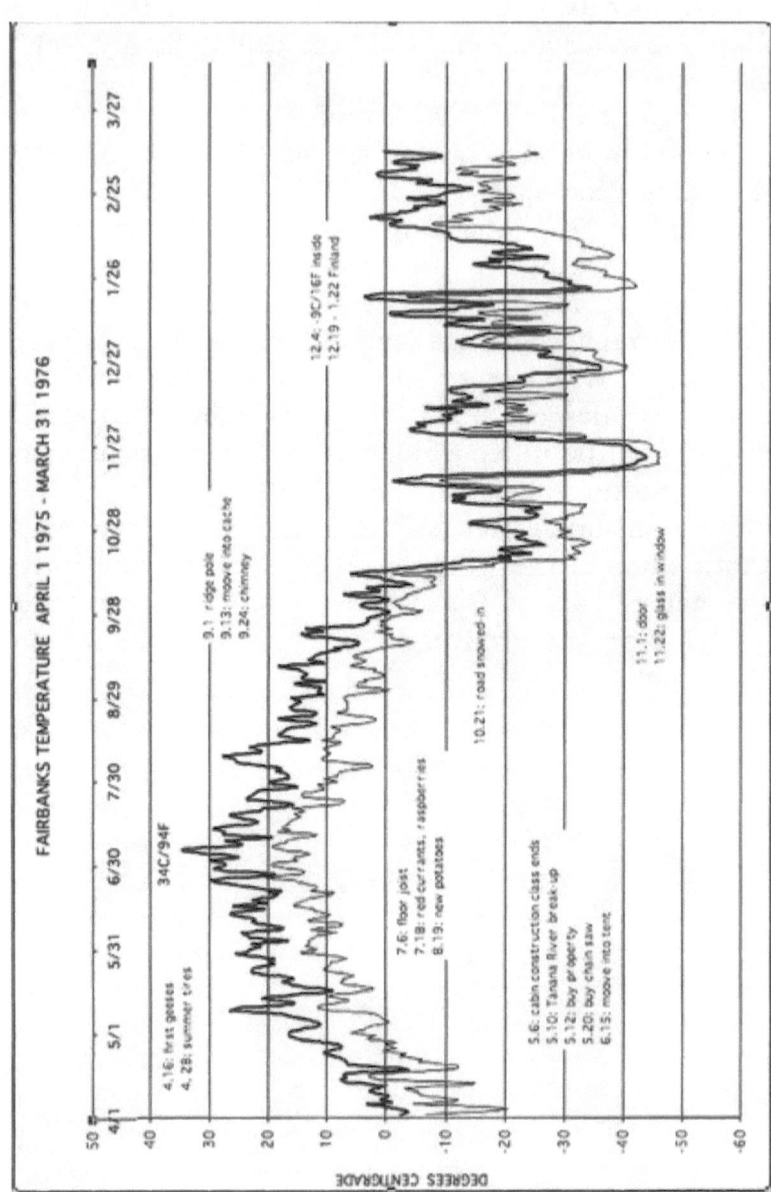

Fairbanks Maximum and minimum Temperature April 1 1975 - March 31 1976

25

Rescued by the US Coast Guard

"Do you want to go on an all-expenses paid cruise?"
Dr. Robin Muench, my boss at the Institute of Marine
Science (IMS), asks me early in 1976.

"Sure, I love to," I reply enthusiastically. "It's below
freezing in my cache when I wake up in the morning
and when I come home from work."

"IMS needs a representative for Physical
Oceanography on the National Oceanic and Atmospheric
Administration (NOAA) research vessel, the R/V
Surveyor, on a cruise to the Bering Sea in March," Bob
says. "You don't need to do much. You just have to
measure oxygen and check that the ship's professional
survey technicians follow IMS protocol for sampling
sea water."

"But I haven't measured oxygen since I was on
the R/V Aranda in Finland. The method has probably
changed in 10 years," I say with some hesitation.

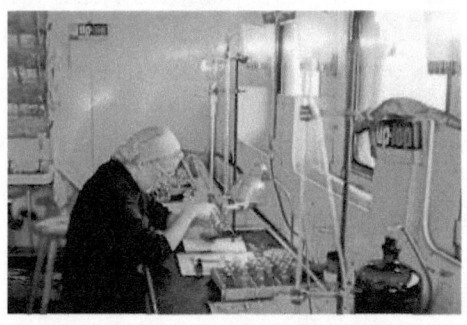

Kristina titrating the Oxygen on the R/V *Aranda* 1963

"The Winkler method for measuring oxygen hasn't changed," my boss replies as if there was nothing for me to be concerned about.

"Is there a machine that I can practice with here?" I ask.

"No, the titration equipment will be sent directly to the ship from the marine station in Seward," Bob replies.

"But I am not familiar with IMS protocol for hydrography," I say. "My recent oceanography cruises have been for marine geology and chemistry," I say.

"We have an instruction book," Bob says.

My oceanography colleague, David Nebert, often goes on cruises. Patiently he answers all the procedural questions I can think of. This makes me feel better prepared when I leave. It takes 10 hours to fly from Fairbanks to Kodiak with a stopover in snowy Anchorage.

It is a sunny and brisk afternoon on March 13, 1976. At the U. S. Coast Guard dock in Kodiak, no one seems to know any details: when we can go on board, when we will sail. None of us six scientists from Fairbanks is in a position of authority and nobody takes any initiative. We sit down on a collection of crates to wait. Twenty-five boxes with scientific equipment are missing. Towering behind us is the white R/V Surveyor, with **05532 NOAA** in large black letters on the bow.

At nine p.m., I enter a very cold cabin I will share with Marilyn Sigman, a University of Alaska student. My large heavy Army surplus parka on the ship's blanket will keep me warm until the heat comes on.

The other scientists on the first leg of this six- week research cruise are marine biologists from the University and the Alaska Department of Fish and Game. They will study everything from walruses to plankton. Their sampling gear varies from rifles to Millipore filter.

I am very curious about the contents in the boxes shipped from Seward and eager to unpack them but don't know where to set up my equipment nor whom to ask.

We cast off the next evening. Bad weather is forecasted. I start unpacking my oxygen equipment and choose a counter in the lab. I have two boxes with calibrated glass flasks, a quarter of which are broken. The swell grows. We can expect wave heights of 23 feet.

Survey Technician (ST), Patrick McKeoun, who has the 4-8 watch, helps me tie down things in the lab. There are two STs per watch and a total of 15 scientists. STs work eight hours per day. There is no time restriction for the scientists.

"How long have you worked as a ST?" I ask Pat, happy to meet my first experienced technician.

"Two months, I've made one IMS cruise before," he replies.

"Are you trained as a survey technician?" I ask. "No, the only thing required is some college classes in science," he says.

Bob Muench promised me trained technicians. I must have met the newest one first, I think, but unfortunately, this is not the case. Only three of seven STs have experience. The best, Tom Chapman, with a degree in economics, has been here for six months.

I am relieved to find the expedition has a chief scientist (CS), Don Day, from Juneau.

"We'll have a meeting at ten where you can explain IMS protocol to all STs and ODs (Officer on Duty)," CS tells me. It is confusing to me that the ship's personnel are referred to by their abbreviated job titles.

I make copies of IMS's CTD-station protocol. The CTD recorder is an instrument that electronically registers seawater salinity, temperature, and depth from the surface to the depth where the recorder stops. It is normally combined with a Rosette- sampler with cylindrical Niskin-water bottles. When the collector is lowered, all bottles are open so seawater can flow through the cylinders. Water samples are taken at standard depths registered on magnetic tape. The CTD records as it goes down and the results are drawn on paper. On the way up, the recorder-collector is stopped at predetermined depths and the bottle closing mechanism triggered. Thermometers can be attached to the bottles to calibrate the electronic readings. When the bottle is closed, the thermometer trips and breaks the mercury so the temperature at the specified depth is preserved. When the whole equipment returns to the surface, the thermometers are read and water samples from the different depths drawn from the respective bottles.

Twelve of us are seated at a round table in the officers' lounge. This is the first IMS voyage for the Surveyor. I find the situation embarrassing as I explain how the water sampling is to be conducted, with the help of a thick manual. I cannot admit, of course, that I have never used this equipment. Now I am to be the expert, when I thought everyone else was.

The swell has grown since yesterday and rocks the ship roughly. The motion has a disturbing effect on me. Soon, I need to excuse myself. The door to the head is conveniently behind my back. The noise from the engines and the breaking waves scarcely drown out the noise of me throwing up. After the intermezzo, I return to the table and continue my talk as if nothing had happened. I hope my face is no longer green. When I finish, the ship's STs want to show their sampling equipment.

The sea feels worse in the chart room two decks up. ST Tom, from the 8-12 watch demonstrates the CTD -recording receptor until I have to interrupt.

"Where's the head?" I ask urgently.

The weather officer escorts me. With my stomach empty, I can smilingly resume my discussion with the CS (Chief Scientist).

"Excuse me again."

The closest man politely opens an appropriate door. Afterwards, I sleep for three hours. Pharmacy maid Mary brings me some Dramamine for seasickness.

"Take four a day and one at bedtime," she instructs. "You're not the only one. Some of the plankton and fish researchers are also sick."

The pill and sleep helps settle me so I can continue to set up the oxygen apparatus. David Brickell, with wide, sculpted face features, is in the lab setting up a Beckman-spectrophotometer for chlorophyll. He is in a bad mood.

"I'm mad at IMS Physical Oceanography. You're the third inexperienced person they send to sea to measure oxygen. They assume I'll be on hand to set up the oxygen equipment and show how to use it. I've taught myself. If you absolutely cannot handle it I'll have to help you too," David ends.

I am intimidated by his emotional blow off and decide not to bother him until I notice a piece is missing. Dave hands me the part and an Allen- wrench. Everything is dirty. I clean what I can with concentrated hydrochloric acid. When was it used last, I wonder.

We are scheduled to reach our first CTD-station after breakfast the second day. I get up at six to have everything ready. We pass through Unimak Pass with snow-covered volcanoes on the Aleutian Islands and enter the Bering Sea. I want calibration thermometers on two of the 11 5-liter Niskin bottles in the Rosette collector. That will tell me the reliability of the CTD temperature recording. When I check the temperature scale on the first thermometer, it goes from 0-60°C.

"The water temperature here is between -2 and 10°C. We need the smallest scale possible to get an accurate reading," I tell ST Pat. He changes the thermometer.

I am not pleased with the other thermometer either in the scale of -10 to 40°C but let it pass for the first station on the recommendation of both CS and Dave.

The sampling starts in the chart room by selecting sampling depth and scale for the electronic registration and entering station data on tape while the water sampler sits on the after-deck. Communication between the two locations could be improved. David Brickell comes to the chart room before the first CTD sampling but doesn't take over. I feel he is just checking up on me.

"Here's a list of the standard depths for sampling," he says as he hands it to me.

"Thank you for your concern," I reply. "Your list is in agreement with mine."

The Philippine chief survey technician, called CR, is friendly and smiling but doesn't concern himself with sampling. I have to fill out all the forms myself and trigger the first bottles at a depth of 400 meters. Dave returns to the chart room.

"The Rosette-Sampler has been on deck for a long time. We can't do anything until you collect the oxygen samples," he informs me.

"I am sorry. I didn't think about that. I thought some of the "experienced" STs would collect the samples," I say. The oxygen must be collected first before any oxygen from the air mixes with the deep- water samples. Pickling reagents containing Manganese and Iodine must immediately be added to the oxygen bottles to bind the dissolved oxygen. After that, the samples can safely sit until convenient to measure or, I run out of bottles. When I am finished, so is dinner, but I get served anyway. The next CTD- station comes at 7 p.m. CS and ST are running to me.

"How do you enter station data on tape?" they ask.

With the help of Tom, I get the thermometer scales I want, -2 to 3°C for the bottom sample and 2 to 7°C for the surface sample. CS is upset.

"The Rosette-Sampler takes too long. It should only take 45 minutes, not 90. You don't need to collect temperature and salinity data when you have electronic recording. Otherwise, we could regress 100 years and use Nansen-bottles," CS says.

"This is only our second CTD-station. We are still not accustomed with the procedure. Initially we need a few actual samples to compare with the electronic registration," I explain. I don't mention that Nansen-bottles are what I am accustomed to using on previous cruises on the Baltic.

I am finally in my cabin, tired and upset after a straining 16-hour workday. Am I trying to do too much? There are a limited number of salinity bottles and ST-resources. I am outside the watch system and appear to be responsible for the results of each CTD-sampling.

CS, the Chief Scientist, and I are the first at the breakfast table.

"I am seriously trying to coordinate all scientific events with the ship's available help. A steam engine is broken. We can only make seven knots and have already lost a day. The CTD broke when you were asleep," CS unloads his concerns.

"I felt justified in sleeping after a 16-hour work day," I say quietly.

I couldn't imagine it would be so difficult to get the oxygen equipment to work. Air bubbles have collected in the glass tubing. I get some of them out after loosening the tie-downs and tilting the machine. If I could turn it upside down, I should be able to get all air out, but it weighs too much and I need more than two hands. David knows I need help, but I don't see him and don't want to bother him. I walk around deck looking for someone to help me. The second time around, I see Dr. John Burns, a sea mammalogist, reading a book. He has a big purple mark on his temple, making him look like a pirate. I wonder if he got too close to a walrus? While John flips the apparatus I can turn the glass faucet and get the bubbles out. Finally, at lunchtime, I am ready to measure oxygen but my stomach is getting queasy. I take a Dramamine in place of lunch and sleep for three hours.

Dinner and the next CTD-station come at the same time. I don't feel like eating. The deck is cold and windy with snow. The Niskin bottles are frozen in the sampler and must be thawed with hot water and pliers. It is difficult to get the event number I have to enter on tape in the chart room before the sampling can start.

"Ask OD," OO and XO on the bridge tell me. I must spell these abbreviations out in my mind to know whom I deal with. OD = Officer on Duty, OO = Officer of Operations, XO = Executive Officer.

"I'm busy checking position, I'll give you the number and depth later," OD says. After discovering an Echo Sounder in the chart room, I can read my own depth but I still need the event number from the bridge. The form for the arrangement of thermometers is incorrectly filled out.

"Tom and Debbie, would you please correct the form," I ask the survey technicians. "After the sampling, I will show you how to collect sea water for oxygen and salinity in the wet lab." Dave, appointed CS for this station, supervises everything in silence.

Next CTD comes at dawn, but I'm running out of oxygen flasks since a quarter got broken in shipping. I have to measure oxygen. I do this with the accuracy of one drop. That's why I cannot allow any trapped air bubbles. It is after midnight when I finish titrating the old samples. At one in the morning I sit alone in the galley with a cup of cocoa. My thoughts go back to my time as a galley girl on the Finnish research ship Aranda. Then I was tired after a 10- hour workday setting tables and washing dishes. In my spare time, I was privileged to titrate oxygen and salinity in the lab since I was a student of oceanography. In those days they didn't accept girls in the scientific party

On the morning of the fourth day, we can see the ice edge at the horizon. The bridge is buzzing with at least seven officers. The entire windshield is frosted, with the exception of three small round viewing holes. No one appears to have seen ice before. The Captain is surprised when John Burns explains:

"The edge consists of thin mush we easily can get through to the dark areas behind, which is open water."

A reconnaissance tour by helicopter is prepared to learn the best way to proceed. A warm battery is carried out. A fireman dressed in silver supervises fueling with fire hoses ready for use. Finally, the helicopter rotors are spinning on the windy upper after-deck but the fueling hoses freeze and the tour is canceled.

The ship moves slowly and carefully into the ice between the Pribilof Islands, looking for a suitable location to anchor for the first 24-hour sampling station. ST Tom reads instructions for measuring salinity with a salinometer while CR looks for standard Copenhagen water for calibration of the salinometer. Water from an oceanography lab in Copenhagen is the standard all salinity measurements are compared to. When I titrated salinity on the Aranda, I was accurate enough to split drops and was used to calibrate the Copenhagen water.

The ship's salt-water evaporator for making fresh water is broken. No more showers allowed.

Our sixth day at sea, March 20, is sunny and almost calm. We float amidst slowly rocking ice floes at the edge of the ice. A curious king eider with a large orange beak swims by. The ship wants an early helicopter reconnaissance; John Burns wants one in the middle of the day when the animals are out.

When I start to measure oxygen, I am disgusted to discover new air bubbles in the glass tubing.

"You must keep the air temperature in the lab constant to avoid bubbles. Leave the lights on at all times," Dave advises.

I get ST Debbie Wencker from the 8-12 watch to help me. While I turn the glass faucet, the wheel bumps into something and the micropipette breaks. I am angry and upset.

"This apparatus should never have come to sea and absolutely not without spare parts," I say.

We see seven large fishing vessels at the solid-ice edge. They raise Soviet flags as we approach. We answer with the American. The ice floes are covered with sea lions. John Burns returns to the ship in a Boston whaler, towing an ice floe with a sea lion they shot.

Thin gray ice-plates start to show between the ice floes as we move further into the pack ice. The plates slide over and under each other as the ship pushes them to the side. The survey technicians (ST) are getting accustomed to the CTD-routine, so I plan on sleeping during the next CTD-station at five a.m. and give ST Pat his chance to solo.

"Pat, by now you know what to do and can take a perfect CTD," I announce for all to hear.

Gradually all ST-watches learn how to handle the CTD and only come to me with questions and problems. I write detailed instructions for everything. I want to give the survey technicians a feeling of responsibility and pride over work well done so I don't have to check everything. I realize STs don't have much time to measure salinity, so I ask Tom to show me how the salinometer works. When CR sees this, he suddenly finds two new boxes with bottles.

OO gives me one of the ship's ungainly life preservers for my first helicopter tour from the ship. Ed Muktoyuk, an Eskimo mammalogist, sits in the copilot's seat to look for seals. The back-seat passengers are interested in sea-ice and to find a way out of it for the ship. I can see ice floes of different age fused together, between leads and large smooth ice floes.

Suddenly the helicopter dives like an eagle and makes a few tight circles around a floe before we land on it. Ed saw a spotted seal, but it had time to dive. Only seal tracks remain on the windy floe.

"It wasn't my intention to scare you," the pilot assures me.

"Everything went so fast, I didn't have time to be afraid, just surprised," I reply.

The hazy swell moves slowly through the new gray-ice. John Burns gets excited about the seals we see from the bridge. Until now, we have seen mainly sea lions. The Boston whaler is launched for seal hunting.

The sun emerges. The large lifeboat with inboard motor is launched for the bird watchers - George Divoky and Doug Woodby. I go along as an observer. The ship sends two deck officers as well - a man to tend the motor and an oarsman. George and Doug sit in the bow with their rifles ready, but the birds have the sense to fly away before we get close. We only have an hour, enough time to make a last run towards the ice-edge. It is interesting to get a closer look at the sea ice. Two white gulls fall into the water after two well-aimed shots. A deck officer retrieves them with a net.

The sun continues to shine after lunch. I get a thin thermofloat jacket that fits under my thick Army parka. David Brickell has invited me to come along on an ice-drilling tour. I take the invitation as an offering of acceptance. I have managed the oxygen without bothering him. Dressed in two coats, padded flight pants and Bunny boots, I have a hard time swinging my legs overboard. The Boston whaler with a Johnson outboard motor has been cleaned up after the seal hunters. Seen from the E-deck of the Surveyor, it looks very small and very far down on the surface of the water. The rope ladder to it seems really long. The ship sends only one man to run the motor.

The boat is slow. With a weak wind from the stern, it is a pleasant tour along the mushy gray-ice with a few rounded white floes imbedded in spots. Birds sit all over the ice and fly along it in large groups. We see a suitable 20-foot ice floe and steer towards it. Carl Tobin jumps on ice with an anchor.

"We come unarmed, as friends," he announces dramatically.

Dave follows with the SIPRE-ice drill. I sit down on the floe and run my S-8 movie camera. What a strange sensation to step out of a boat and feel the "ground", rock under me. The swell makes the floe and the entire area of ice rise and fall slowly. Curious sea lions pop up their heads around us. We see four seal heads in the background. They must have heard Carl's greeting. "Don't let the seal-hunters come here. You are our friends," Carl tells the seals.

The first core is a foot long. The underside of the floe is white. The algae bloom has not started yet. Dave bends over the edge of the ice floe to take a closer look under the water with a plastic bag over his head.

We can see the ice edge at the horizon on our 12th day at sea. The sea mammal researchers make long reconnaissance flights and see seals all over, at times hundred in a place. I finally have the time to start the Bible correspondence course I brought along. It gets more fascinating with time. My cabin mate, Marilyn, works on her master's thesis on moose.

Our beautiful days are almost over. A low pressure over Kamchatka and another south of the Aleutians will soon bring us normal Bering Sea weather. The swell grows. Both Marilyn and I go horizontal. Our cabin is at the water's edge. The noise is awful when the ice floes scrape against the side of the ship. Our work at the ice edge is over and we leave the Bering Sea.

Ahead of us on the port side, the snow-covered coast of Unimak Island with mountaintops approaching 10,000 feet comes into view on March 31. We meet a freighter carrying timber in hazy Unimak Pass. The ship steers straight for us at a good speed. We change our course a little but the other ship doesn't see us until we send out thick black smoke through the smoke stack. On the Pacific side of the pass, we begin to feel the promised storm, and the ship becomes unstable. I try to finish my report for CS about the physical oceanography work during the voyage before the rocking gets worse. We took 28 CTD-stations, most of them in the vicinity of the ice edge.

To my surprise, I feel fine on April 1, though the ship continues to rock. Sometimes it is as noisy as when we passed through the ice. I take a nap after dinner but am violently awakened by the ship's alarm. Fire, amidships in my quarters! Sleepily, I observe the events in the lounge until XO speaks to me:

"You are supposed to go to the officers' lounge. Look out for the fire doors."

Just then the doors slam automatically. I save my log cabin construction book, but I'm too tired to read. Two men are missing. Dave checks. He shakes life into Carl and Ken, who didn't hear the alarm. They thought it was an April fools joke. Interesting to have this drill the day before landfall — after 19 days at sea.

The NOAA-ship, R/V Discoverer, is in port. ST Debbie's sister is one of three female officers on board. Debbie offers me a tour. Compared to the Surveyor, the Disco looks more like a passenger ship with wide corridors, large cabins, comfortable lounges, exercise equipment, and a large laboratory. It even has an operating room and dental office.

A man stands in the doorway. I concentrate on listening to Debbie's sister and ask questions with my characteristic accent. I must have been watched for a while.

"How long do you need to recognize me?" the man with a neat reddish beard asks and gives me a hug. I am surprised. It is my ex-husband, Tony, whom I haven't seen for eight years after he asked me to return to Finland, since I wouldn't change to his liking. He has matured, looks better, and appears content with life. He waits for me after the tour. We take a brief walk.

"My new wife would like to meet you. It would be nice to see how you live," Tony says.

"My wall-tent is vacant since I moved into the cache. You are both welcome to stay in it," I extend an invitation.

"Thank you, but I don't have enough vacation time," Tony says. I am pleased to learn he has made a new happy life for himself.

An engine problem on the Surveyor was discovered yesterday. Two specialists arrive from Seattle. They can re-file the gear axle in five days.

New scientists arrive for the second leg of the cruise. Chemists Bob Barsdate and Margie Young look at my broken oxygen equipment.

"The pipettes are wrong. One of the three arms in the glass faucet is too long. The equipment must have broken before and been repaired in the wrong proportions. We can order all the parts needed by air freight so you can measure oxygen again," they tell me.

"Why didn't anybody check that the apparatus worked before they sent it?" I ask.

After a two-day delay and a test day at sea, the Seattle mechanics leave the ship by helicopter. The second leg of the voyage to the Bering Sea has started. We expect to reach the first station at 2 a.m. on April 15. After Unimak Pass, we reach the first CTD-station in the Bering Sea. The depth is 2,700 meters but the ship's winch has only 1,500 meters of wire. In the chart room, I get radio earphones so I can talk directly to the bridge and the winch operator on the after-deck. The competence and cooperation of everybody has increased noticeably and the work runs efficiently. Almost everyone, including the captain, observes the taping of data in the chart room for the first CTD-station. Holding a handle in the instrument wall, I stand firmly. We lower the CTD-fish to a depth of 1,500 meters without complications and wait five minutes for the thermometers to stabilize before we flip them and close the sample bottle. I fill bottles with 2.5°C water for 16 oxygen samples. Five hours after the start of the station, I have the oxygen bottles secured with reagents. By 11 p.m. the samples are titrated. At 3:45 a.m. a crewman pulls the blanket off me.

"We're arriving on station at 4:30," he says.

On the afternoon of April 16, we reach the ice edge with its familiar banging and scraping. We are surrounded by beautiful white ice floes. The sun is out again after clouds and blowing snow. I have no problems measuring oxygen with correctly functioning equipment. Filtered samples from the under side of ice floes show the phytoplankton bloom has started.

On April 21, we run a line with frequent CTD-stations. The survey technicians in the chart room are new to the task, so I supervise everything and handle the oxygen sampling. My workday extends to 23 hours. I am exhausted and discouraged over the loss of the STs I had trained on the first leg.

The seal hunters bring banded seals aboard. There may be only 100,000 of them. Eskimos seldom catch them. It is unknown where they spend their summers. Kathy Frost from Fish & Game tags white seal pups with large brown eyes. She has no trouble finding helpers.

After dinner on April 24, the gear axle breaks again and the ship is adrift without power. Rumors run wild but the weather is good.

On April 25, I decide to sleep in but am awakened by ST Pat for a CTD. The ship is drifting at 0.8 knots through dense fields of small ice floes. STs Tom and Debbie try to cock the stiffly frozen closing wires of the Niskin bottles with the help of the helicopter mechanic and a 500-degree heat pistol. They could have launched the whole Rosette- Sampler with this method The white

U.S. Coast Guard vessel, the Boutwell, and a Coast Guard plane arrive at lunchtime the next day. The scientific part of the voyage is finished. Towing starts at 8 p.m., north east of Unimak Island. I write the position: 55°26.3'N; 163°33.8'W on a piece of paper I put in a bottle with a request that the finder contacts me at IMS. It will be interesting to learn about the further drift of the bottle, should it ever be found.

The ship is towed through Unimak Pass at a speed of four knots on April 27. During the night, the speed increases to eight knots as we reach the Gulf of Alaska.

During the towing, I finish measuring the oxygen samples, calculate the results, and write a report. I continue the Bible correspondence that intrigues me. I feel slightly guilty enjoying the free time I don't have at home. When the junior officers get too loud with singing and guitar playing, I switch to my cabin construction plans.

Watched by sea lions on April 30, the Boutwell turns over the responsibility for the Surveyor to the family-owned tugboat Kodiak King. It is surprisingly hot on the sunny deck, 77-degrees.

It is amazing how long hours I had to work on a cruise where I was told I didn't need to do much. Being a scientist I am accustomed to finishing a project regardless of how much time and effort it takes. On this cruise, my mission became to accomplish a job despite faulty equipment and untrained personnel. In the end, I felt satisfaction of having successfully managed to measure oxygen and teaching others how to do a job well. The fringe benefit of this scientific cruise was experiencing exotic events and nature.

26

Building My Cabin

The fall of 1975 was a race against time. Would I be able to move into my cache or not? Competing with the building project was the urge to bring in what I needed for the foundation of my big cabin, while the road was still drivable. I want to start the main construction as soon as spring begins, without having to wait for the road to dry.

I outline a 16 x 24-foot area for my cabin with 2 x 4-inch boards in preparation for the gravel delivery. I put the boards at the height I want the foundation, and level them with a water-filled garden hose with glass tubes at the ends. The next day, the hose is frozen.

On October 7, I receive eight truckloads, each of nine cubic yards of coarse tailings. The pile is impressive. How on earth can I get it spread out? I wonder. Some rocks in the pile are heavier than I can lift, and the thought of doing it with a shovel is mind- boggling. I hire a man with a caterpillar tractor to spread it out. When he is finished, I realize I don't have enough. Snow powders the ground by the time the last loads are delivered. Bob Sullivan made such a big deal of the necessity to compact the foundation for the cache with the birch pole he made. This time, I rent a gasoline-powered compactor. The vibrating box-like noise-hammer with handlebars jars my arms in a very unpleasant way, but I endure the discomfort for efficiency. Now the foundation is prepared for construction.

The corner of the cache roof wasn't finished, because the stores ran out of 2 x 6-inch tongue-and- groove boards last fall. I have been thinking all winter about how to finish the roof and get myself successfully off it. A small birch tree, growing next to the edge of the cache roof, gives me the idea to build a ladder, using that tree and a birch pole and nailing thinner birch poles as cross steps between. This makes a sturdy ladder.

The stores are re-supplied with building materials for the summer of 1976. In May, I buy a red Ford Courier pickup for $3,700, which simplifies transporting supplies. It feels almost like treachery to sell my 9-year old faithful Volkswagen for $650.

In July, I have a "cache warming," with 10 people in my new 49-square foot home. The last person, however, has to stand on the 16-foot ladder. I serve birch mead, because birch sap was more accessible than water when I brewed the mead. With this many people, it is no problem to erect the power pole my sourdough friend, Walt Peirce, hauled in on his boat trailer. I previously dug a 5-foot deep hole.

A few days later, I am connected to the power grid with an outlet on the pole, just in time for the Olympics. I have lived without electricity for a year and the first thing I connect is my sewing machine in the woodshed. The cache is 100 feet from the pole. With many extension cords tied to birch trees, I have electricity.

Kristina watching TV again in 1976 after a year without
electricity.

The next necessity is an outhouse. Common sense
dictates to dig it deep so it doesn't have to be emptied.
I don't know what is an appropriate depth, but six feet
sounds like it should last far into the future. I select
a secluded spot among the willows downhill from the
cabin site and start digging. After three feet I encounter
an ice lens and frozen clay. That's to be expected on
a north-facing slope in Fairbanks, where the mean
annual temperature is below freezing. Progress is slow
as I am using only a pick, iron bar, rock chisel and
sledge hammer — until I get the idea to build a fire in
the hole. This is the same technique the gold-miners
used, I was told later. After each fire, I can dig a little
deeper. Soon, I have to build a ladder to get down into
the hole. By the end of August, it is done.

To keep it from caving in, I line it with boards. A
house over the hole makes it comfortable. A mosquito
net in the door opening keeps undesirables out but
doesn't obstruct my view. In wintertime, it gets a bit
chilly, but a Styrofoam seat provides some comfort.

The summer of 1976 flies by as I finish the cache,
garden and dig the hole. It doesn't hurt the cabin
foundation to go through another freezing and thawing
cycle — in fact it should stabilize it. The logs I bought in

the summer of 1975 will also benefit from another year of drying.

One day in March 1977 it feels like spring, when the sun warms the daytime temperature to 60 degrees but at night, the temperature still sinks to 15 below zero. With my own electricity, I can plug in the car, and so I have been able to drive home all winter. I hope to start cabin construction early this year, but the site is still covered by two feet of snow.

In the middle of April, I spread wood ash over the cabin foundation to speed up the last snowmelt.

At work I have a new boss, Dr. Tom Royer, whose specialty is Gulf of Alaska oceanography. Once a week, I still drive out to the Gilmore satellite tracking station to check the weekly harvest of satellite pictures. When I come to Gilmore in the beginning of May, the station has a new director, concerned about following *all* government rules.

"Do you have a new purchase order with you, with money to back it up?" he asks me.

"I have requested one. The university will mail it. We have the funding to cover it," I reply.

"We can't give you new pictures until we have the purchase order in hand," he says.

Ken Meyer, the efficient photographer of the tracking station, has booked time to work with me but he isn't permitted to do anything. I show him the plan for my cabin foundation.

"You ought to put the foundation timbers on a concrete foundation or at least have them supported by concrete blocks," Ken advises me.

"My road cannot support a concrete truck," I reply.

"I saw a small wheelbarrow cement mixer in Sears' catalog," Ken says. "If you buy it, I'll show you how to use it. When you don't need it any more, I'll buy it from you for half price."

This was an unexpected outcome to my visit to Gilmore. I need to discuss the new foundation ideas and Ken's proposal with somebody who understands these things. My friend Carol Hagglund and I visit Erkki Kotelainen, the carpenter who re-filed my drill. Erkki has established himself as a professional builder in North Pole south of Fairbanks. We discuss my cabin plans and are treated to a sauna. On May 16, I order the cement mixer from Sears. I also special order extra long logs from Four Star Lumber, so I don't have to join the first and last log course. On May 18, the birch leaves break out. Summer is almost here.

I order a truckload of sand for my cement mixing. The heavy truck backs into my driveway on June 3. At the most narrow place, between a spruce and a birch, the ground starts to vibrate and heave in waves under the back wheels.

"We can't get as close as you want," the truck driver says. "What do you want us to do?"

"Dump the sand where you are," I say, concerned the ground may split.

The 7-foot pile of sand blocks my entry completely. Fortunately, my car is on the outside.

Charlette Chastain, my colleague from Douglas Marine Station who now works for the Department of Environmental Conservation in Juneau, calls me with an offer of manpower. In return, I let her assistant Ken Imamura, coming to Fairbanks for fieldwork, camp on my land. I also feed him. During dinner at my sewing machine table in the cache, Ken hands me a sealed envelope from Charlette. I unfold his recommendation written on the tiniest piece of paper.

"He is harmless," it says.

I cannot keep from laughing. Despite Ken's curiosity, I don't feel inclined to share his boss' evaluation of him. I wash the dishes in a cup of water and use another cup to rinse them.

"You certainly know how to conserve water," Ken says with amazement.

Summers are short and the ground is cold, so I thought it would be a good idea to grow vegetables in an isolated box. I built the walls with double layers of slab wood, stuffing sawdust in between. The bottom is covered with 2 inches of blue foam. I plan to fill it partially with musk ox manure as fertilizer. The evening is beautiful enough to visit the Musk Ox Farm after dinner. In the pickup, I happen to have two shovels handy.

Ken Imamura might be harmless, but he is certainly a good worker. I have a large wheelbarrow made from plywood on two bicycle tires. The sand is heavy. It takes both of us to handle it. I have to get the pile of sand moved to the construction site, so I can drive my car in, but it looks this will be a long project; I will do a little at a time.

The cement mixer from Sears comes on June 8. It fits inside the canopy-covered pickup box, so I can load six 20-foot 2 x 12-inch boards on top. With a board like this as a ruler, I can easily get all 2.5 x 2.5-foot cement forms on four straight lines on the well-compacted gold tailings. I built the forms from 8-inch boards. Ken Meyer, the satellite station photographer, visits with a surveying scope so we can adjust the forms to the same height, pushing a vertical rebar rod in the center. Ken ties rebar crosses to the rods for additional support. I am ready by June 15 with a large pile of sand, six bags of cement and several 5-gallon containers filled with rainwater. Ken arrives to show me how to mix cement.

Ken's recipe for cement (single portion)

1 gallon water — pour into rotating cement mixer
3 shovels sand — add
1 shovel cement powder — add and mix well
2 shovels sand — add a little at a time.

With the cement mixer rotating, Ken pours the contents into the first cement form, while I agitate it with a shovel to remove the air bubbles. The surface is smoothed with a plastering spade dipped in water. We cover the form with wet newspapers and a plastic sheet and leave it to harden for six days. The form is removed after two days.

Construction progresses slowly, since I also have a regular job at the University. On June 16, two unknown men, Dick Peterson and Andy from Colorado, visit me at work.

"I was a roommate of Ed Szafran at the University," Dick says. "You invited your marine geology student colleagues for Christmas dinner in your trailer and Ed took me along."

"I remember," I say. "Ed was the guy who ate all my cookies one night and put a note in my office drawer requesting more."

"We plan to build a log cabin and spend the winter," Dick says. "We are prepared with a riverboat loaded with supplies. Now, we are just looking for a suitable spot we can reach by boat."

"It's OK for you to park your boat on my property while you look," I offer. "In return, you can help me to move a pile of sand and saw some rebar." *How lucky can I get!* I think.

Dick shows up a week later, alone. His partner, Andy, has returned home. We pour a cement form before he hooks up his Jeep to the riverboat and waves goodbye, heading for his Alaskan adventure. A canoe and a sled top his load.

I celebrate the summer solstice of 1977 alone, removing and building cement forms. The sun goes down, but still leaves enough light for me to work past midnight. Ken returns for a couple of evenings with his 15-year old son, Craig. We fill five forms.

Proud of our accomplishment, we date and initial them.

"Craig will be alone over the weekend. It's OK for you to use him," Ken volunteers.

Early, on a sunny Sunday June 26, 1977 I pick Craig up. He has become an expert cement mixer under his father's tutelage. My faithful friend Carol visits me frequently. She and Craig manage to empty the cement mixer with joint efforts. In between, Carol peels logs while Craig and I work on the cement footings. Craig makes a good impression on us. After a productive day pouring four new cement blocks, he handles the barbeque on the cache landing. Soon, we enjoy steaks and corn on the cob. I am very pleased with my birthday, although Craig didn't know the significance of the day.

As a result of my Bible correspondence course on the R/V Surveyor, I had found a special church with loving and concerned members. On June 29, friends from that church visit: Dennis Gentleman, Ralph Dow and Roy Morey. Together we pour a double footing to support the pointed western wall of the cabin. I have chosen that shape because I want windows facing both the sun in the southwest and the view in the northwest.

After getting all 14 cement footings poured, I get the idea to dig a root cellar under the house. I start to dig between four cement blocks that are supposed to support my 4 x 8-foot entryway. Digging would have been a lot easier before the tailings were spread out. In the same fashion as I did the cache foundation timbers, I treat the 10 x10 and 8 x 8-inch timbers with creosote as a preservative.

Four men from church arrive for a work party on July 10. Dennis takes the lead. He is good with a chainsaw — obviously has worked construction before. Roy, with Ralph's assistance, specializes in drilling holes in the timbers to match the rebar sticking up from the center of the cement footings. Roger Lewis helps

Carol's colleague, Joe Thomas, dig my root cellar deeper than I could. Carol peels my last eight logs while I make movies and get things.

Marilyn Gentleman and Toni Dow, together with seven children, arrive with lunch in the middle of the day. A pile of seventeen 1-1/8-inch thick sheets of tongue-and groove plywood makes an excellent lunch table. The wives and children leave after a satisfying and relaxing lunch. We continue to lay three 20-foot long rows and one eight-foot long row of 8-inch timbers perpendicularly across four rows of larger timbers. We lay double layers of timbers to create airspace under the cabin to prevent the heat from the house melting any permafrost that might be in the ground. The vertical rebar in the cement blocks are long enough to go through both layers of timbers with appropriately drilled holes. In an earthquake, the foundation should stay together. We staple metal netting on top to prevent unauthorized entry by squirrels from below. Squirrels steal fiberglass insulation if they can. Next morning, a 4.5 Richter magnitude earthquake shakes me awake in the cache.

On Sunday, a volunteer crew of six people shows up at 8 a.m. All stay until 8 that night except Guy Ramsey, who flew in from Clear, 100 miles to the south. He landed his plane on the airstrip of the original homesteader on top of the hill. The wives, Marilyn, Toni and Judy, provide lunch so I can concentrate on construction. The day is very productive. I am elated to get the entire floor done with 2 x 10-inch joists, fiberglass insulation, a 6-mil visqueen vapor barrier and tongue-and-groove plywood. The floor is 20 x 28 feet but part of it will be outside decking On July 24, a work crew of five shows up.

"I have enough long logs for the first course," I say. "I would like the corners joined by notches."

"We can do that for the first course," Dennis agrees.

"Some logs in the cache have split on the inside while drying. A colleague advised me to saw a groove on the underside of the log with a double circular saw blade," I say.

"I can try that on the long logs," Ralph says.

The plan has the main floor as 16 x 20 square foot with a pointed wall to the west and a 4 x 8-foot entry in the southeast. We start by outlining the location of the walls with strips of 1 x 6-inch fiberglass sill seal. We lay out 22-foot logs along the north and east edges of the plywood decking. Dennis cuts notches with a chain saw to join them in the corner. Then we lay a 22-foot log 16 feet from the log along the north edge and notch the end to the wall in the east. We had previously poured a double cement footing to support the point of the western wall sticking out three feet.

"This will make my cabin a pentagon," I exclaim. "Will notching the corners be too difficult?" I ask Dennis.

"It will be good practice for starters," Dennis says confidently.

In the afternoon, I can improvise a dance of appreciation and joy as I balance on my first log course with a hatchet in one hand and a sledgehammer in the other.

Between work parties, I work alone. When I wake up in the mornings, my hips and back hurt but the pain goes away later in the day.

Generally, I do things the same way I learned when building my practice house, the cache. I have tried to think about all the details. I have read everything relevant and discussed procedures with people more experienced. In addition to knowledge from the log cabin construction class taught by Axel Carlson, I have perused his book *"Building a Log House in Alaska."*

In the cache, some logs have shrunk lengthwise, which they were not supposed to do. I butted them square in the corners, but I notice the fiberglass insulation is loose. Since I cannot prevent shrinkage, I try to lessen the effect. Where the end of a log butts in a corner, I cut an inch-deep indentation. I join with diagonal cuts the logs needing lengthening. To make perfect cuts, I build a short miter box with one end square, the other at a 45-degree angle. The box fits over the 6-inch 3-sided logs

On August 7, I am ready for my second log course. Roger Lewis arrives at 8 a.m.

"I don't know anything about log cabin construction," Roger says. "The only thing I know, I learned in woodworking in school."

"It's OK. I can use the chain saw. The rest we'll figure out together," I reply, glad to have an assistant.

Without wives bringing food, lunch is simple: a sandwich and salad from my garden. George Lajunen and Helli West, Finnish friends of Carol, arrive after lunch and carry peeled logs from the road to the cabin. The next evening, George and Helli bring a third Finn, Vilho Kangas. Together we get course three in place.

On August 11, there is smoke in the air from a 120,000-acre forest fire 250 miles from Fairbanks. Alone, I saw one log for course #4 while a squirrel in a large nearby spruce peels cones. Every time I start the chain saw, the squirrel replies with chatter.

When Carol arrives on the 14th, I have help smoothing the corners and to nail vertical guide boards for the walls. We get three logs in place for the fourth course. When I work alone, it takes a lot longer to move a log, since I have to walk from end to end until I have it adjusted correctly. I use a pry bar and other tools and boards so I don't disturb the inch-thick strip of fiberglass until the log is perfectly placed. If I am unlucky, the log drops off the cabin. It takes me a week to finish this course as a side job to my work at the University. The wall is now two feet high.

Friday evenings, I sometimes go to Helli's — she has a sauna. Often, I meet other Finns there. On August 21, I cook a pot of goulash, expecting Finnish construction help. Nobody shows up except for two Jehovah's witnesses who are unsuitably dressed for work.

"Are you building a log cabin by yourself?" one of them asks.

"You are welcome to help me," I invite them as I prepare my chain saw.

They look at me with bewilderment as they quickly depart.

Carol comes to help me after work the following four nights. I serve her goulash every night. In the cache, I have a small refrigerator I rented for the summer from the University. We complete courses 5 and 6. To drill holes for the rebar that peg the logs together, it is necessary to stand above the log. As the walls grow it becomes risky, until Guy Ramsey lends me a log horse he built. It straddles the wall, and has two sturdy boards to stand on.

It took the cache until the next summer to dry out after the wetness of construction. To keep the insulated cabin floor dry, I cover it with visqueen at the end of each workday. As the walls grow, I drill a large drainage hole in the area that is to be my kitchen. There, I put a funnel in the hole and drape the plastic to guide the water. In reality, I end up bailing most of the water. The summer was warm and dry until September.

When I built the cache, I didn't have electricity, so it was a big problem to drill holes for the rebar. Now it is difficult to pound down the ten-inch rebar cut by machine and slightly bent in the ends. Carol's friend Joe Thomas saws 40 rods and even sharpens some of the ends.

Half of the cabin will be two-story with a small bedroom upstairs. I plan to make a spiral staircase around a large log that will support the ceiling. I drive to the Four Star Lumber sawmill to find a suitable log.

"I want seven feet of your biggest spruce log," I tell the owner.

"OK, let's walk through the yard until you see something you like," he tells me.

"There is a good-looking tree," I point. "How big is it?"

"It's 28-inches in diameter."

"Can I have exactly seven feet of it? The ends must be perpendicular," I order.

Five days later, the owner's son, Bob, shows up with a 7.5-foot log with one uneven end.

"I ordered exactly seven feet. How will I be able to cut off the excess evenly with my 14-inch chain saw?" I ask with frustration.

"You won't," Bob replies. "I'll be back."

Bob returns with a 24-inch chain saw. He measures seven feet, makes a small mark, starts the saw and calmly saws perpendicularly through the log. I am impressed. I count the tree rings and deduce the spruce was 125 years old.

Fall is here. The birch leaves glow in shades of yellow. It rains often. There isn't much more I can do on the cabin before winter. The important thing now is to get it covered. Despite pouring rain, Carol Hagglund and Jack Hakkila come to help me for two evenings. We are all members of the Sons of Norway, which was recently chartered in Fairbanks with 460 members. Carol and Jack are third generation Finns and even speak Finnish. Jack is strong and doesn't want help to move a 22-foot log. He just puts it on his shoulder and walks, a handsome man with curly blond hair and blue eyes. We complete course 10 and work on the window opening on the north wall.

On a hazy September 18 morning, the day before I leave on a six-week trip, church friends drive down at 7 a.m. We complete course 11 and part of 12. The walls are now six feet high. It is obvious it will be a cabin. A week earlier, OK Lumber had a sale on 2 x 6-inch tongue-and groove boards. I bought 58. With the boards and a tarp, supported by 4 x 6-inch timbers, the cabin is well covered for the winter. Inside it is dry and light enough to continue working. The upper part of the pointed western wall is still open. The cabin has to rest for another winter until I can continue construction. I still have to live in my 49-square foot cache on poles.

During the winter, I have the usual problems with the car getting stuck in the snow. Now I can drive all the way home along private, unnamed roads that aren't routinely plowed. At times, I have to ski to work. I can keep the temperature in the cache pleasant with the sheet metal wood stove and an electric heater, even though it is 30 below. Often, I stand on the deck and look into my unfinished cabin and imagine a warm fire burning there.

One evening in December, I plan to drive to a Laundromat. I am warmly dressed in thick Army surplus winter clothing. Socks of reindeer skin inside seal skin mukluks that an Eskimo in Barrow made for me keep my feet warm but *they are very slick.* The car is running to warm up as I climb down my 16- foot ladder with my left arm around a large laundry basket. With double wool mittens inside the long Army padded gloves, my grip is insufficient when my foot slips on the ladder. I feel the back of my head hit the ground. After that I don't feel anything, until I wake up on my stomach in the snow.

I hope I haven't broken anything.

Carefully, I start to move limbs and assess the situation. My right calf and thigh are sore but nothing appears to be broken. I don't know how long I lay in the snow, but the car is very warm.

This was a scary incident, but I drive to the Laundromat. While the wash is spinning, I go to the nearby Lamonts clothing store. I feel dizzy and totally uninterested in any of the goods. In the warm ladies room, I survey my injuries. Despite the heavy padded flight pants, I have impressive colorful blue marks on my leg.

In early April 1978, the temperature rises to 50 degrees although the snow cover is still thick. I shovel the snow from my temporary cabin roof while a snowshoe hare, with large ears and feet, chews willow twigs. My outhouse hole fills with water as a sign of spring. *I have got a water closet, WC*, I muse. After a rainy night, the birch leaves come out on May 6.

I make plans to build a ladder I can use without the help of hands. It takes me a month to build the staircase from 2 x 12-inch boards with inserted steps. On May 14 I get it in place with the help of a pulley when Carol and her sister Karen Hagglund visit. Everyone knows I built the ladder myself, but they are amazed I really built the staircase. I must have learned something in three years.

Kristina in sealskin parka on new staircase to cache,
January 1979. Note original 16-footer ladder and upright
birch ladder to the roof.

When I peel the 7-foot old log in early June, I notice two different kinds of morel mushrooms. The pointed true morels I can eat immediately. The rounded brain morels I dry until they loose their poison. The log is large and heavy but I can peel all sides by rolling it with a long pole as leverage and kicking in wedges under it. Eventually, it will stand on the middle of the floor, cradling a log and supporting both the ceiling and a spiral staircase. I recall my old geometry from high school to calculate and measure the appropriate locations for 10 steps around the log. Then I saw and scoop out notches.

Kristina moving the large log with a leverage rod and
kicked wedges in 1978.

The pointed, western wall is three feet high with six
log courses that will support two windows, one facing
southwest the other northwest. After a lot of thinking
and consulting, I decide to surround the windows with
vertical logs, because the areas are small and I think it
would look good. I notch the log ends to fit 2 x 2-inch
horizontal supporting strips both at the bottom and top.
Joe Thomas, Carol's colleague, has cut screw grooves in
the ends of four, yard-long metal rods that will tie the
vertical logs together. All I need to do is drill straight holes
through two sets of six logs. I measure very carefully
before I drill, concentrating on keeping the drill-bit
perpendicular to the log. When I have the six logs drilled
for the northwestern wall, Dick Peterson drops by.

"Hi, you survived the winter," I greet him. "Did you
manage to build a cabin by yourself?"

"I didn't need to. I found a mining claim with an old
cabin," Dick replies.

"You arrived just in time to help me guide these rods
through the logs," I say.

We pile the six 34-inch long logs on the horizontal strip. While Dick holds the logs I guide the rods through and tighten them with nuts. Good machine work by Joe Thomas!

"That went easy. I'm impressed!" Dick says.

"I take pride in doing my job exactly," I reply, pleased.

On August 13, 1978 it stops raining at 7 a.m. when the participants in the first work party for the year arrive. In preparation, I have sanded and varnished all tongue-and-groove boards while I could walk on them as a floor on the cabin roof. In the cache I learned varnishing boards in the ceiling causes varnish to drip in the eyes and run down the arms. Dennis Gentleman and Roy Morey take down the temporary ceiling. With the help of Mark Thoennes, they wrestle the large log into the cabin through the window opening in the southwestern wall. The notch I made in the base fits exactly over the horizontal supporting log on the floor. Dennis climbs to the top of the log and shakes.

"Wow, this log doesn't go anywhere," he affirms.

Marilyn Gentleman and Flossie Morey come to inspect the progress bringing lunch and children. In the afternoon we get one log up above the window openings and another above the door.

"This is a new milepost of significant progress," I declare with joy.

I need many 22 and 24-foot long logs as rafters. When Dennis and Ralph, the first participants in next week's work party arrive in the drizzle, the logs aren't here yet.

"Four Star Lumber promised to deliver them on time. I told them I would have workers here at seven Sunday morning!" I assure my helpers.

"Are you sure they believed you?" Ralph asks.

At 7:30 Four Star backs in and rolls the long logs from their flatbed.

When I am alone I survey the result. My spirits fluctuate between hope — the cabin is almost ready to move into — and frustration. There is still a lot to do with detailed fittings with angles and slopes demanding plenty of patience. Towards the end of August, I get the rafters in place with the help of Mark and Ralph.

In the middle of September, the tongue & groove boards are once more on the roof, but this year they are varnished and nailed in place. Below them, all walls are completed, but the door and windows are still missing.

OK Lumber has 3-sided 20-foot logs that are 7 inches thick. They cost and weigh more than Four Star's 6-inch logs, but should provide better insulation. I order 880 linear feet of them for the loft. I need two windows for the kitchen. Unfamiliar with brands, I order two different kinds for comparison.

There has been a smell of fall in the air. While the first snow falls on September 20, I harvest my potatoes and carrots. The earlier harvest is stored in my root cellar, where a light bulb keeps the temperature above freezing. My faithful volunteers have their own fall chores and Roy will move to Anchorage. My neighbor, Joyce Allen, has moved back and helps me get plywood sheets up on the roof. My neighbors, Joe Enzweiler and John Wagner, who are building their own log cabin, sometimes help me lift logs. I complete two log courses for the loft. After scraping ice from the covering visqueen, I fill the area with fiberglass and cover everything for the winter. A 2 x 12-inch 20-foot board that I try to get up slips, but misses my car when it falls down.

I continue to work with the window openings downstairs. When the windows finally arrive, after months of waiting, they are too big for the openings. That's a detail I easily fix with the chain saw. I treat all logs with oil. In the beginning of October, I get my east kitchen window in place. I cover the other openings with visqueen. Craig Meyer, my cement mixer, visits after school and starts to dig a ditch between the power pole and the cabin. Eventually, I will have a buried power line and maybe even a telephone.

It snows all day on October 10. When the sun shines on the 12th, I drive home from work at 1 p.m. and sweep the snow off the tarp that covers the deck above the cabin. It is 18 degrees when I start to saw a hole for the chimney and put down the first layer of Thermax sheets. I am eager to do as much as possible while the deck is uncovered and free of snow. When the sun sets, I bring up a photographic tripod, attach a lamp and connect it to the power pole with many extension cords. When electricity fails due to frequent outages, the moon rises. At 11 p.m. I finish with the help of a flashlight. Temperature has dropped to 12 and I am tired. Every time I can continue the roofing job, I must first sweep off the new snow. At times, the preparatory sweeping can take two hours. I lay a second layer of insulating sheets on the roof and surround them by wooden nailing strips for the covering plywood. After that I don't mind if the tarp gets snow covered. Now I have a warm roof.

Early November I start to work on the door. It will be 6 inches thick as the walls, with a round porthole on top. A kerosene-drinking Aladdin heater makes the job reasonably pleasant although it is 7 degrees outside. Sometimes I work at home while it is daylight, and go to work in the afternoon. After a good morning, the vibrations and noise from the fans in the adjoining Mineral lab are less disturbing in my new working area.

The Northern Libraries Colloquy in France invites me to write an article about Arctic sea ice. I want to know how thick it is. At the University Library I check out the original Norwegian edition, printed in 1897, of Nansen's "Fram over the Polar Sea." I am the first person to borrow it! As I read this old book in my cache, I can relate to Nansen in his cabin on the S/S Fram and am fascinated by him.

To get my Norwegian cast-iron Jøtul heater into the cabin and more logs up on the roof, I organize a preliminary cabin warming for November 12. Two cars get stuck in the snow. With two Aladdin heaters and two Coleman lanterns, the cabin temperature rises to 52 degrees. Eight guests stay to drink hot- spiced wine and help me move and lift everything I need. A blanket that has become heavy laden with beautiful snow crystals covers the door opening. To prevent more warm moist air from condensing on the blanket, I add a sheet of visqueen on the inside as a vapor barrier.

It wasn't difficult to install the chimney but it is worse with the chimney pipe indoors. It is too long and the pipes don't fit together. Disappointed I go to Woodway, hoping they would come home and do the job for me.

"We can order a sliding pipe for you so you can adjust the length. You can borrow this tool to crimp the pipes to fit," the man at Woodway says as he hands me the crimper.

Before the end of the year, the windows are installed and the door is built, but it is too heavy to lift. I celebrate New Year's Eve alone by lighting a fire in my newly installed cast-iron heater. I put a bottle of champagne out to cool while I set the table on two long boards over a couple of sawhorses. To my surprise, the champagne cork ejects discreetly, without the usual bang and bubbles. Despite the fire, the champagne is too frozen to pour. After some coercing it emerges in timid drops.

On New Years day 1979, I wake up in a brilliant mood in the cache. Everything I try this day is successful. I am strong enough to lift the door in place — and it fits! I don't want to move from the cache until the cabin is finished. It is a lot easier to work, if I don't drag in all the things that seem necessary for living.

Carol Hagglund will graduate in May from business administration. Her Department of Fish and Wildlife will move to Adak in the Aleutians. This inspires me to finish editing my construction movies, so I can show them to her. On April 15, I have a first- floor cabin warming. Two men want to see the cache. "I will give you a tour and then you can take the refrigerator to the cabin," I tell them. We lower it with the attached block and tackle.

When the guests leave, the fire still burns invitingly. The temptation is too big. I move in and spread out over 304 square feet for four days. What a luxury compared to 49 square feet in the cache.

I go to a remote sensing conference in Michigan, where I give a presentation about using satellite imagery to study the surface temperature of seawater and the distribution of sea ice. When I return home, I cannot get in. The key won't turn in my new door lock. Maybe we had an earthquake shaking the cabin? It is too late to disturb a neighbor. What can I do? I wonder. A small window in the entryway is still covered with visqueen. It is at a height of 7 feet. I wonder if I can fit through it? I step on a sawhorse and get the top half of my body in. It is a tight fit. I hope I don't get stuck. It would be embarrassing and probably very uncomfortable. The acrobatics are exiting, but the outcome is worth the exercise. My reward is to sleep in my own bed.

Truck driver Roy Morey, who moved to Anchorage, visits in May.

"Some of my former roofing colleagues owe me. I told them, I have just the perfect small job for them," he says looking at my sun deck.

The timing is well chosen, a beautiful sunny day. Spring in Fairbanks is normally dry when snow melts, until the first rain in early June. The plywood roof I built as a deck over the living room of the cabin has survived the winter below the tarp. The roofers arrive with a small asphalt kettle on wheels. They work efficiently and cover the deck with tarpaper. In three hours, I have a hot asphalt roof. I am impressed and thankful.

It rains a lot in July. The tarp over the loft construction doesn't always do its duty. Many times I have to bail water from the kitchen. Despite the rain, people come to help me with the logs. I teach Ralph Dow's 12-year old son, Dan, to peel logs. On July 29, Dennis, Ralph and Dan arrive already at 7. We work with log course four on the loft when Toni Dow races in with rocks flying.

"Dennis!" she shouts, "Marilyn is in the hospital giving birth!"

I lose one worker. Together with Ralph, we complete course six while Dan peels logs and digs a little in the power ditch Craig started.

Another friend from church, dental technician, Vickey Hodnik stays with me for two nights after work and helps me with courses seven and eight. With her experience as a dental assistant, she is ready to hand me the drill where I stand on the eighth log course at a height of four feet. With electricity, it is easy to push the 5/8-inch drill bit 11 inches through two logs. When I return the drill to Vickey, she hands me a piece of rebar and a sledgehammer. I don't need to ask her for anything. She is an alert assistant. When I work alone, I try to keep all tools at hand. Sometimes they fall from the log. At times even the log drops to the ground.

One evening in August, Martti Sorvoja visits with a friend and a 6-pack of beer.

"How have you got all the logs up?" Martti asks with curiosity.

"No problem. I'll show you. Here's a long log on the ground. Can you lift one end, Martti, and your friend the other end? Now follow me to the cabin."

My neighbors, Jim and Marty Baldridge, help me lift logs for course 11 when we hear a gun shot from my closest neighbor. Soon Joyce comes running through the woods.

"I just want to warn my neighbors," she pants. "The door in my trailer was open and a large black bear stepped in. My rifle was above the door behind the bear. Besides, I didn't want to shoot it in the house. The bear looked at me with puzzlement, as if it knew it wasn't invited. I promised not to shoot it, if it just stepped out. The bear obeyed, but started to rummage around. I grabbed my rifle and shot into the air to scare it, and it finally ran off."

"This is surprising," Jim says. "We haven't seen any signs of bear lately."

"Do you remember yesterday?" I ask. "My compost crate by the outhouse had tipped over and you helped me carry compost to the garden. What surprised me then was that I couldn't find any of the salmon scraps I threw there a few days earlier."

"You have attracted the bear here," Joyce accuses me. "It loves salmon."

In August 1979, the loft walls are six feet or 12 logs high. Three large, 20-foot purlins lie by the driveway waiting to support the loft roof. How will I get them up? While thinking about it, I cover the loft with a tarp. I will be gone for a while attending the POAC-conference in Trondheim, Norway.

Three 20-foot purlins ready to support the loft
roof in August 1979

At the train station in Oslo I meet a colleague. Dr. Bill Sackinger is one of the organizers of the meeting. He previously advised me to target my presentation to the interests of the oil companies, when I told him I didn't have any funding to attend.

"Show them the risks of navigating the sea ice on the route to Prudhoe Bay. Hopefully, they will pay your way."

"That's easy with my access to satellite imagery," I reply.

I book my ticket on faith, prepared to pay for it myself. Why doesn't Sackinger say anything? I wonder, assuming the worst.

"Have you heard if the oil company will pay my trip?" I finally ask.

"I was just wondering how long it would take you to ask," Sackinger says. "Yes, your trip is paid!"

I take a breath of relief and joy.

During the train trip, we have time to talk about — my logs.

"It's no problem to get them up," my engineering colleague assures me.

I return to Alaska, exhausted after an 18-hour flight. The tarp has blown away and the kitchen is flooded. Water is still dripping through the kitchen ceiling/loft floor. The bed by the far western wall is dry, but most of everything else is floating. I am too disturbed to go to bed. Instead, I climb on the roof and bail out 35 gallons. The support lines in the tarp corners are torn. It seldom blows hard in Fairbanks. I reinstall the tarp. In the cabin, I only manage to bail 8 gallons. The rest has seeped through the plywood floor.

I contact Sackinger.

"Would you mind coming to show me that it isn't any problem to get the big logs up," I ask.

To be on the safe side, I also invite my volunteers from church and closest neighbors. Sackinger brings two of his sons. It takes eight men to carry one purlin to the cabin. From there, Sackinger handles them alone with two come-alongs tied between diagonally running wires from the ends of the purlin to the back corners of the loft walls. As the engineer he is, Sackinger elegantly and exactly guides the logs to the rooftop. From there, two are immediately lifted to the wall of the loft.

Sackinger engineering the raising of the ridgepole

Now I need to notch the purlins into the walls, but those who could help are busy with their own construction projects and moose hunting. I have saved the improvised log scriber Laitala made me for the cache, and scribe the purlins shallowly into the 12th course. The difficulty is to check the fit and to roll the purlins off the notch for fine adjustments. A purlin might weigh half a ton. It is time consuming to move it alone with the help of rope, wedges and leverage rods. Once I am pleased with the seating in the 12th log course, I trim the logs in the 13th and 14th courses to fit tightly between the purlins.

Now it is time for the ridgepole. I invite friends and neighbors for the ridge raising on September 16. The rain stops when ten people lift and roll the largest purlin to the ridge top. Victoriously, I climb on top of it, open a bottle of champagne, pour a little on the ridgepole and the rest into glasses for my helpers to toast with. Jim Baldridge nails a small spruce to the end of the pole.

I buy plywood and tongue-and-groove boards for the roof. The fumes from varnishing the ceiling boards drive me to move back into the cache for ten days. I notch the ridgepole but don't have time to cut the gables appropriately before winter is here again. I cover the loft for the winter with the plywood and a tarp. Fiberglass bats cover the floor. Now, the first floor is securely covered and insulated.

For relaxation, I have been digging in the power ditch Craig started last fall. Power company code requires it to be two feet deep. Two of my neighbors are electricians but they are not part of my volunteers. They charge by the hour. I hire Jim Ferrell to connect the cable between the power pole and the fuse box in the cabin. While he installs some wall outlets, I assist by handing him tools and ask a lot of questions. With Reader's Digest "Complete Do- it-yourself Manual" I plan to do the rest of the electric myself and hire Ferrell to inspect the results.

On a University organized tour to China last spring, I roomed with a Yup'ik Eskimo girl, Barbara Nick. She comes to help me pull electric wires under the cabin. I enjoy talking to her with her different cultural background. When I drill a hole in the floor, water squirts out.

"Where did that water come from?" Barbara asks surprised. "It is 14 degrees."

"It must be rainwater that seeped through the plywood and collected on the visqueen below," I reply. "Now I understand why there wasn't more water in the kitchen when the tarp blew off."

"What do you think about the day, Barbara?" I ask, pleased after all the chores we have accomplished.

"Would you rather have stayed at the University to study?"

"This was a lot more fun than studies. Almost as fun as fish camp."

I am concerned about the water below the floor. How much is left after all the floods? If it freezes, it will crack the plastic and destroy the fiberglass insulation. Ken Meyer at the satellite tracking station is a problem solver. I ask him for advice.

"I have a shop vacuum that sucks water. I can make you a pipe to attach to the vacuum cleaner. Then you just drill a hole in the plywood and suck up the water," Ken says.

"Thank you, Ken. That sounds easy."

Carefully, not to damage the vapor barrier, I drill a hole under the kitchen table and suck up—17 gallons. I probably have water reservoirs between each floor joist. My exploratory drillings pay off handsomely. I recover — 90 gallons! Maybe I have invented something; insulating the floor with water.

During the winter I think about the construction of the spiral staircase around the old log. I custom order a 2 x 16-inch board of rough lumber from Four Star and saw it into 2-foot pieces for the steps. I make the acquaintance of electronics technician Rick Lamb who is interested in fine carpentry.

"I plan to saw a tongue into each piece of wood and insert them into the pole," I explain to Rick.

"It would look better if we made the steps pie- shaped, and widened the outer edge to 20 inches,"

Rick suggests. "I can figure out a way to support the steps. I do have appropriate tools."

In the beginning of May 1980, Rick brings me the last step.

"You have done a good job sanding and varnishing them," he says as he runs his palm over the smooth, shiny surface.

Rick picks up a step. The narrow end fits into the notch I made in the log. The elegantly curved support attaches to the step with dowels and to the pole with a thicker dowel.

"This is an inventive piece of engineering and a lot better looking than my original plan," I say with admiration.

In the summer of 1980, the loft roof is uncovered again. I start to saw down the gables diagonally as Laitala showed me on the cache wall five years ago. I have nailed a 2 x 4-inch board as a guide and T&G boards over the protruding logs to sit on.

A sunny day on August 4, I kneel on the edge of the roof close to the ridgepole, nailing T&G boards over the loft. I can see down into the kitchen through the opening surrounding the spiral staircase but feel comfortable on the edge. A knot on the ridgepole prevents the board from laying flat. Thoughtlessly I stretch forward, hacking at the knot with my hatchet. The knot is tough but suddenly it breaks. Alarmed, I feel how I slowly rock forward on my knees towards the opening two floors below.

"Help, God!" is my brief panic prayer.

The next moment, I feel invisible hands on my shoulders pushing me back.

"Thank you, God!"

Shaken, I contemplate my mortality. I could have been crushed on the floor two stories down. What happened? I have never felt anything like this before. Was it my guardian angel that intervened?

In the middle of August, I have trimmed both gables of the loft by myself and nailed the last T&G board in place. Dennis and Ralph arrive to help with the roof.

"First, we need to attach a metal screen for ventilation along the edge of the roof," Dennis says.

"I weigh the least of us three and can staple it in place if you make sure I don't fall off the roof," I say as I tie a rope around me.

"Ralph will guard you with his life," Dennis says as Ralph ties the other end of the rope around himself.

Securely belayed, I sit safely on the edge of the roof above the highest part of the cabin. After the netting is in place, we cover the T&G boards with a visqueen vapor barrier, attach 2 x 12-inch rafters with 2 x 4-inch nailers perpendicularly across. A new couple in church, Tom and Paula Davis, deployed to Fairbanks by the US Air Force, wants to come and help with the fiberglass insulating bats. We start to nail plywood. Walt Peirce, my sourdough friend, helps me to continue. My colleague, Terri Paluszkiewicz, helps me nail the last sheets.

Terri once walked past my office at IMS, three moves after the bulletin board hideout in the basement. I was in the Irving II building with a view of Denali. Terri got so interested in the satellite pictures I showed her with eddies along the ice edge in the Bering Sea that she chose that as a subject for her master's thesis in Oceanography. Terri accompanies me to Gilmore Satellite Tracking Station every week to learn what I do, until that grant ends. My last day at Gilmore, in September 1980, ends as it started with the A-shift in 1974.

My boss at IMS, Tom Royer, ex-boss Bob Muench, and a few others treat me to a farewell pizza. Again, I get to move offices, this time to a large southeast-corner office on the third floor of the Irving II until IMS hires a new professor. Soliciting among my previous colleagues at the Geophysical Institute, I gather enough funding to support me half time. Gerd Wendler supplies 25% to study the relationship between the extent of sea ice and weather in the Bering Sea.

Since February 1981 I have been asked to move, but not told where. It is full everywhere. Tom Royer pays me with leftover money to write a report summarizing everything I know about the use of satellite imagery. He reviews it with the following comment:

"Kristina: Very Good Report!! I enjoyed reading it. Tom"

The unusual praise makes me feel good. In March 1981, IMS publishes the 91-page report: "Surface Temperature Enhanced NOAA-Satellite Infrared Imagery for the Bering, Chukchi, and Beaufort Seas and the Gulf of Alaska."

On March 18, I have a note on my desk from the IMS office manager:

"Pack out!"

The librarian empties a dark storage area for me. They install electricity.

On April 6, I work on an IMS seminar lecture about "The Effect of the Atmospheric Circulation on the Location of the Ice Edge in the Bering Sea." There is a knock on the "darkroom door." A middle-aged man dressed in a suit, which is uncommon in Fairbanks, enters.

"I am Zygmunt Kowalik from Poland," he introduces himself. "I will work a year for IMS."

The name sounds vaguely familiar, but first I cannot recognize the man. My thoughts go back in time.

"You were one of four Polish scientists who came out on the Finnish research ship Aranda for a week in 1962," I recall.

"That was 19 years ago, when you visited Gdynia and we met," Zygmunt says.

In the summer of 1981, I enlarge my vegetable garden, since my job situation is uncertain. I build my bed on the loft and can finally move up. Now I have 469 square feet in my large cabin with a solid roof over my head. This gives me a feeling of security. Zygmunt has built a house in Poland and knows how to mix cement. We mix cement in half a lengthwise cut oil barrel. Then we set black slate stones in the cement as a support for my cast iron Jøtul heater.

Until the summer of 1987, I continue with inside cabin details. Ten years have passed since I poured the cement blocks for the cabin foundation.

I send out invitations for a formal cabin warming June 26-28, without any hidden plans for help. Fifty of the invited show up unaware that it is also my 50th birthday. I serve them mead brewed from birch sap as I did for the cache warming in 1976.

Never could I imagine that the construction project — building a cache and a cabin I planned to finish in one summer would take me 12 years. Log cabin builder Laitala did know what he talked about when he said that I could be proud of myself if I could finish the cache the first summer.

27

Silver Anniversary for Gold State

A reproduction of the gigantic Liberty Bell in Philadelphia chimes 49 beats outside Alaska's Capitol in Juneau on January 3, 1984. It did so also 25 years ago, in 1959, when president Dwight D. Eisenhower officially signed the declaration that made Alaska the 49th state in the Union.

The Russian fur trader, Grigorij Shelikhov, established the first colony in Alaska on Kodiak Island in 1784. Towards the end of the Russian period, when both Alaska and Finland were governed by Russia, two of the Alaskan governors, Adolph Etholen (1840-1845) and Hampus Furuhjelm (1859- 1863) were from Finland.

The United States of America bought Alaska from Russia in 1867 for 7.2 million dollars, which equals 2 cents per acre. At the time Alaska was considered worthless since the sea otters with their valuable pelts had been exterminated. It was five years before gold was discovered near Sitka and 30 years before the Gold Rush, when everything that could float from Seattle headed for Alaska.

As an American Territory, Alaskans had the duty to pay tax and serve in the US Army but no right to vote. The first initiative on statehood was taken in 1916, when Alaska tried to get control over its future. The U.S. Congress, however, didn't approve.

In 1954, Alaska's Territorial Legislature convened a Constitutional Convention at the University of Alaska in Fairbanks. Representative delegates were chosen from all parts of Alaska. The result was a brief and powerful constitution that was approved in 1956.

William Egan, the chairman of the convention, and Ernest Gruening were chosen as unofficial senators. Uninvited, they were sent to Washington, D.C. together with the official, but also vote-less delegate, E. L. Bartlett. Their work finally bore fruit three years after the signing of the constitution. On January 3, 1959 Alaska was admitted as the 49th state into the United States of America. William Egan became the first governor, 1959 - 1966.

A new stamp is issued in honor of the event. Appropriate celebrities attend. I buy a first day cover with the stamp canceled on the day of issue and ask for governor Egan's autograph.

"I came to Alaska in 1969 and lived in Juneau when you were governor for the second time," I tell him.

"I remember meeting you," he says.

That's the way to express yourself when you are a diplomat. We never met officially but once had dinner at the same restaurant.

Since the Constitutional Convention was held in Fairbanks, it is appropriate to organize the main festivities for the celebration of Alaska's 25th anniversary in Fairbanks. Of the original 55 delegates, 27 are in attendance.

In the afternoon the public is invited to a free reception at the Travelers Inn. The announcement to the 60,000-person population in greater Fairbanks has gone out over both press and radio. A ton of wild meat from different parts of Alaska will be served.

When I arrive around 5 p.m., it is impossible to find a parking place in the vicinity.

The glittering gala room is stuffed and the free libations evaporated. I manage to find the serving table loaded with food but there are only small tea- plates to put it on. The only silverware provided is a toothpick. I get bison, halibut and sweet-and-sour moose and deer. The rest of the dishes I cannot reach in time after ending up in a confluence between two lines. It's obvious you are not supposed to dine. This is just a reception. A dinner for especially invited follows. I heard there was even room to dance in the dining room.

28

𝒫leistocene 𝐵ison on the 𝒨enu

In the summer of 1979, Walter Roman was thawing frozen silt in a canyon north of Fairbanks to reach the gold bearing gravel below. The hydraulic giant with its powerful water canon slowly thawed and washed down the embankment when a hoof emerged. Professor Dale Guthrie of the University of Alaska's Institute of Arctic Biology (IAB) was notified. Together with his wife, Mary Lee, they started to excavate and eventually found the whole body of a frozen bison. Its neck flesh was still red. The bison in Alaska became extinct 500 years ago but this specimen, when carbon dated, proved to be considerably older.

Mostly intact animals are seldom found. Only three have previously found their way to museums: two woolly mammoths from Siberia are on display in St. Petersburg, Russia. A woolly rhinoceros, preserved in a salt mine, resides in Poland. Consequently, there is little expertise in the field of conserving and mounting ice age animals.

The conservator of the Zoological Museum in Helsinki, Finland, Eirik Granqvist, is called upon to mount the bison for display. This makes the University of Alaska museum in Fairbanks the only one in the western world that can take pride in displaying an animal from the Ice Age, a steppe bison (Bison Priscus). There are, however, some complications in mounting the animal. The hide is soaked in muck, torn by an ice age cave lion (Panthro Leo), partly devoured on the back, besides being a bit weakened by its age.

"Jesus walked on earth 2,000 years ago, the pyramids in Egypt were build 4,000 years ago, and a bull steppe bison was killed by a lion in Alaska 36,000 years ago." This is how Eirik Granqvist muses when I drop in on him at his temporary workspace at the IAB, in March 1984.

Eirik, with wavy brown hair combed sideways over his wide forehead and a trim short dark beard, is only here for a short time due to meager funding. He brought his hunting knife and fishing yarn as tools. He splits the wet hide with his knife to make it thinner and more pliable to work with and sews up the tears. Lack of suitable tools, material and time forces Eirik to accomplish the impossible in record time. He is an inventive artist and craftsman.

"I know this will be one of the star attractions of the museum," Eirik says with frustration.

I visit regularly, interested in following the progress of this unique enterprise. Every time I see a new phase in the work.

"The next step is to create a body to fit the hide," Eirik explains. Guided by a small bronze sculpture Guthrie made, and existing bison bones, he makes a plywood silhouette. Attached to that he builds a body of chicken wire and covers it with plastered fabric and clay.

"Now I will become a sculptor," Eirik says as he starts to scrape off excess clay with his hand made tool consisting of a wire loop attached to a pin. "The final result will be a body showing the contours of the muscles of the bison."

"Why do you have the bison lying on its knees?" I ask.

"The bison was found in this position," Eirik explains. "After all these years, I think it would be too much to ask, to demand it to stand up."

Eirik runs out of modeling clay in the middle of the project. In Fairbanks it isn't always possible to run to a store and buy what you want.

"I don't have time to wait for an order from "outside". Besides, I don't have money to buy more clay," Eirik says. "I planned to make a plaster mold around the entire clay body to get a negative body. Now I have to do it in pieces. When the plaster hardens it can be taken off. The pieces make the mold for the final body that will be cast in fiberglass. When one area is finished I will have to scrape off the clay and move it to the next body part."

"How do you know that the hide will fit the casted body?" I ask.

"I have made the body slightly smaller so that the hide, that has been kept wet all the time, will hang loose. The old bull will get to keep all of its wrinkles," Eirik says.

After more sewing and nailing that would have made a tailor or shoemaker proud, the hide fits as the custom made skin it is.

"Why have you left the back uncovered? Did you run out of skin?" I ask.

"No, that's where the lion feasted. You can see the marks of the lion's claws and incisors in the hide that still has hair in places. It was already so cold that the lion broke a chip off its incisor tooth. I found the chip in the hide. That's why the bison wasn't completely devoured. The body continued to freeze harder during the course of the winter. During spring break-up the bull was buried by down-washed silt according to the recipe in Björn Kurtén's book, *How to freeze a mammoth.*"

"This is a fantastic revival project," I say impressed, "but I find the nails in the hide disturbing."

"The job isn't finished yet. I will cover the nail heads and the seams with wax. The whole hide will get a wax treatment," Eirik says.

"Is it necessary?" I ask. "It looks good."

"We want it to continue to look good also for posterity. I will use the same waxing method as the French used when they repaired the mummy of Ramses II in Egypt," Eirik elaborates.

"The horns look good," I say with admiration. "They are epoxy castings. Professor Guthrie has made them well. The original head with horns is preserved for research in a freezer," Eirik says.

"Why is this bull bison called Blue Babe?" I ask. "When the animal was excavated, the hide had a bluish hue resulting from phosphorus in the animal's tissue and iron in the ground that united to form the iron phosphate mineral, vivianite, that oxidized and turned blue when it came into contact with oxygen in the air. This bison will get its blue color back after I brush it with iron phosphate," Eirik says.

Dale Guthrie and Eirik Granqvist with "revived"
Pleistocene Blue Babe bison.

"This is your last day, Eirik. Will you get Blue Babe ready before the museum closes?" I ask.

As Blue Babe is carried out into the corridor of Arctic Biology by five men in a festive procession, Eirik bursts out in loud singing. The moment is unique. Eirik has finished his project with honor. Two minutes before closing, Blue Babe arrives at its new resting place in the near-by museum.

Have you used a computer to create the body?

Eirik expects some German to ask.

"No, I couldn't find the BISON-button on the computer," Eirik plans to reply, until I get an idea.

"We can modify the program I use to depict the ice edge in the Bering Sea from satellite imagery. I can create a data register, AK_BISON_36,000. The result can be a resting bison with its heart in the middle of Alaska where it was found surrounded by the coastline of Alaska."

"This sounds good. I can draw the bison." Eirik says.

"I need to know how the bison tastes to get the inspiration for the data work!" I exclaim.

The meat protected by the thick neck hide was deep frozen, of course. Except for the small piece that Professor Guthrie tasted in the gold mine, the rest was placed in the freezer for future occasions. I have heard rumors that such an occasion was planned to celebrate the revival of Blue Babe, Eirik's 40th birthday and a visit of Björn Kurtén from Finland. Professor Kurtén came to Fairbanks to lecture about the hunting methods of the Neanderthal man. Despite my interest in the bison project I have not been invited. I have nothing to lose by asking Eirik to be included.

"It isn't my party, but I'll ask Guthrie," Eirik promises.

Eagerly I guard my telephone all afternoon until I go home, disappointed. Listlessly I look in my refrigerator when the telephone rings.

"This is Dale Guthrie. May I speak to Kristina? If you have time this evening, you are invited to a small party in our house."

"Thank you very much, I will be delighted to come," I reply politely with my heart beating with excitement as I spring into some dance steps.

It is an unusual April evening when everyone's thoughts have already turned to spring. The temperature has risen above zero. The new snow for skiing I have waited for since March has finally fallen.

In honor of the occasion, the Guthries have prepared a Mexican meal to serve their Finnish guests. A well-seasoned stew still simmers on the stove in Burgundy wine with Pleistocene bison. Dessert is served after the dinner. Have they forgotten the bison? I wonder concerned.

"I haven't yet figured out how to properly serve ice age bison, I wonder if bowls of Chinese rice China would be appropriate?" the hostess, Mary Lee Guthrie, says.

Solemnly Dale Guthrie ladles a little bison stew into our individual rice bowls. He makes sure everybody gets at least one little piece of meat. The spices do not conceal the taste of ancient refined mud. It is a powerful stew that even an ice age cook could have been proud of. The aged Pleistocene bison stew with Polish bison vodka for cheers is the highlight of the dinner.

The old bison immediately becomes the new highlight of the University of Alaska museum as Eirik Granqvist predicted. Blue Babe rests peacefully in a glass cabinet behind the impressive 10-foot high Kodiak brown bear, Otto, who welcomes the visitors on his hind legs.

Mary Lee Guthrie writes a beautifully illustrated booklet, *Blue Babe, The Story of a Steppe Bison Mummy From Ice Age Alaska* that is sold at the museum.

29

Visit by President and Pope.

Pope John Paul II plans to make a stopover in Fairbanks on his way from Rome to Korea on May 2, 1984. President Ronald Reagan with wife Nancy, on their way home to Washington D.C. from China on May 1, decide to stop in Fairbanks and wait for the Pope. This will be the first time a pope and a president meet outside of the Vatican or the White House. Fairbanks has two months to prepare for The Visit.

Rumors run wild about the arrival of President Reagan in "Air Force One." The city has two military airports in addition to Fairbanks International. The time and place are continually changed. For security reasons the President pulls the stunt of arriving in two identical planes that land at different airports. Only the initiated know in which plane he is. The White House has flown in 300 security agents to assist the local police. I don't know whether the agents are supposed to be secret and blend into the public, but in Fairbanks nobody else dresses in a beige trench coat or a dress suit with white shirt and tie and a shining round badge on the lapel of the jacket. In addition, they have eagle's eyes that don't rest for a moment.

While waiting in Fairbanks, the President will give a speech and have lunch at the university. I position myself strategically at the entrance to wave in the company of interested students. The security agents on the sidewalk sharpen their glances further and stare at us when the impressive row of black cars with flying flags approaches. Four attentive honor guards in black dress suits stand on the wide running boards of the presidential car. I get a fast glimpse of both Ron and his beautiful Nancy.

The whole airport and surroundings gets closed off for The Visit. My colleagues, Greg and Hedy Kaspsuk live inside the closed-off area. They invite me to spend the night. In the cool morning haze on May 2 we start to walk towards the airport. No private car traffic is allowed. We are comfortably warm after an hour of walking. The airport is divided by ropes into different sections. We have to pass through a security control to get in. Greg and Hedy have passes from the Catholic Church that admit them into a section close to the stage. When the guard lifts the rope for Greg, I follow.

The airport is packed with people and more arrive by buses from town. Half of the Fairbanks city population of 30,000 is at the airport. Some were let in already at 6:30 in the morning. Far in front of me I can see an imposing 10-foot high platform draped in blue with a podium flanked by the American flag to the left and the yellow-white flag of the Vatican to the right. The seal of the President of the United States adorns the podium. I can see well from the back of the enclosure that still is empty in front of me. An oil barrel supports the dividing rope. Intentionally I place my backpack with warm clothing and cameras on the barrel to reserve it for later use. The waiting period turns long and cold despite entertainment by many volunteering groups. I manage in a long down coat with chemical hand warmers in my pockets while 35 less well prepared are treated for hypothermia by the first aid crew.

A red carpet is rolled out at 9 o'clock triggering the security guards into heightened attention. Blinking red lights are seen in a distance at the airport. President Reagan's armored limousine is approaching, surrounded by security guards on the running boards. Governor Sheffield, Senator and Mrs. Murkowski, and prominent representatives of the Catholic Church greet the President and his wife. Excitement among the public increases. We no longer notice the drizzle and cold when a chartered white-green-red Alitalia DC-10 descends from the clouds with roaring engines. The public greets the plane with shouts and applause. Somebody waves a large Polish flag. The airplane stops at the end of the red carpet. Archbishop Laghi, the ambassador of the Vatican in USA, and Bishop Whelan of Fairbanks climb up to welcome the Pope. The Pope dressed in white, followed by the black and red dressed men slowly descends to the red carpet where President and Mrs. Reagan welcome the Pope to USA. The public cheers, cameras click, the atmosphere is charged. I feel happy and honored to have the opportunity to witness the meeting between these world leaders.

Both climb up on the platform so the public can see them. The President wears his trench coat nonchalantly open despite the drizzling rain. In a mighty voice he proclaims:

"More can be accomplished through the simple prayers of good people than through the statesmen and armies of the world."

Pope John Paul and President Reagan at the Fairbanks
airport 5.2.1984 (Photo Earl Roemer)

Pope John Paul II starts with a shout: "Praise be to Jesus Christ!"

After their talks, both walk together to the air terminal disregarding the waiting limousine. In a room prepared specially for The Visit, they discuss world problems for 20 minutes. After The Visit both are driven to the waiting "Air Force One" where they say goodbye. After a final wave, President and Mrs. Regan are on their way back home to the White House.

To see better I have climbed the barrel I reserved as I had planned. The barrel stands at a walkway, the full importance of which I don't immediately understand. After The Visit, guards with equipment and a dog pass along the way.

The Pope and Bishop Whelan step into an open black car where they stand in front of the back seat. The Pope has exchanged his small white scull cap for a wide-brimmed red hat. The procession with a smiling, waving Pope gets into motion along the staked walkways through the crowds while security guards run along as dogs. This car doesn't have running boards as the presidential limousine. I stand on my barrel by the route with my movie camera and record the excitement, feeling highly elated in my lofty position during the papal drive-around.

Service from a tall black platform next to the blue one follows. The event starts with the well- known hymn, "A mighty fortress is our God" and ends with "America the beautiful."

The historical visit ends with a last papal waving to the public from the stairs of Alitalia. Before the plane has even taxied to a runway, the frozen but spiritually enriched crowd stampedes from the airport. Shortly thereafter it starts to snow.

I feel blessed to live in such a unique place as Fairbanks where politics and religion can meet peacefully and draw a crowd.

30

Finding the Perfect Ice Floe

Nearly everybody has a vision about an ideal place of work, a secluded getaway where no one will distract you, a place of limitless horizon and boundless opportunity but without disturbing phone calls, junk mail, air pollution, traffic congestion, complaining neighbors, etc. To this idyllic picture must be added uncommon details: this place has to be on an ice floe in the Arctic Ocean — a big floe, steady as a rock yet drifting slowly with the winds and currents towards the west, following the general ocean circulation of the Beaufort Gyre.

So much for the dream. The reality is that my job situation hasn't stabilized. I continue to fish for small contracts wherever I can. During a phone conversation with my co-author for a research paper, Dr. Gerry Garrison at the Applied Physics Laboratory (APL) of the University of Washington in Seattle, he mentions the following requirements:

"We need to find an ice floe of suitable size and strength to carry a scientific research camp. The floe has to be strong enough to take the abuse of curious scientists for two months without cracking up; a multi-year floe would have the required strength. The floe also must be accessible. We want to get to it after the middle of September 1984 by the U.S. Coast Guard's *Polar Sea* icebreaker. We want the floe to be far enough away from the coast to be secluded but still within helicopter range of Barter Island. The floe also has to be in position for a rendezvous with the icebreaker when the time comes to break camp."

"That's quite a shopping list," I reply "but with my experience as a remote sensing specialist I can find you a perfect floe," I say confidently, hoping for some paid work.

"I can pay you three weeks salary for your search," Garrison offers.

"Thank you. I will select a suitable floe within 200 nautical miles of Barter Island and track it with satellite imagery. I will also select a route for the icebreaker to reach the floe from Barrow both before and after the experiment," I promise.

I feel excited and energized after the call. This will be a fun and interesting project. At the Northern Remote Sensing Laboratory (NRSL) of the Geophysical Institute we have access to satellite imagery both from the National Oceanic and Atmospheric Administration (NOAA) weather satellite and the special Landsat Quick Look receiving station that we run at the Gilmore Tracking Station. The NOA-AVHRR satellite gives us multiple daily passes over the Arctic Ocean in a scale of 1:7 million. Those pictures are suitable for general surveillance. The Landsat pictures in a scale of 1:1 million are ideal for detailed research but are not available daily.

I spread out a chart of the Arctic Ocean coastline and draw a semi-circle with a radius of 200 nautical miles around Barter Island. I must find my floe inside this area. I draw in all relevant future Landsat passes and request the tracking station to record them.

On the first Landsat image that I study for August 13, 1984, I find a 9 x 16 mile large floe, 188 miles northeast of Barter Island. This is ideal. Was it really this easy to find the perfect ice floe at the first attempt? Enthusiastically I call Garrison.

"I have found the perfect floe for you," I say.

"Good, then I don't need to pay you. Your contract doesn't start until August 15," he replies.

The following two weeks are cloudy, which is normal for the Arctic Ocean in summer. The next time the ocean can be seen, the "perfect floe" is nowhere to be found. Other large floes that I located northeast of Barter Island have drifted about 60 miles to the southeast, toward the mouth of the Mackenzie River where the ice edge is farthest from shore. Those floes were beyond helicopter range to start with. They are in danger of melting once they reach the open water along the coast. The images from the September 1 Landsat orbit show a strange cluster of small floes. After some comparison with NOAA imagery, the mystery of the disappearing "perfect floe" is solved. Some floes build up internal stress to the point that they can suddenly disintegrate, and that is what happened to the first- choice floe.

I contemplate the virtues of a smaller floe. A floe that has been around for a while without changing its size might last longer, a matter of considerable interest to people intending to camp aboard it. The multi-year floes that have survived at least one winter have more rounded edges and appear brighter on satellite imagery because they consist of denser ice that reflects more light. The promising floes are labeled so they can be documented and discussed. From September 6 to 11, floe "G" drifts toward the southwest. It looks promising, but just before it comes within helicopter range its direction of drift changes. The importance of selecting the right floe becomes more serious as the deadline approaches. I start to feel the pressure of my promise to find the "perfect floe". Floe "F" is a bit small but seems to be in the proper place. On August 30, it is in the location where the "perfect floe" was first spotted. While I watch floe "F", it drifts about 45 miles toward the northwest in nine days, coming to the edge of the access range. This was not expected; according to all rules, the floes should drift toward the west. None of the floes considered so far have drifted like "F".

Garrison calls. "We must avoid the influence of the Mackenzie River outflow. Try to find a floe as far inside the pack ice as possible — yet not so far that there is danger of its drifting outside the access range."

NOAA imagery no longer shows any large old floes within that range. The project leader flies to Prudhoe Bay to do air reconnaissance. Satellite imagery flies from Fairbanks — via airmail — to Seattle and at the same time by overnight courier express to Prudhoe. For orientation purposes I flag a small bright floe in the middle of the access range on the images as "3" so that we can use it as a reference for future planning.

Time seems to be winning over technology. On September 17, members of the main crew pass through Fairbanks on their way to Barter Island, where they will board the icebreaker. A suitable destination floe has not yet been found. The assistant project leader, Gerry Garrison, visits the NRSL. He and I systematically scrutinize each floe on the satellite imagery until past midnight, trying to find a suitable floe. For the previous six days all of the floes have drifted toward the north-northwest, and they continue to do so. Garrison himself travels on toward the north-northeast and joins the icebreaker. The Landsat Quick-Look program tries to sense through clouds to find a suitable floe. The U.S. Air Force takes over communications between the icebreaker and the NRSL, and radios the drift of some of the floes to Garrison.

September 24, I get a surprising phone call from a lieutenant at the U.S. Navy submarine command in Pearl Harbor, Hawaii.

"The icebreaker *Polar Sea* works for us," he says.

What have I got myself involved in? I wonder with serious concern. The feeling of responsibility grows for my little project that started out so light heartedly.

I have promised to talk to a school class from North Pole that will visit the Geophysical Institute at the end of the week. It will be easy and fun to talk about the search for the "perfect floe" — until the phone call this morning. Many of the children's parents may work for the Air Force. My talk might be too interesting. I better be on the safe side and show them pictures of penguins.

September 25 is a day of hectic action in Fairbanks. Both the Navy in Hawaii and the Air Force in Fairbanks contact me — at the same time, one by phone the other by radio through the same phone line. This is very strange to me. Cloud-free imagery from the Gilmore Tracking Station shows the last identifiable piece of the "perfect ice floe" at the ice edge. Two Navy pilots visit. In the afternoon I attend a special lecture on sea ice but don't have the time to stay to the end. Unknown men in dress suits attend the lecture. While analyzing the last satellite pictures from Gilmore, I hear the voice of ice expert, Bill Sackinger, in the corridor.

"Kristina has probably left for the day since it is past 5 o'clock," he notes.

I meet the dress suits from Washington D.C. and two Navy ice observers.

"Hello, Kristina! Do you remember me, Carl Newton? We flew together in Antarctica."

I show them the latest satellite images and point out the promising ice floes. Carl takes a small piece of paper with latitude - longitude notes from his pocket.

"The positions of these ice floes are classified!" Carl says looking puzzled.

"I didn't know that. I generated the numbers you have on your paper," I respond.

"Tomorrow we will fly over the icebreaker in the Beaufort Sea," Carl says.

"Great, can you air drop some pictures?" I ask.

I put the latest satellite imagery in an envelope and address it "Coast Guard Icebreaker *Polar Sea*, Arctic Ocean." The next day, September 26, that imagery lands on the deck aboard the icebreaker.

The remotely sensed ice floe "3" is selected and quickly occupied. The floe is eight foot thick and is imbedded in 1.5-foot thick ice. On one side is open water with chunks of ice 20 to 40 feet in length floating around. While the floe continues to drift, the sea ice closes in and starts its slow expansion toward the south.

On October 25 new ice reaches Point Hope southwest of Barrow. On October 28 the area is cloudless, and the manned ice floe is found on a 4X enlargement of NOAA imagery.

The scientists are busy collecting samples and taking measurements for a total of 45 days, if in not quite the serene seclusion they had imagined. All the polar flights between Alaska and Europe pass above the vicinity of their personal ice floe. There are at least 50 flights per week, and each leaves a contrail behind. People come and go by helicopter, and day- by-day ticks off in busy routine — with occasional bits of excitements. A crack opens 300 feet from the camp, running right across the landing field. It soon re-closes. The floe stays discreetly on a conservative westerly course, and drifts 75 miles in 38 days.

On November 11 the icebreaker keeps its rendezvous and picks up the scientists from their frozen isolation. They return to trees and traffic in Seattle, leaving the Arctic Ocean — and their wandering ice floe— far behind.

For me, this 3-week fun project became an interesting challenge for three months. I had generated my own funding and did accomplish my promise to find the perfect ice floe.

31

Fishing Bears

The water foams white between the rocks of the McNeil River Falls where the river splits into many small rapids. The Kachemak Air Service Beaver floatplane lists 45 degrees on its right wing. We are only three passengers. All seats are on the left side of the plane. I release my seat belt and move to the right side kneeling with devotion on the floor by the first window scanning the falls with my camera on high alert. There they are: one, two, three, many, more! There are bears all over. While the plane circles, I rapidly try to count them. There are at least 35 grizzly bears at the falls and further down along the river. What a fantastic sight! I am so impressed by the bear assembly I forget I am in the air. The thought makes me dizzy and a bit apprehensive. We have come to visit all these bears in their own fishing territory. I have taken the headphones off because the wire was not long enough to reach the window on the opposite side so I cannot hear the pilot. The plane is too noisy for conversation. Soon my friend, Carol Hagglund taps me on the shoulder and points to my seat. We are about to land.

The Beaver lands softly on the water and taxis towards the shore of a long sandy cape filled with driftwood, polished white by the waves. A few bald eagles take to the air. The floats bump against the beach with a small jostle. The pilot, dressed in hip boots, steps out on a float and throws a line to a man on shore. Balancing along the float we reach the shore with our boots dry. The plane is rapidly unloaded. The timing is crucial. The pilot must land and return while the tide is still high. He jumps into the water, pushes the plane out and is in the air almost as fast as he got down. The evening is beautiful and peaceful.

Larry Aumiller and Polly Henning, biologists with the Alaska Department of Fish and Wildlife, help us with our gear. We follow the driftwood cape until we reach a higher grass covered shore.

"You can pitch your tents here," Larry, with thick black curly hair and beard, says as we reach a small meadow, covered with wildflowers and surrounded by tall dense brush.

We have come to the camping place for the McNeil River State Game Sanctuary. This is bear country and we are guests.

"We have made the camp totally unattractive for bears," Larry explains. "Everything edible is placed high up below the ceiling in the cook shack. The garbage is burnt and the dishwater thrown into the ocean. If a bear accidentally walks into camp, it is politely asked to leave."

The rapids, where we saw the bears fish are two miles from here. You need a permit to go there and they are only granted to 10 people per day. Lots are drawn in the spring among those who have submitted applications. Carol and I tried last year but without success. This year we take our chances without a permit. There are 22 people in camp including nine without permits. The chances to get there once are good if you are patient. Two of the nine have already been there once so they must wait. The remaining seven will compete for two places.

Excitement builds up. How will this end? I wonder. Everyone wants to go and everybody wants to go now. Somebody gets a pack of cards and mixes them painstakingly. Carol pulls the Joker, and I the ace of clubs.

The sun is setting at 10:30 p.m. We pitch our tents. They flutter lightly in the wind. Everything is peaceful.

Tuesday morning dawns cloudy but it doesn't rain. We lucky winners walk away at 11 a.m. led by Larry Aumiller.

"The one carrying the heaviest pack can lead," Larry says. Without dispute he takes the lead with his large pack labeled "This is Bear Country" and a camera tripod over one shoulder and a rifle over the other. We start out following the beach. On the other side of the bay we already see a few bears. Everyone, except for Carol and me, have hip boots. They can easily wade across the small bay while Larry ferries Carol and me in a skiff. A short Japanese lady joins us although she has hip boots reaching her armpits.

"I feel safer close to Larry's gun," she says.

We walk up a slope covered by tundra with the estuary of the McNeil River on the other side. The vegetation is mainly large grassy tussocks and brush. We see bear droppings on the trail and a tuft of soft bear wool on a bush. We are concerned that a bear could hide anywhere.

"Don't worry," Larry says. "I am convinced that all bears are at the river."

We reach a hill after a brisk 45-minute hike. The McNeil River with its fishing bears lies in front of us. We don't stop to look nor reflect but continue straight down along the trail through low bushes to a small gravel patch above the falls.

"Five of you can stay here while the other five can go to a narrow cliff shelf below," Larry says. "If there are too many of us in one place, the bears get anxious."

The gravel-covered area is our territory. Here we can do almost anything and the bears don't care. We try to act so the bears are neither threatened nor attracted by us. Most of the time the bears ignore us. Aumiller has visited this place for 11 years and many bears have come here for as long. He knows most of them personally and has even given them names. During all these years he has never had a need to use his rifle.

Suddenly we see bears in front of us. It is so natural that it doesn't even scare us. Instead we are so overwhelmed by the sight that the cameras start clicking. A large bear with its back towards us sits at the largest rapid on the other side. Another one sits submerged to the neck in some calm water. Often it seems to have a salmon between its paws and takes a bite now and then. Other bears make rapid visits to the falls to snatch a chum. Surprised, we realize the green slopes are covered with bears.

The large bears step sure-pawed into the falls, grab a fish, take it to a cliff and start eating. The discriminating ones only take a couple of bites; the gourmets only sink their teeth into the roe so the caviar splashes, while others only eat the skin. What is left is soon snatched by a bear with less fishing experience. The gulls feed on the last remains.

The salmon are plentiful. Tens of thousands of fish swim up the river. It is mainly chum salmon but also a few kings and Sockeye or red salmon. This is the same river where all the chum salmon were born three, four or five years ago. The age of the king salmon varies from one to seven years. The salmon have spent the preceding years at sea. Now they are grown and mature enough to spawn and start a new generation. Their meat gradually turns patchy red, although taste isn't immediately affected, as they purposefully swim up their native river. The rapids constitute an obstacle, but most of them get through the bear ambush. Those who survive the fishing bears, instinctively find their birthplace where they spawn and die. By then their color is dark red. It is so crowded at the combined place of birth and death that you can easily see red.

A young bear stands all day below the falls and occasionally hits the water with his paw. The technique isn't effective. Eventually he manages to catch a fish but a bolder bear immediately steals it. A charming, shaggy, silver sparkling young bear sits decoratively on the sloping beach below the falls. Occasionally she makes some testing attempts to get to the water but is easily scared away by larger bears. This must be her first summer alone. Eventually, Silver gets braver and dares to go all the way to the beach where three bears are busy eating. One raises his head and looks at Silver but continues to devour his salmon. Another raises its paw and Silver jumps aside but changes her mind and approaches very hesitantly. Does she want to share their meal? She must be hungry and possibly afraid of the water. The wind blowing from the falls is chilly, although it is warm further away in the bushes where the bear are resting. I wonder how many there are? I counted 35 from the plane but there could be three times more. The slopes are filled with bears and we are right here with them.

A group of three bears walk up the hill towards us as if they had a purpose in mind. I feel a little bit apprehensive but nobody else appears concerned. It is a large female with two big cubs. She approaches leisurely and lies down on her back in the grass only 15 feet from us. The cubs start to suckle while we watch in amazement and take pictures

Grizzly mother suckling her two cubs at McNeil River.

The roaring of the falls over-powers the shrieking of the gulls as well as everything else. The water splashes in blue-gray when a dark, almost black bear with light edges on its ears high jumps through the water while another one tries to dive from a jump. Others take it easy and stand seemingly well anchored on the slippery rocks in the fast moving water until dinner swims by. The grizzly bear has very long claws.

Females with cubs permit their offspring to share their meal with mild protests. Many have cubs from last year that now are one and a half year old. A female generally has two cubs and permits them to stay with her for two or three summers. After that, they are kicked out to fend for themselves so she can start a new litter. The cubs are born in hibernation during the winter.

A female with two small dark half year-olds suddenly descends the slope. She ends up in a fight with a threatening male on the cliffs. The female is very protective since males can kill and eat small cubs. The cubs get scared and run away. They are also afraid of the water so they run towards the cliffs where we stand on a 3-foot wide shelf. The mother follows. Somebody claps their hands to scare away the cubs as we were instructed the day before. I follow the example.

I applaud with such enthusiasm that my palms burn but besides that I don't have the time to feel afraid. I just try to inspire the cubs to turn around and return to their mother who stands with gnashing teeth 10 feet away. Carol doesn't appreciate the show enough to applaud. Instead she tries to take a picture but for some reason her hands shake so badly that the picture gets blurred. She moves to the platform above.

"Stop clapping your hands," Larry shouts from the slope above where he stands with his rifle.

The bears have retreated. Larry comes down and crouches sideways in front of me. I assume he does it because there isn't room for him to face forward and he doesn't want to stand up and block my view.

"I know most of the bears personally," he says "but I have never seen this one. It was wrong to clap your hands. It was an aggressive action, unsuitable since the bear already was agitated."

The female approaches again. This time she doesn't have a reason. It looks like an attack. I photograph enthusiastically feeling safe behind Larry's back. The bear appears very nervous. This is a dangerous situation. Bear are unpredictable and guard their cubs aggressively. Somebody with less experience of bears might have shot the bear in so called self-defense but Larry tries to convey confidence and non-aggressiveness. Bears that bluff attack sometimes stop and turn sideways to show how big they are. It is a signal to the offender to disappear. In our case, we want to gain the opposite. Larry crouches and turns his side to show how small, submissive, and non-threatening he is. The female accepts the sign and turns around. Somewhat shaken, we return to camp after an eventful day.

The next day we don't have a chance to go to the falls. We take a beach walk instead. This time Carol and I are alone.

"What do we do if we meet a bear?" we ask Polly Henning.

"Just wave your arms and say, Hello bear" she replies. "Chances are the bear will run away. If it doesn't, just step to the side and give it room."

The shoreline is dramatic. A precipitous cliff rises behind a narrow sloping edge of sand. First it resembles the wall of an ancient massive fortification with coarse columns. The waves have scooped out caves between the pillars.

A light haze covers the ocean. Thirty miles to the northeast you can distinguish the steam that still rises from the Augustine volcano. It erupted this spring.

We plan to fly out the next day but there is only room for one of us on the plane. I take the chance to stay behind. The opportunity for a bear visit on Friday is good. We draw lots for three places among five interested. My prayers are again answered.

We walk to the falls around eight. Fishing is already in full swing but all bears haven't arrived yet. The place is busy. Bears sit on the beach watching. One scratches its ear with its back paw. Some sniff each other friendly. Others eat and some wait to be fed. Two almost black half year-olds stand up on their small back paws to look for their fishing mother. A cub from last year sits down behind its mother and lovingly leans its head against her wet fur coat. Two dark brown cubs fight. A bear wanders searchingly among the rocks at the falls. One walks carefully up-river, another down-river. The bold grizzlies snatch their salmon quickly and devour it on the beach. Meanwhile, a careful female closely followed by her small cub rushes up the slope with her salmon. A large bear wades decisively into the flowing stream, grabs a salmon by the tail and brings it to the beach.

One large cub immediately approaches to share the meal, but another is pawed away until it has retreated backwards all the way into the water. Larry takes half of the group back by noon.

"High tide is early today," he explains.

We follow Larry in a single file up the slope through the dense brush with sleeping bears. The view is better from the top. Suddenly there are five bears in front of us. It looks dangerous. What do we do now? I wonder. We stop. All the bears have seen us so we don't need to announce our presence. I am last in line. We seem to have time although the plane is expected anytime. The bears determine our motions. I take my backpack off and use my movie camera. The closest bear behaves properly and runs away. A female is in front of us. Her medium brown silhouette with the characteristic grizzly knob on the neck is outlined against the green grass on the slope. She watches us carefully while her three dark brown half year-olds roll around playfully. Fortunately, the cubs and the mother are on the same side of us so the situation isn't threatening. We make a roundabout and part with mutual respect.

We return to camp a little late. I take down my tent in a hurry while the noise of a plane grows louder. I make it to the beach before it lands on the water.

I am the only one returning to Homer with the red floatplane. The other passenger aboard is a woman with a dog going to a fishing boat. I relax with my XTRATUF rubber boots on the seat-back in front of me while enjoying the great coastal scenery. It feels a little sad to leave the land of the bears. It has been an intense experience I will long remember.

32

Meditations in Storm

R/V Alpha Helix, the 133-foot long research vessel rolls violently from side to side somewhere in the Gulf of Alaska. The bow struggles to penetrate a hard ocean that resists with force. When biology professor Scholander at Scripps Institution of Oceanography in San Diego, where I was a graduate student at the time, had this ship built in the mid-sixties it was considered a wonder. It was built specifically for research along rivers in South America. Now, University of Alaska owns the Alpha Helix. I am excited to finally have an opportunity to get better acquainted with his ship.

My bunk is furthest to the bow, a location of minor status since the days of the sailing ships. In my younger days at sea it was still unusual to have women aboard. Often I was the only female in the expedition, sometimes one of two. Then I was always assigned one of the best cabins. It was a sign of man's respect for woman. Equality between the sexes has ended this respect.

On the Alpha Helix we have a crew and a scientific team of seven persons each. Among the crew, three are women: a marine technician, a deckhand and the cook. The only ones who have to share a cabin are the two female scientists. We get the worst cabin in the bow. In the harbor the cabin looked very cozy with its three bunks on the leaning bulkhead. Two bunks have a round porthole above them. The third is a suitable stepping stool to the top bunk that I choose.

At sea the sound in the steel changes. My cabin is next to the bow propeller that takes a screeching, hissing swing when the ship approaches a station, where we try to hold our position to take water samples. The ocean billows with a mighty roar and the anchor chain rolls with a bang from side, to side, to side behind my closet. The closet door swings open and shut and open again, until, in frustration, I tape it closed. At times a large wave hits the keel. At first it feels as if it momentarily stops the ship that vibrates a little but then continues to chisel its way through the wave while rolling in all directions, apparently at the same time. The next wave lunges with a hissing against my porthole. I am a little concerned but expect the porthole to continue to withstand the force of the ocean. A little water trickles through but it runs down between my mattress and the bulkhead.

I lie in my bunk being thrown back and forth. I have lost track, a long time ago, of how many times I have thrown up. All good preventions with seasickness pills have come up, even four times in succession with calming intermissions. After each session on my knees in front of the head (marine toilet) I brush my shoulder against the wall in the corridor for support and balance, to get back to my cabin. When the ship lists towards my bunk, I take a power dive to get up into it.

Soon I am totally exhausted with no energy left and my mouth coarse as sand paper. It is cold with a steel bulkhead as a barrier against the aggression of the ocean. The only thing I have the strength to move are my thoughts.

It would be warmer if I pulled the blanket over me, but I don't have the strength to touch it. It is at my side.

A towel in the porthole would prevent the water from trickling down into my bed, but I don't have the energy to reach for it at the foot end of my bunk. After planning and freezing for a long time I muster the strength to pull the blanket over me. I have a vial with seasickness pills under my pillow. I should have thrown up all I can. Maybe a new pill would calm the vomit reflex? A plastic bottle with water is also within reach. While lying down, I get a pill out and manage to close the container. Then I lie for a long time with the pill in my hand planning to swallow it. Nothing interests or concerns me.

I haven't felt like this since my first voyage with the Finnish research ship Aranda in August 1959, when the water of the Gulf of Bothnia was turned upside down, because the thermocline, which is the division between the warm surface water and cold denser bottom water was destroyed by the storm. At that time the wind blew at 10 - 11 Beaufort (50 – 60 knots). I lay on the floor in my cabin on the Aranda and was cold because I didn't have the strength to rise and pull the blanket from the top bunk. All loose items from the table and shelves dropped on me but I didn't care. Through the corridor I heard the crew a deck down throw up and second mate, Nordberg, lecture about the strength and seaworthiness of the ship. The ocean roared and the waves reached above the tops of the masts. Had we been wrecked I wouldn't have had the strength to get up. It was then — a long time ago on another ocean when it was a real storm and others were in actual peril. I didn't find out the details about that until my colleague Palosuo came to help me build my cache.

This time it is mainly I who am sick. Others don't feel too well but they can work and eat. I have never before experienced a storm lasting this long on such a small ship. In the past I have managed with over- the-counter seasickness remedies. This time I use prescription medicine from the University doctor. It didn't occur to me then that this might have been my problem.

"When is it pleasant to be on the Gulf of Alaska?" I ask the captain.

"June, July, August, that's it." Now it is February.

After a three-day nightmare I can no longer stand the noise in my cabin. I take my pillow and blanket to the library one deck up and mid-ship. My cabin mate has already lain there on the floor for a long time although she is one of a select few who doesn't get seasick just drowsy. The marine technician also lies here because her bunk is along ship and she feels it is less tiring to sleep cross-ship. Here on deck now rests the entire female contingent of the scientific expedition.

Compared to the storm on the Gulf of Bothnia I still think this isn't anything to talk about. Winds of 40 knots with gusts around 70 but no tall giant waves and no mighty roar. The waves gather up at times into individual boiling piles but there are no organized rows with hissing foam. Maybe this ocean is too vast to concentrate the waves? Yet, although not obvious, the waves were supposedly 30 feet high. There are three round tables in the mess hall but only the four chairs around the captain's table are loose and slide around unless weighted down by a body. To balance a plate of food, it is easier to sit down on the floor with my back against the bulkhead and my feet spread out as a brake. I try a banana and a can of soda water but my eating is slow. The decision to eat is not enough. I barely have the strength to take a few gulps of water.

After five days in the storm we set course for the closest land, a leeward bay along the northeastern coast of Kodiak Island, to give everybody a chance to sleep. As soon as the wind calms to 35 knots I feel a little bit better and start to enter data on the ship's computer. As the anchor descends, we can all admire the view of the precipitous green slopes through the rainy haze. The engines are stopped for the night and I can enjoy my first dinner on board even sitting at the table. Fried fish with corn-on-the-cob. What a delicacy!

What occupies my thoughts when I am physically disabled? Old memories, especially people I have met a long time ago and of course, comparable experiences from my time on the research ship, Aranda, almost 30 years ago. Although I have been at sea in bad weather on many ships and oceans since then, it is the oldest memories that affect me the strongest.

Events of my past are enclosed by walls that reflect my thoughts. The scenery where my thoughts roam looks like a park at dusk. There are large deciduous trees with dense, long branches that almost sweep the ground. My thoughts only visualize the closest groups of trees. For days they haven't even noticed the walls in the background but run around as if they didn't exist.

I have now lain for 24 hours since the Alpha Helix re-entered the storm. The night on some couch pillows on the floor in the library, the day on the sofa. When the ship heaves I slide around on the floor but it is nothing to be concerned about. All items are securely attached. I always try to get up in the morning but as long as the storm continues my attempts only lead to a repetition of the routine from the day before. Throwing up is the first order of the day after getting on my feet. With an empty stomach I can move around for a while and go to the lab and the mess hall a deck down. I return to the library with a banana and sit down on the short sofa where I cannot stretch out. Eleven hours later I have gathered enough strength to eat the banana when my thoughts are distracted by a booming bang. It was the window to the winch hut on upper deck that was smashed. The wind is 50 knots most of the time and the ship lists 30 degrees. I get up to go to the head and throw up but a wave makes me miss the door. I land on the floor just before being thrown against the bulkhead 24 feet away. This is a weird existence I am starting to get accustomed to. I have no sense of danger. Praying for protection every day gives me an inner feeling of peace in the storm.

One evening, after almost two weeks at sea, the wind decreases to 45 knots. Once again we turn the bow towards the closest land. The temperature has dropped; there is a danger of icing. We can expect to reach Kodiak in one to one and a half days.

At home, four days later, my bed is still rolling when I turn around and there is a ringing in my ears. My weight has stayed constant although I barely stressed the ship's food supply. My metabolism must have sunk close to zero. That's why I only had the strength to move my thoughts and to freeze. I wonder if patients in a coma are in a related condition? Can they think, hear and feel without having the strength to move the smallest muscle in reply? I wonder if I would have gone into hibernation as a bear if the voyage had continued?

How much is a 50-knot wind? It is 10 Beaufort, the unit with which I am accustomed to relate wind strengths. The strongest winds we had at 70 knots equal 12 Beaufort. No wonder I didn't feel well. The gusts were worse than on the R/V Aranda that is about twice the size of the Alpha Helix. In the Gulf of Alaska this is normal, especially on expeditions led by my boss, Tom Royer, commonly called Dr. Storm.

Why was I invited on this voyage? It was scarcely a pleasure cruise. Nobody, especially myself, expected me to react the way I did. I have never been this sick before nor have I taken prescription medicine against seasickness.

The main reason Dr. Royer asked me to come along was probably that he is so busy. On land we seldom see each other. We even work in separate buildings. He had secured a three-year research grant from NASA to study the circulation in the Gulf of Alaska using imagery from a newly launched Landsat satellite. As the remote sensing expert for the project, Royer trusts me to do the work essentially independently. He is supportive with positive advice when I ask. It takes a year before we get the first useful image, but it saves our project. Thanks to new advanced sensors on the satellite, we discover a multitude of mushroom-shaped eddies never seen before in the Gulf of Alaska. My responsibility on board, except for the routine work, was to write a manuscript about the eddies.

Eventually, we publish three research articles. The main one: "Multiple Dipole Eddies in the Alaska Coastal Current Detected with Landsat Thematic Mapper Data" by Kristina Ahlnäs, Thomas C, Royer and Thomas H. George in *the Journal of Geophysical Research*, vol. 92, November 1987. NASA invites us to give a presentation at a space conference in Finland and Royer sends me. He is pleased with my work. NASA is pleased with the results of our research and uses a color picture of "our" eddies in their advertisement. EOSAT, a company that sells satellite pictures, does the same. They even use one of my color enhanced eddy pictures on the cover of their publication.

Despite the success, the grant ends and I am on the verge of loosing my job. The personnel office has already mentioned the word unemployment. The grounding of the tanker Exxon Valdez in March 1989 saves my job. New research grants are immediately released to study how the 11 million gallons of crude oil that leaked into Prince Williams Sound spread. Using satellite imagery I can tell where it is safe to fish without going to sea. Next time I do go to sea, I will be prepared with ginger; no more doctor prescribed pills for me.

It is comforting to know that I did gradually acclimatize and could function when the wind decreased to 35 knots that is still a respectable gale. The memories and feelings from my ordeal, being too weak to put my thoughts into action will remain with me and remind me there can be thoughts in a body that cannot move. Being out on a small ship in the roaring storm we were at the mercy of the elements. Thanks to the mercy of God we all returned safely.

33

Mission with Dates

It is cold in Fairbanks in late January 1993. My 1985 Jimmy has been plugged in all day at work. The car starts thanks to a battery blanket and an engine block heater. I unplug the extension cord and let the car warm up while I ponder life in the garage of the Geophysical Institute. At 43 below it is too cold to sit in the car and wait. I have worked nine hours and am looking forward to cooking dinner in my cabin.

The phone rings while I am still peeling off layers of winter clothing.

"This is Jack. I just hitched a ride back to town from North Pole. My car broke down. Could you give me a ride back to the car?"

"I just got home from work, I am tired and I haven't had dinner yet. Can't you find someone else to help you?"

"I cannot get hold of anybody else. If I don't get back to the car soon, it will be frozen in for the season. It is a lot colder in North Pole than in Fairbanks. It is at least 55 below there, but I believe I can still start the car if I get back to it now," Jack says.

"Why did you leave it in the first place?" I ask somewhat puzzled.

"The car will only go for a short distance at a time. I need someone with emergency flashers behind me to warn other traffic. My emergency lights don't work. I'll buy you dinner at the Elfs Den," Jack says with pleading persuasion.

"OK," I say will resignation, looking forward to a meal in a restaurant. "Where do I meet you?"

"I'm down town at the Polaris Hotel," Jack says. "My car is still warm so I can start immediately.

I'll be there around seven."

I dress in my warmest clothing: Eskimo sealskin parka, padded US Navy surplus flight pants, white Army surplus Bunny Boots and double pairs of wool mittens inside leather gloves. Visibility is poor in the dense ice fog that forms around 20 below when pollutants in the surface layer of the air freeze. When it is this cold I only do minimal driving.

Jack is waiting outside the Polaris Hotel dressed in a long parka. Traffic is light. Due to the heavy ice fog, we appear to be almost alone on the road since we don't see any other cars until they are next to us. As we head south along the Richardson Highway, we notice many abandoned cars along the edge.

"You are not the only one with car trouble, Jack." "A cold snap like this is a good test and will screen out cars unprepared for winter driving," Jack says with experience.

"I was a bit apprehensive to venture out in the cold tonight and drive all the way to North Pole," I say "but I am pleasantly surprised over how well my 8-year-old Jimmy is humming along. I feel a lot more confident by now."

"You have nothing to worry about with your almost new car," Jack says.

We turn off on Badger Road and cruise through empty roads looking for the Fire Department where Jack left his car. Visibility is poor. All street signs are covered with frost. There is no one around to ask for directions. I feel frustrated and annoyed.

"You don't remember where you left your car," I accuse Jack.

"I know where I left it," Jack says. "It's just a question of finding it."

We finally locate Jack's 1972 Cadillac by a big pile of plowed-up snow. After some tinkering, Jack gets the car started.

"Let's go and have dinner," Jack says. "The car needs some time to warm up before it will move."

We drive further south to the central part of North Pole where the Elf's Den appears to be open. There is one car in the parking lot. A couple comes out as we enter. We now have the place to ourselves. I drape my fur parka over the back of my chair but soon have to peel off both my padded pants and Bunny Boots as I start to heat up. The menu is limited this late at night. We get chicken and mashed potatoes.

"Food is good here," Jack says with starved appreciation.

Jack doesn't invite me out every decade, only on rare occasions.

"Jack, do you remember last time you invited me to your favorite eatery on South Cushman?" I ask.

"Oh yes, the place with the delicious ribs."

"I never saw ribs before. When they arrived I was shocked. I didn't know your finances were so stressed that you could only afford to order dog food."

"The car should be warmed up by now. We are on a mission and better get back before it runs out of gas," Jack says to end our reminiscing.

The car is still running when we get back to it. "This is a good sign," Jack says. " I want to drive it to Quick Lube in Fairbanks. This shouldn't take too long. It is only ten miles from here."

"It is already 10 p.m.," I say. "I doubt they would be open this late."

"I will leave the car outside and be there when they open," Jack says optimistically. "Would you please turn on your emergency blinkers and follow me."

Jack maneuvers his 72 Cadillac out on the dark empty road. He drives very slowly but confidently— for 100 yards. It wasn't even far enough for me to figure out how to turn on the blinkers. We both get out of our cars. The snow squeaks under our steps. The cold has pulled all the moisture out of the air and condensed it in thick crystals of hoarfrost on the tree branches. Without traffic the ice fog has dissipated and the stars shine brightly. The wolf ruff on the hood of my sealskin parka has a strip of wolverine next to my face. It doesn't collect frost. Despite 55 below, I actually feel comfortable the way I am dressed

"Why don't you order Santa's elves to come out and push," I suggest. "We are still in North Pole. What's wrong with your car anyway?"

"The diaphragm for the modulator valve is leaking. The car needs to recharge before it will run further," Jack explains. I don't understand what he says but am not interested in hearing more so I keep quiet.

After enjoying the winter postcard setting for ten minutes, Jack's car makes an advance. Eventually it will go for half a mile before it needs a recharge of 15 - 20 minutes. As we enter Richardson Highway we occasionally see another car. For safety we drive along the edge of the road because we are so slow and visibility is too poor to let other cars see my blinkers until they are almost on us.

"We are stopped to recharge for longer than we drive," I point out to Jack, who gets into my car every time we stop, because his heater doesn't work either.

"I really appreciate your help," Jack says. "We are making good progress. We are already on Cushman Street. Let's hope we get through the intersection without having to stop."

The lights are green but making a 90-degree turn onto Airport Road is too much for Jack's Cadillac. It gives up in the middle of the crossing with me right behind. Jack gets into my car while the lights turn red and green and red and so on. This is one of the busiest sections of town but there are few other cars tonight.

"I wonder how long it will take the Troopers to interfere with our date?" I tell Jack, slightly amused at sitting here chatting in the middle of the intersection of Airport and Cushman.

"I doubt there are too many Troopers out past midnight at 50 below," Jack replies.

"Let's give them 20 minutes to catch us. By that time my car should run again." It did start again.

By 1 a.m. we finally park Jack's Cadillac at Quick Lube. We had spent three hours driving two cars ten miles. We could have walked the distance in this time but missed out on all intriguing conversation stops and excitement anticipating somebody dropping by to investigate. This was truly a mission with many interspersed dates. — Alaska nightlife at its best!

34

In Anna's Shoes Through The Gold Rush

Anna needs new shoes. They have to be old-fashioned high-laced shoes but they must be comfortable and should not cost too much. My eyes scan along the shelves of shoes at *Value Village* second-hand store. Finally I find a pair that fits *me*. Why do I choose shoes for me on Anna's behalf? Anna will go traveling to talk about her life during the Gold Rush 100 years ago. This is a piece of magic I need to help her with by stepping into her shoes so to speak. The story started a year ago. In the summer of 1997 the University of Alaska museum in Fairbanks planned to open an exhibit, Threads of Gold, about women in the Gold Rush. During a meeting for the museum docents, the education coordinator, Terry Dickey, said: "Our museum is already one of the top 10 tourist attractions in Alaska. We want to try something new and present living history. We need a few volunteers. You choose whom you want to present."

Pioneer seamstress Anna DeGraf intrigues me. She is enshrouded in adventure and drama. At age 55 she hauled her sewing machine over the Chilkoot Pass. She spoke German, a Germanic language like Swedish, my first language. Perfect, we have a similar accent. I decide to be Anna, reincarnated in new shoes.

"Anna has written a book about her life in the North country," Dickey says. I read it thoroughly.

June 12 is *the* day for us. We will give our 10- minute presentations twice every Thursday morning for the rest of the summer. To our relief, the museum is almost empty. This will be good practice. My "speech" isn't quite ready and I feel unorganized. I am overwhelmed to become Anna for a moment when I have her whole life as background in the book she wrote. Physically I am ready. I have a long skirt in three tiers in shades of green, blue, white, and olive. A cornflower blue high-necked silk blouse with ruffles and long puffed sleeves matches the blue in the skirt. A wide, laced, black velvet belt separates the two. The blouse is adorned by an Indian beaded necklace in shades of blue. The crowning glory is my wide-brimmed straw hat I decorated with a long blue strip of feathers, silk flowers, and green tulle.

Kristina and Anna DeGaf at the
University of Alaska Museum

"When the Gold Rush is mentioned, most people think about strong, tough men. Few know that 10% of the luck seekers were women. Only the light- footed entertainment brigade has won notoriety. Little is known about the women who came to do a decent job accompanied by their husbands, brothers or alone. We hope this exhibit will remedy this lack,"

Some buses arrive. To our horror, tourists pour in. A docent introduces me dressed as Anna DeGraf. I am the first presenter. Convinced my first impression is striking, gives me confidence to step up on the small platform with a microphone.

"In 1982 two great-grandchildren of Anna rummaged through her steamer trunk in San Francisco and found — a manuscript. Ten years later, on the 100th anniversary of Anna's first arrival in Alaska, the book, *Pioneering on the Yukon 1892- 1917* was published — and here I am, Anna DeGraf," I say as I put on my hat and curtsy, holding my skirt.

I have thought for a long time about how to present Anna. She impresses me through everything she has done, her fast thinking in critical situations, and her dramatic way to describe her experiences. At times I feel I can read the un-mentioned between the lines as I have been in similar situations. I can empathize with Anna and try to become her in my presentation. It is no longer theater; I talk about my own experiences in Anna's shoes. When I can, I use her own words from her book:

"I went through fire and water and hardships, that seem almost unbelievable, as I look back on the 25 years when I went in and out of Alaska and Yukon looking for my son, until I was 78 years old and a great grand-daughter was born in San Francisco."

As Anna, I tell about my son who left me in Seattle. Looking for the lost son runs as a red thread through my life. I go to Alaska, hike the Chilkoot Trail twice and float down the Yukon River. On the way I encounter a variety of adventure and trouble.

"Your story flowed well, Kristina," Dickey says with appreciation.

Our audience has barely left before a new bus arrives. This group is smaller. I feel unorganized when a man falls asleep on the couch in front of me. He is no inspiration. I become confused and forget what I said an hour ago or think I already said it. I cannot use a manuscript since I talk about my life.

"Consider this good training," Dickey says. "Tomorrow, the exhibit: *Threads of Gold* will open with invited guests, among them the University chancellor Joan Wadlow and the authors Claire Murphy and Jane Haigh, whose book: *Gold Rush Women* is the foundation for this exhibit. You will only have two minutes each to perform your life histories."

I carefully rehearse my presentation in front of the mirror with many direct quotes from Anna's book. There is no reason to be nervous. I know what I will say and how long it will take. It will go well, I assure myself.

Afterwards many thank me. Some are touched to tears.

"Your Saxonic accent was very good."

"Thank you, I have practiced it for a long time," I reply.

"Would you please autograph the new Klondike scrapbook with pictures from your Alaska collection," I ask Candy Waugaman.

"You still speak with Anna's accent," Candy says surprised.

"I am still in Anna's clothing."

Fairbanks Daily News Miner prints a large headline: THREADS OF GOLD SUMMER GALA, an elegant evening with dinner and dance to celebrate the centennial of the Northern Gold Rush. A gourmet dinner with five courses, fine wines and champagne in a Grand Pavilion Tent with a view of the Alaska Range on June 26, 1997.

Ticket price $125 is to benefit the museum extension campaign 2002.

"I would love to attend this gala but I have already promised to meet my friend, Carol Hagglund, who arrives in Anchorage on June 25," I say.

My only honorable possibility to attend the museum gala is to get Carol to Fairbanks.

"You be a gold rush woman, Carol."

"You lived in the same house as Amalia Hill who came from Finland and mined gold in Ophir. The newspaper wrote about her in 1979. I saved the obituary," I say with persuasion.

"Good, I also have a clipping from Amalia's time in Ophir," Carol says.

"This gala will be an experience we don't want to miss. We planned to celebrate our birthdays in Anchorage, but imagine what a party we can have in Fairbanks instead. We can pretend this gala is just for us," I add the extra alluring temptation.

Claire Murphy attends a meeting where we plan how to dress for the gala. It is her book that pictures most women as they dressed during the Gold Rush. Anna is shown leaning against a pile of rocks wearing a long shawl wrapped around her head, a skirt of gunnysacks and her feet wrapped in rags.

"We don't need to worry about Anna's clothing," Claire says.

"Anna was a seamstress who made clothing from silk and velvet imported from Paris. She knew how to dress for a gala," I say annoyed as I continue to defend Anna's sense of clothing until I realize I am criticizing Claire.

"Excuse me, I forgot you wrote the book," I apologize.

Two Fairbanks theaters lend us clothing.

At the gala the tables under a large red and yellow striped tent are set beautifully with rows of crystal glasses, triple sets of cutlery and fresh flowers. A lady in a Gold Rush dress is assigned to each table.

Archaeological excavations, mandatory before building on state land, are conducted behind the tent. I have learned the basics by participating a day per week.

"Come Carol, I'll show you what I've done," I say enthusiastically.

We rustle through the grass in our long skirts with wine glasses in hand to look down into the arbitrarily chosen one square yard holes. My colleagues, who still dig and sift, eagerly talk about the rock chips they found as evidence of people living here before.

Carol and I have birthdays two days apart. "What a birthday party we had, Carol!, All these 250 people were here to honor us although they didn't know it."

At the end of the summer my presentation is canned so to speak and it has expanded to 15-20 minutes.

The US Forest Service in Cordova invites the gold rush docents to perform in Prince William Sound in 1998. By now a group of three performers has crystallized. We are all so passionate about our characters that we call each other by their names.

Returning from a visit to Homer, I take the ferry from Whittier to Valdez where I meet the others. We perform at the museum. Next morning we take the ferry from Valdez to Cordova and perform at sea. This is fun with supportive company. It was intimidating to do it alone coming to Valdez.

This is the first visit to the small fishing town of Cordova for all of us. Unfortunately, the ferry only stays for a few hours before returning to Valdez. This is not enough for me. I stay until the next ferry goes to Whittier. The others don't want to wait for five days.

I get lodged at the U.S. Forest Service bunkhouse for summer workers. In return I get to talk about my life as Anna. I will be the only program at the old courthouse and plan to expand my talk to 45 minutes. I hike up the ski slope into the mountains above Cordova where I can practice undisturbed. Talking loud is also good notice for the bear that I am here.

"It is fun to see you transform into Anna in front of us" Terry Dickey and other docents have told me.

***

I am filled with admiration for Anna, who literally went through fire and water. Despite all adversities, she never lost her ability to survive and start again. Stepping into her shoes has given me another life to talk about, a past life so to speak.

Visiting Juneau in 2004 I looked through old newspapers in the library. To my delight I found an ad in the *Alaska News* from June 1894:

Fashionable Dressmaking Parlor Assisted by my daughter, Mrs. Hobbs, I am prepared to do all kinds of Dressmaking in the Latest Styles.

MRS. A. DE GRAFF
Seward Street
Juneau, Alaska

This advertisement authenticated the existence of Anna. There are one hundred years between Anna and me. Both of us left Europe in our late 20's and chose to go to the unknown of Alaska we learned to love. Faith in God led us through our hardships and gave us the courage to trust we would be protected and blessed. Although my life hasn't been as dramatic, we share a few experiences that have made it easier for me to present "Anna."

Anna	**Kristina**
Born in Saxony in 1839	Born in Finland in1937
Speaks a Germanic first language: German	Speaks a Germanic first language: Swedish
Leaves for USA @ 28 in 1867	Leaves for USA @ 26 in 1963
Married in Seattle	Brings feather bed from Norway
Lives in Juneau in 1892- 1894, 1915-1917	Married in Seattle
Hikes Chilkoot in 1894-97	Lives in Juneau (Douglas) 1969-1971
Ore cars on Skagway 1897- bound train breakdown blocking track. Miss boat	Ore cars on Skagway-bound train too heavy to make Pass. Miss boat
Stranded in Skagway 1897 lodging from person she knew in Juneau	Stranded in Skagway in 1971 lodging from person she knew in Juneau
Very seasick in storm on the Bering Sea	Very sea sick in storm on the Gulf of Alaska
Wrote book about life in Alaska and Yukon	Wrote book about life in Alaska

35

U Da Naa - Long Ago

"Are you the actress?" a woman asks me at a party. "What do you mean?" I ask surprised.

"Yes, I recognize your voice," she says. "You performed living history of the Gold Rush in my school."

Ever since I presented Anna DeGraf I have wondered if I have a talent for acting. A mailing from Fairbanks Drama Association (FDA) announces auditions for "U da naa." Gina Kalloch has written an original play based on traditional Athabascan stories about Raven. I am intrigued by native culture. This could be interesting and educational. Curious and a bit apprehensive I go to the auditions at the FDA Warehouse in mid-December 1998. There is only one car outside. Is this it? With hesitation I enter the huge warehouse and find a lone woman.

"I'm Gina Kalloch," the tall woman with luscious long dark hair says. "I want you to read something. Pick a book you like," she says and points to a basket with children's books. None of the books are familiar to me since I grew up in a different culture. I pick a small book with a cute skunk on the cover. Gina sits down cross-legged on the floor as an eager kid expecting to hear a good story. I start reading to her with all the feeling I can muster, not knowing what comes next in the story.

"Thank you. That was good," Gina says. "I'll contact you later."

How did I really do, I wonder? Was I good enough?

Three weeks later Gina leaves a message on my answering machine, "come to rehearsals tomorrow night at the Glass Bead."

A total of nine people, including three men, arrive on January 5th.

"Raven will be the only specific role in the play and for him we need a native male," Gina says. "The rest of you will play many different roles. For now I want each of you to read a part of Grandmother, who will be a puppet head, narrating the story."

At next rehearsal on January 7, only four people show up. We learn about stage lingo seen from the actor's point of view standing on stage.

"It's important that you know where to stand in each scene and from where to enter and where to exit. USR means upstage right, DSL, downstage left," Gina says.

"ACT II starts with dancers entering the stage singing," Gina explains. "Three women want to go berry picking and Raven gives them a ride, one at a time, in his canoe. Kristina, you are Woman #1," Gina says as she hands out the manuscripts. We practice reading our parts.

At the January 8 rehearsal we are six with three new women including a stage manager. It is five weeks to opening night. Gina appears flustered.

"We still need four more people and specifically a Raven, the main character," Gina says. "I better go to the University trolling for a native male."

Gina catches a tall good-looking native engineering student, Ray DeWilde, and persuades him to play Raven. Ray studies ravens by the dumpsters at Safeway and soon learns to hop like one. Ray grew up in a cabin outside Huslia and remembers his grandmother telling stories. He will make a perfect Raven.

On the second week of rehearsals we meet five times. It looks like we have all the characters needed.

We look at a book with pictures of native dancing. To my surprise, some pictures show Athabascan dresses at the National Museum in Helsinki, Finland collected by Etholen when he was the governor of Alaska during the Russian era.

"I could make dresses like that for us," Bernice Dahl, a graduate of Indian arts, offers. "I can buy a suede-like fabric that looks like soft leather."

On January 16 we meet in Gina's shop, the Glass Bead, to practice native dancing and singing. A couple of girls know the words to some songs. After a lot of encouragement from Gina, they shyly start to sing the Good Luck song: "Aaliia, aaliia..."

The poster artist, Will Biedemeyer, brings in his design of a raven sitting on the edge of the moon. Gina is pleased. Will is a tall outspoken man from Eagle. "Your soul is in dancing," he says, and starts to dance.

"Come and dance with me," he invites the watching women. "I am looking for a wife. I'm a good provider. I have a fishnet and will bring you a moose per year." No one is bold enough to take him up on his offer.

Gary Pitsenberger, the technical director, leads the set construction. The design is intriguing with slanting plywood islands on wheels that can be moved apart or together as needed. His crew finishes the first island on week three. The show will open on February 12, the sixth week of rehearsals.

We practice the berry-picking scene from ACT II. It starts to feel more real, standing on one island, asking Raven to ferry us across the river to another island. Raven respects age and paddles me across first. As I reach the other island it feels natural to pick some berries and hand them to Raven. It was not in the script but is added since the script is still evolving. Similarly, parts of the dialogue change as we practice and get inspired.

On January 19 we practice ACT I, Scene IV where a Great Doyon, a powerful chief, has stolen the sun and the moon from the sky. Raven and the villagers are in distress in the darkness. I have a few lines as a concerned villager. Raven promises to help if he gets a good meal first. The stage goes black.

Matt Reckard, a short man with little fur on his head, is an experienced performer with many theatre productions in his past. He is the Great Doyon. He already plays without notes. I am asked to read the part of his wife with the daughter who gets tricked by Raven.

On January 21, three weeks before opening, the posters advertising the play are ready. Raven gets his large head with a long beak. It is a feat to carry it and to act as if it belongs. Bernice measures us for the fringed costumes she will sew. Both Raven and Matt act without notes. Gina asks me to be the mother and Chief's wife.

Raven, now well fed by the people in the dark village, ponders how to help them and get the sun and moon back. I am sewing inside the Chief's skin house lit up by the sun and the moon on the wall. As my daughter goes out to fetch water, Raven gets the idea to become one of us. The second time our daughter goes for water, Raven throws a feather in the water and wills her to drink it. She becomes very sick. Her father is worried. I, as the mother, am amazed. Before we have time to get her married off, she gives birth to Raven's baby. The baby grows fast. The Chief, not recognizing the origin of the baby, is very proud of his new grandson and lets him play with his toys, the sun and the moon. As the baby is left alone with the toys, he turns into Raven and throws the sun out through the smoke hole and frantically starts to tear the moon into pieces, naming each one for a month as he throws them out. The Chief returns, not giving Raven time to name the last month so it is thrown out with no name. Raven rushes out kissing the astonished Chief good-bye. "See you Grandpa!" Raven flies through the house ending ACT I.

The rest of us enter the back stage dancing and singing the Dogmushing song: "Djii hia, hia hia heej" to the beat of a drummer.

"This is the last week you can use notes," Gina says as we enter the fourth week of rehearsals. "On Monday we will run the entire ACT I, on Tuesday ACT II." A schoolgirl who doesn't show up for rehearsals one night is replaced. Lou Ann Rose, who is 13 years old, will be the new Willow Grouse and Goose girl. Temperatures drop to 40 below. We need motivation to come to practices at night. On Thursday we run the whole show. I try it without notes. I feel insecure not to have the script as a back up but the lines aren't that difficult. After four weeks of practice we know the stories and the dialog is supposed to come naturally. Gina hands out the last rehearsal schedule for the month of February.

"We're running out of time and have lots of work to do so please make it to all rehearsals and please be on time," Gina says. "From here on all rehearsals will be at the Alaskaland Theatre where the performances will be."

This is good since it got very cold in the warehouse when the temperatures dropped to 40 below and colder.

Raven gets his black, fringed shirt on February 1 and the animals get their heads. We wear the extra identifying heads as hats.

In ACT I, SCENE II, Great Raven asks Raven to build a raft to save the animals from a big rain that will flood the whole world.

"This sounds like Noah's flood in the Bible," I say. "These are old Athabascan Indian stories," Gina replies.

Raven builds a raft and herds the animals on. I am a wolf. Gina watches from the audience.

"You look cute with your heads on," she says. However, we have a hard time keeping them from falling off. We say our lines as practiced. In between, the voice of the Grandmother puppet narrates the story. After floating for a long time, Raven orders Seagull to help him look for land. While they fly around throughout the theatre, the animals on the raft sing the Seagull Song: "Aalaliia he-eah lia hee ..." "Did you see anything?" Raven asks Seagull. Seagull (indicating the audience) replies: "I saw some strange animals with fur only on their heads."

After more floating around, Raven indicates he is hungry, to the disgust of the others. Raven decides to make land and sends Otter to dive to the bottom and bring up some mud. Otter cannot hold his breath long enough. Beaver gives it a try but also comes up empty-handed. Muskrat offers to try, to the amusement of the other animals. He is gone long enough to be feared dead when he finally returns, paws filled with mud. Raven takes the mud and remakes the earth.

On Thursday of week five it is close to 50 below. Bernice traces our feet to make moccasins for us. Grandmother's large puppet face is taking shape.

I have my most significant part in the last scene of ACT II where I, as a grandmother, confront the Chief who killed Raven. Eddie Stevens with a theatre minor has performed in many plays. He is the Chief and wears a necklace. We all wear similar suede dresses with fringes around the hem and shoulders.

The scene starts with a village council meeting where everybody is upset with the tricks of Raven. The last straw was him eating a whale. The Chief feels it is his responsibility to kill Raven and scatter the pieces to the four winds so he cannot come back. Suddenly there is chaos. Women notice the river disappeared. The lake dries up under some duck hunters. One villager turns to me, as Grandmother, asking what terrible thing could have happened to cause this?

I confront the Chief. "It is what you did. It was killing Dotson Sa' that has done this. The water is disappearing everywhere. Even from our pots as we cook. You must find a way to bring him back or we will all die!"

The Chief with the help of the villagers collect every scattered piece of Raven and bring them to Grandmother. When I have everything, I carefully wrap them up in a skin while singing the Raven Good Luck song:

"Aaliia aaliia aaliia aaliia
hoohe hoohe-ehe hiia
hoo-oho hiia, hoo-oho hoo-oho hiia hoo heej!"

The others join in singing the third line. Raven reappears in all his glory. There is water everywhere.

We get critiqued after the performance. I am told to:

"Speak loud and articulate. Speak to the back of the audience. Don't sing too loud. Sing, don't read."

I have trouble remembering the words that don't mean anything to me in these native songs. It helps after I get a tape and can write them down in the way I would pronounce them. The tone is another story. I feel it is a joke for me to sing solo to an audience. In school I had zero in singing. I was forbidden to open my mouth during singing lessons from the age of 10 to 12 after which there was no more singing. I haven't told Gina about this. As the director it is up to her to put a stop to my solo singing. I am curious to see how long she will let me continue. It's a week to opening night. It helped when David Engles, the drummer from Minto, sang together with me yesterday while marking the beat on his drum.

Next day there is wet paint on the stage. We get introduced to stage makeup. I get suntan beige in a shade darker than some of the native girls.

On Sunday we practice for the benefit of the technical crew so they can adjust the lights, music, improvisations of water etc. The goose luggage is ready for the Goose Girl scene in ACT II. I am one of the flock of migrating geese.

Tuesday February 9, three days before opening night, we rehearse in costumes and makeup. My dress is roomy since I wore heavy cloths the cold night we were measured for size. I don't wear my glasses since they don't fit into an Athabascan story happening U da naa or long ago. Gina is agitated. The goose wings don't sit right. The cloth moccasins are slippery as we run all over the house as migrating geese. It is frightening, as I don't see well without glasses. The Chief's daughter with Raven's baby has quit. Gina finds a replacement with theatre experience, Levi Tyre. She has a lot to learn in a short time.

The show starts in darkness with the puppet Grandmother speaking in Athabascan and English telling the story of the Sun, his brothers the Stars, and their sister the Moon. The Moon goes looking for a husband all over earth followed by her brothers. They continue up into the sky where they die without finding the husband. I am one of the Stars. We walk down the steps in the dark theatre and climb a scaffolding back stage while everything gets covered in smoke and fog until we become the lights in the sky. The smoke sets off the fire alarm outside of the script.

In the final scene I do my singing better than ever, I feel. Practicing singing many times with David Engles is working.

Gina, who has observed us from the audience, gives us feedback.

"There is too much giggling. If the audience laughs, pause for a while. Don't correct yourselves when you make a mistake, just keep going. Improvise if necessary but stay in character. When you are flying as geese, keep flying all the way until you are out the door."

We have practiced every day the final two weeks. The last four days we have been going until 10.30 at night. My life has been on hold for the past 6 weeks as rehearsals have taken all spare time. It feels as a relief that opening night is finally upon us. All technical problems have been solved. Our animal heads are steady as we are saved from the flood. Our goose wings and packs stay on as we migrate. I can now see clearly, wearing my old, forgotten contact lenses. The moccasins are less slippery with patches on the soles. We know what props we need for each scene and from where to enter, and our lines are part of us now. We are ready. Let the curtain rise. The butterflies left in our stomachs will just help us to fly better.

Our first serious dialogue comes as we sit on the raft as animals. The lights are so bright in my eyes I cannot see the audience. It feels as if we are in our own world far away, U da naa—long ago. In the last scene I sing my song with confidence as Raven comes back to life with a flash of lightning. The villagers sing and dance.

The voice of the Grandmother puppet has the last words: "And that is why we never kill Ravens. They are greedy, and tricky, and sly, but they are also powerful. We always respect Dotson Sa' for all of the things he has made, and all of the things he has done for us. — I thought the winter had just begun, and now I have chewed off part of it."

We run a total of six shows for two weekends. The public is appreciative but it is getting tiring towards the end.

What did I get for all my efforts? I got to experience other worlds. It felt as if I actually lived in them for a while. I learned how a show evolves through group cooperation, interaction and a lot of hard work. There is a special camaraderie in the dressing room. I learned some Athabascan songs and dances and I got to sing solo in front of an audience against my wildest dreams. This was really fun. Maybe I do have a talent for acting. I soon get supporting evidence when the director of FDA, Barbara Pitsenberger, calls and invites me to audition for the next show: "I Hate Hamlet." "We need a female over 50 with a German accent representing Shakespearean actors," she says.

This if anything is a compliment to my acting. I must have talent!

36

Slavig in a Yup'ik Village

"Do you want to come home with me and celebrate Slavig?" my Yup'ik neighbor Sarah Ferrell asks me as we are picking the last blueberries of the season on Murphy Dome. Sarah is an impulsive short and slim Eskimo from Kwethluk on the lower Kuskokwim River. I raise my eyes from the blueberry brush. The rolling hills around tree line are already turning into the autumn shades of reds and yellows.

"I would love to," I answer, intrigued to experience customs in a native village. "What is Slavig?"

"It's Russian Christmas. You go from house to house and eat for a week. People in every house give you gifts. You need to bring a big bag to carry them," Sarah says with an excited grin on her bespectacled face rimmed with short black hair with streaks of gray.

"I am not sure that I would like to eat in every house," I say hesitantly.

"You don't have to, in some houses they just distribute gifts," Sarah says.

"Do you have to be Russian Orthodox to attend this festivity?" I ask.

"Oh no, everybody in the Yukon-Kuskokwim delta celebrates Slavig."

There are still four months to think about this but basically I feel intrigued. As departure time gets closer, more questions pop into my mind. Every time I pass

Sarah's house on my way to pick up my *Fairbanks Daily News-Miner,* she happens to be outside and accompanies me for the walk.

"If people give me gifts, how many return gifts do I need to bring?" I wonder.

"No, it's only the people whose houses you visit who give gifts. They prepare for this all year by ordering gifts from catalogs and gathering food. They consider it an honor to give," Sarah explains and teaches me some Yup'ik words. *"Kuyana,"* thank you. "However, do not ask so many questions, that's not tradition," she says.

The Orthodox Church follows the Julian calendar where Christmas is 13 days later than customary, starting on January 7. We fly to Bethel on January 6, 1998. It is 15 below but I am well prepared with clothing for cold, wind, and rain.

Bethel with a population around 5,000 is the cultural center for Southwest Alaska. The city lies 60 miles up the ice-covered Kuskokwim River. Boats and barges lie frozen-in along the shores with a grid of low houses spreading inland.

Kwethluk is half an hour away from Bethel. The next evening, we get a pickup ride on the dark plowed ice road over the frozen river. It is snowing. We will stay in Sarah's nephew, David Epchook's house where we unload our luggage.

Kwethluk has a population around 800. The city stretches along the river and is divided into two parts, appropriately called Downtown and Uptown. The flat landscape is covered by two feet of snow, not enough to conceal boats, barrels, and other paraphernalia lying around. A conspicuous scale leaning against a pole shows a high water mark at five feet and a recommended building elevation at six feet. Most of the houses are built on pilings to protect them from the annual flood when the ice on the river breaks. Some have large disc antennas for TV- reception. The large white church with turquoise trim has onion domes and Orthodox crosses on each of its three parts. It stands on sturdy pilings with a dense support of bracing boards.

Russian Orthodoxy is the oldest religion in Alaska. It was well accepted because it is adaptable to local customs and language. During pre-Christian times people in the delta area gathered for feasting and visiting in winter. Their Messenger festival combined with the celebration of the birth of Christ became Slavig, a unique time of feasting and gift giving. Slavig is derived from the Slavonic word Selavig that means starring. The Yup'iks sing Orthodox Church songs and carols from the Carpathian Mountains in Eastern Europe. They retain more old folk songs than the locals in the Carpathians.

The program for Slavig in Kwethluk lists 137 houses open for visits during seven days. Each house has its scheduled time. We walk to the current house of activity. A table is covered with food of all kinds looking like a potluck. People sit crowded around it eating as we enter the house. Older women wearing colorful headscarves, sit on a couch and on the floor. The rest of the people stand tightly packed everywhere. As soon as a couple of places open around the table, Sarah pulls me there.

"It's OK, you are an elder," she tells me. "They eat first. Do you want moose or otter stew?" she asks. She hands me a bowl. The pieces of moose are large and tough. When everyone has eaten, the people move to the next house.

Returning from the last house for the day, we talk until three in the morning with our host family. Sometimes Sarah refers to her nephew David as Grandmother. I am confused. I thought I understood her Yup'ik accent well.

"David's Yup'ik name is Aanaluq. He's named in honor of my grandmother," Sarah explains. "It is spiritually powerful to cross-name children after ancestors.

When we step outside in the morning on the second day of Slavig, Saint Nicholas Orthodox Church across the road appears empty. We don't waste time to look inside.

Hastily we walk through town to the first house for the day, Uptown. We arrive before the crowd. Three young girls, Anna, Vanessa, and Jessica, entertain me with games of hand clapping and string puzzles while waiting. Two boys carrying stars, about two feet in diameter and a crowd of 60 arrive an hour later. Maybe they were in church? All the snow machines and 4-wheelers people use for transportation might have been parked on the other side of the church.

The serious young boys carrying the Bethlehem stars wear striped dress shirts. They line up facing the people by the Christmas tree. Both 5-pointed stars are white with decorations. A ring of gold surrounds one; the other is edged by glittering red tinsel. As the boys twirl the stars, seen going clockwise by the public, everybody starts to sing "Glory to God in the highest..." One song follows another in rapid succession in English, Yup'ik and Slavonic for half an hour. I only understand the English part "Christ is born in Bethlehem and Mary is his mother." The choir chants the invocation for the people in the house to live many happy years.

After singing, most people squat down, maybe because this is how they normally sit when no chairs are available or because the floor is wet from all the snow from people's boots. I scoot down on the floor in a dry corner with the three girls. They all have short black hair with bangs to their eyes. When nothing happens, they play with my hair. I have a ponytail.

"Your hair is so soft, it's like fur," Vanessa says. "That's a nice compliment," I reply. "It sounds a lot better than saying I have thin hair." These are smart 10-year olds. They have answers to most of my questions.

The master of the house gives a spiritual message with a Bible in his hand. Timidly I only have tea and bread. I pass the hand-stirred marinated salmon but find the *akutaq* or Eskimo ice cream appetizing. Anna hands me a morsel of delicacy, chunks of fish head. I don't find anything edible on the bones but put it in my mouth.

The visit in every house always ends with the occupants passing out multiple rounds of gifts. There are special gifts for men, women, and children. Everybody gets candy.

After the priest's house the stars will separate to tour Downtown, and Uptown. Symbolically, we follow the star of Bethlehem.

In the next house there is only singing and gifts but no food. There is a guard by the door to make sure no children leave the house unattended. We skip the last house for the day and walk back to Aanaluq's. Vanessa and her sister Jessica walk with me.

"We want you to meet our dad," they say. "He will come to pick us up."

Boris Epchook is the brother of Aanaluq. He is the new mayor of Kwethluk, an articulate young man with a pleasant smile below his thin black mustache. Water is the most obvious problem for me in this village of honey buckets. Indoor "facilities" consist of a 5-gallon plastic bucket in a closet. A house near by has a large proud sign: Kwethluk WASHETERIA 1986, Public Watering Point. That's the place to go when you want a shower. People drive up to the faucet on their snow machines pulling a trailer with a plastic barrel they fill with water. I ask the Mayor about the water problem.

"We do have a 10-year project to provide Kwethluk with water," Epchook says. "The closest place for clean water is the Kilbuck Mountains 50 miles away."

We attend vesper at five. After church we follow the star to the house of Sarah's aunt. There is not room for all to get in. The door is open to include people on the porch. Buckets of food and soup bowls stand on the floor. A 9-year old serious boy twirls the star with the red tinsel edge while his 12-year old brother holds a lit candle by his side. The choir and people sing, interrupted by a few scripture readings from the audience. After eating, the family members pass out candy, socks, gloves, washcloths etc. from big boxes and bags. All women around me get a small package. Thinking it is licorice I stretch out my hand. Everybody laughs. How did they know I don't chew tobacco?

The proceedings in this house take two hours. Some people leave after eating but all re-appear at the next house. It is hot. Tired of standing I try to crouch against the wall with my parka and backpack on my knees. Anna hands me a bowl of salmonberry *akutaq*. It is good.

When the star is carried into Aanaluq's house where we are staying, I sit comfortably on the couch. People crowd into all available floor space including the arctic entry with the door open. No wonder the linoleum is well worn with this foot traffic. By now I recognize the routine, starting with half an hour of singing in three languages, blessing of the family and rules in Yup'ik to respect the home and its occupants by proper behavior. Merry Christmas. Christ is born.

The residents in the first house on the third day of Slavig welcome us with good china and a choice of food consisting of fish, bird, black bear and beaver. The black bear is cooked soft on the bones. The large vertebras are visible in the pot. My favorites are the salmon soup and salmonberry and blueberry akutaq with seal oil. When the seal oil is fresh it has a very mild taste. The drinks are coffee, tea and juice but no alcohol. Kwethluk is a dry village in more than one aspect.

I see the name Hautala on the house list. That is Finnish. Sarah points out the house as we pass. Later I go back alone. Mrs. Cindy is home with a baby with large brown eyes and two small twin boys.

"Please come in. My guests just left and there is still food on the table," she says. As a stranger, I am surprised to be invited in to eat.

"I used to work for an airline. I even know some Swedish a pilot taught me," Cindy says. "My husband Jim's grandfather came from Finland. Jim is out dog mushing."

Jim drops in. He is a blue-eyed, slim, energetic man in too big a rush to sit down.

"I'm training dogs for the 150-mile run in Bethel in two weeks. Do you want to see my dogs?" he asks. We step outside.

"Jump on," Jim says and points to his snow machine. With a jerk we speed out to his large kennel.

The star hasn't arrived at the next house in turn, Uptown. The crowd is waiting.

"Do you want to come for a walk so we can talk about girl secrets?" Vanessa and her friend Anna ask me. This sounds intriguing. I like the small girls.

"You should have a Yup'ik name," Vanessa suggests. "Star" sounds nice but the girls are not pleased with my pronunciation.

It is time to enter the house. The congestion is great. A baby scrapes me on the back; two small boys push each other by my legs. The smell from pots of uncovered beaver soup on the floor doesn't trigger my appetite. Most people passing out gifts squeeze between without *seeing* me. In other houses Sarah has pointed at me when she feared I would be forgotten. A girl gives me a plastic container with panties and clothespins. Despite her generosity this is no longer fun. I am not accustomed to crowds like these. I want to go home. I get a ride on a 4-wheeler to Aanaluq's house where it is peaceful until the family returns at midnight.

Jim, the dog musher, calls me Sunday morning and invites me for a visit.

"What do you do in Kwethluk?" I ask him.

"I'm teaching math and science in high school for the fourth year."

"Do you want to take a shower?" Jim asks me when I am ready to leave.

"What? Do you have a real bathroom with water?" I ask amazed. Thankfully I take him up on his offer.

Sarah doesn't want to miss any of Slavig and escorts me back when I return from the visit with Jim. She makes sure that I taste a variety of native foods including seal, beaver, and otter. The beaver has a pleasant sweet taste. To my surprise I see some Norwegian decorations in the sixth house for the day.

"My grandfather came from Norway around 1900 to teach the people how to herd reindeer," Elizabeth Spein tells me.

This is a big house that can pack in about 200. "There is *Kass'aq* food on one table," a tall man tells me. He is a Kass'aq, as they call non-natives. It amuses me to be referred to as a Cossack. I have turkey and salmonberry akutaq.

"Thank you for eating in my house," the hostess tells me when I leave.

It is past midnight when we enter the eighth house. I end up with 18 others in a small bedroom. Few gift givers find their way here but I can sit on the bed. Three-year old Katherine falls asleep sitting on the floor with her goodie bag as a cushion between her knee and face.

On the sixth day I visit 12 houses between noon and 2:30 a.m. Sarah drafts me to pass out gifts in a small house belonging to her niece. It is fun to be on the giving side. This house only has room for the star and the choir. The rest of the people wait in a bigger house for their gifts.

When I come downstairs on the morning of New Year's Eve, January 13, 1998, Sarah, dressed in black as usual, is in the process of cooking wormwood in a large kettle. The rising steam gives the scene a mysterious look.

"This should heal your cold," Sarah says. "Besides, it will protect you so you don't get sick when we give you a Yup'ik name."

"Please sit down and take your socks off," she says and hands me a mug of steaming brew. It tastes like bitter herbal tea. Sarah performs a ceremony.

"Congratulations, Ayapan," Aanaluq and Boris greet me.

"Ayapan was the name of our father's uncle. He stuttered like you. You must have got too much wind in your face as a baby," Aanaluq says.

"I wasn't aware that I stutter," I say surprised "but I could have got a lot of wind in my face. When I grew up in Finland it was customary to put babies in sleeping bags and let them sleep outside every day to get fresh air."

This is the last day of Slavig. Both stars meet in the last house. It is packed like an elevator. Suddenly part of the crowd rush out into the dark. Sarah and I follow. I am prepared with a flashlight. I have no idea where we are going as we briskly walk up a small hill. On top is a cemetery. The cold wind blows through my coat. My face is protected by the wolf ruff I added. Unfortunately, people don't crowd here. The stars twirl, the congregation sing and wish the dead a Merry Christmas and a Happy New Year.

Shortly before midnight the church bells ring. I follow the invitation with 40 others. There is room for plenty more. To be unobtrusive, since I am not Russian Orthodox, and comfortable, I sit down on the old women's bench in the far back corner. The felt liners in my Sorrel boots are damp from condensation. I had no idea I would wear them for seven days straight going from house to house. I remove the liners hoping they would dry a little. Now I can enjoy the singing and sermon. Everything is in Yup'ik. I meditate in my own

341

thoughts. Afterwards, four women and Aanaluq extend their hands to wish me a Happy New Year.

Slavig has come to an end. I have eaten in a lot of houses and visited even more. It has been a unique and rewarding experience. My favorite food and staple for the week has been the akutaq made from local wild berries and sometimes fish. In addition to 90 gifts I got 10 pounds of candy. I am overwhelmed by the harvest and give part of it to Aanaluq's family. He gives me a smoked and dried salmon filet.

On New Years day we are ready to return to Bethel. The icy wind shakes the house.

"I hope someone will offer us a ride back but I don't want to ask," Sarah says.

"I will pay for a river taxi, just order one," I say eager to get going. "Why doesn't it come?"

It is dark when the taxi finally arrives crammed with people. The ice road starts out good until we come to a bend in the river where the blowing snow roars like a stormy sea. I stay calm assuming the lights I see through the windshield are Bethel. The other windows are covered by thick ice. The taxi gets stuck. By slowly backing and trying again we get through the wind drift and reach the first light — an abandoned car. The next light comes from a stuck car. It looks serious. How long will this continue? How much gas do we have? We have two babies in the car. Nobody says anything. The third car ahead is not stuck. Men from there help us get through the drift. My intense prayers are answered. We are free. Praise God!

In Bethel I go to the cultural center and library to educate myself on the history and significance of Slavig. According to Fr. Michael Oleksa, Slavig in Western Alaska is a synthesis of three elements: Russian Orthodox liturgy, Ukrainian folk tradition, and ancient Eskimo practices including the Bladder and Messenger Festival.

I feel grateful and honored that I had a chance to experience this unique festivity and was so warmly received in this native village that they even gave me a Yup'ik name, Ayapan. Kuyana, thank you.

37

Kobuk Sand Dunes

When our satellite project was new, I was asked to investigate why NOAA infrared satellite imagery showed hot spots in Alaska. I made an exciting discovery; they were sand dunes. On a thunder patrol by Leer jet in 1974, I saw the Great Kobuk Sand Dunes from the air. Too remote and inaccessible to ever visit, I thought.

When Ramona Finnoff of ABEC Alaska Adventures announces an exploratory trip for June 2002, with Kobuk River canoeing, sand dunes and Cape Krusenstern, I cannot resist. I feel very personally attached to those sand dunes. I *must* walk on them.

I better not postpone a river trip with Ramona any longer but give it a try while I still think I can. I contact her.

"Paddling is no problem, I can put you in a double canoe," she says. "My concern is your backpacking. Are you strong enough to carry your personal gear for five miles to the sand dunes?"

"There is time to build up that strength," I say and sign up for the full 15-day adventure.

Now I have a good incentive to ski and walk. I make a list of everything I need for the trip and weigh each item on my kitchen scale selecting the lightest options. Just my backpack, sleeping bag, and camera gear weigh 20 lbs. Taking pictures are part of my enjoyment. With other items I must have for the 3-day exploration of the sand dunes, my pack weighs 42 pounds. When the snow is gone in May I start hiking with a backpack, gradually increasing the weight until I can walk 2.5 miles with a 40-lb pack. I get exhausted but I am confident I can somehow double the distance.

Ramona, with her long dark hair in a ponytail, greets Joe, Bob, and me with a warm smile as we meet on June 16 by Ambler Air's shiny blue charter plane on the east ramp of the Fairbanks International Airport.

"I'm sorry I cannot come along on the trip," Ramona says. "My white water skills are better needed on another trip. You'll be in experienced hands with Joe Durrenberger as your leader," she says.

Joe is tall and athletically built with brown- reddish hair. He is dressed in a yellow T-shirt over a navy long-sleeved turtle, tan Carhart pants, Xtratuf rubber boots, and an olive ABEC cap. He smiles confidently.

"I work as an engineer for the Denali National Park but like to lead a trip a year for Ramona," Joe says.

Bob Butterfield is retired as an interpreter for the Park Service. He is dressed in Xtratufs, a red fleece jacket, grey corduroy pants, and a white cap shielding very dark sunglasses.

I get the co-pilot's seat but the windshield is too high for me to see through so I look through the side window. A two-hour flight to the northwest takes us across the Yukon, Koyukuk and other meandering rivers until we land in Ambler on the Kobuk River.

The other participants in the tour, Ben and Shirley Schmidt, Richard Beck and Greg McCarthy fly in by way of Kotzebue.

Soon all our gear is assembled on a flat gravel pad above the river. It is very hot. Kids splash around in the river with their clothes on as protection against the mosquitoes.

"We have three Ally Pak canoes and an inflatable kayak," Joe says.

All are conveniently stuffed in large sacks. Ben and Shirley grab one of the canoe bags, Bob takes another. Greg is a psychiatrist. He takes the inflatable. I don't know what to do or whom to paddle with so I take pictures. Ben and Shirley pull out a lot of aluminum tubing. The canoes are puzzles.

"Let me show you how to assemble an Ally Pak canoe," Joe says. It is obvious that the oval shaped gray foam pad goes on top of the rubberized green material that is stretched out on the ground. Two sturdy rounded tubes support the bow and the stern. Some of the bent aluminum tubing snaps out to make eight long rods. Two are threaded through the top sides, the rest are laid along the foam to support the bottom. Shorter pieces of tubing tie them together. Two seats are anchored by tubing. Everything snaps securely together with the enforcement of a rubber mallet. A local man watches in amazement while scratching his ear.

"You can take a break while I figure out what to pack where," Joe says.

"Let's take a look at the village of Ambler," Shirley says. She has curly black hair. Both she and Ben are short. They are dressed in shorts over black leggings. Ben is slim and trim with some white hair showing at the back of his blue cap. We start walking up a hill at an exuberant pace. I keep up but try to hide my breathlessness.

"You are in good shape," I comment.

"We walk, jog, bicycle or ski four times a week," Shirley says.

"What do you do for a living?" I ask.

"We are both retired from General Motors," Ben says. "I was a technical writer and Shirley a data specialist."

It doesn't take long to look around Ambler. Boats lie around everywhere, many well past their useful life on the river.

"Kristina, you paddle with me," Joe says when we return.

"That's a good choice," I say and change into my Xtratufs. We all put on life preservers. Joe steadies the canoe in the shallow water while I step into the front of it.

We are off at five, paddling against a modest westerly wind. None of us has been down this river before. It is a new adventure for all of us. Our only deadline is to be ready for pick up by a floatplane in eight days, where a tributary from the sand dunes enters the Kobuk River. The sun is shining and there are no mosquitoes on the river. The low riverbanks with willows and a few black spruces float peacefully by at three miles per hour. We see a cow moose and a calf at a distance. After two hours we encounter a long sandy beach.

"This is a good place with no bugs. Let's camp here," Joe decides.

I put up my small tent close to some bushes facing the Jade Mountains on the other side of the river. My face got burnt from the sun. I must use sunscreen tomorrow.

When I get up, Joe is in the process of preparing breakfast on a two-burner Coleman kerosene stove. By 11 we are ready to leave. The northerly wind piles up whitecaps as we round a bend in the river turning to the north. After three hours of paddling we are ready for a break and go ashore. The meals for each day are pre-packed in dated plastic bags. On June 17, Joe spreads out lunch 17 consisting of beef salami, cheese, crackers, almonds, pumpkin seed, dried banana slices, and cranberries. We settle around it, comfortably sitting on our life vests. For dessert, Joe opens a bar of Belgian chocolate.

"For adults chocolate is not an option but a right," he declares.

For drinks we each have our bottles with filtered water from the river. We carry a stainless steel filtering pump that is easy and efficient to use.

The wind gets stronger after lunch. There is a strange funnel-like cloud formation ahead.

"It cannot be a hurricane?" I say doubtfully to Joe.

"I think it is blowing sand," he says. The southern riverbank is a 30-foot high steep sloping sand wall. A thin layer supporting a forest of small spruce trees covers the top. Some lean over at the edge. I wonder if this is part of the sand dunes further south. The funnel-like feature is a gorge in the sand wall where the wind blows the sand above the forest.

Greg has a hard time alone in the purple kayak. He is a colorful sight in his yellow rain gear, orange life vest and red, wide- brimmed hat that protects both his neck and face, neatly rimmed by a full brown beard. Ben and Shirley also tag far behind in the wind. A bird flies by as we wait for them.

"That's a long tailed Jaeger," Joe says.

We go ashore to look around Onion Portage. Bear, wolf, and caribou have left their tracks on the beach. Some of the first people entering Alaska used this site, an area with low shrub, blueberry bushes, and voracious mosquitoes.

We set up camp on a small sandy island where there are less bugs. We have paddled 11 miles today at speeds between 2 mph against the wind and 5 mph floating a rapid current. The men look rough with dirty faces. It is obvious that Joe has stopped shaving. It is late night when he serves Caesar salad and moose steak.

"I shot the moose last fall," Joe says.

Greg washes the dishes after dinner and brings water from the river to filter. I get horrified when I look at myself in the mirror. My face is grimy with silt, red from wind and sun. I am definitely not looking my best. This is beyond cosmetic cleansing. Armed with soap and a washcloth I balance my way to the water's edge.

The morning is cool and cloudy. The bugs are so bad that we walk along the beach while eating granola,

Tang, English muffins and hot tea or coffee. Joe and I have Canadian bug shirts with netting that cover our faces and ventilate our sides. The others have head nets but you cannot eat through netting. We don't linger long this morning.

The river is calm. It feels cold. I wish I had put on my longjohns but it was hot yesterday. It starts to drizzle when a cabin appears on the bank ahead.

"These things don't happen on my trips," Joe says.

"I pray for guidance and protection every day," I explain.

"This is a fish camp," Joe says as he studies the site with his field glasses. "There's a small cabin and a shack with a door hanging diagonally from one hinge. We can take shelter there for a while."

We enter just as the rain shower turns the faucet. Inside is a sturdy table for cutting fish. Excellent for lunch! We have paddled for two hours and are hungry. Joe pulls out three types of crackers, canned chicken spread, Colby cheese, horseradish, dried apricots, almonds and dark chocolate. The rain stops when we are finished.

"Do you want me to bring your duffel bag with warm clothing?" Joe asks. I hesitate, not wanting to be a nuisance since everything is tightly stuffed and tied down in the canoe.

"Just say - Joe, I want it - and I'll get it for you." It feels good to get my fleece longjohns and dry socks on. It was a mistake to put my rain pants inside the rubber boots.

The river is calm as a mirror. After an hour we come to a steep bluff.

"I planned to camp here," Joe tells me "but we've made a lot better time than yesterday when we had the wind against us. Let's climb this slope and look for the sand dunes."

Joe is always the first ashore. As his partner I am straight behind him. It feels good to be in the lead. The slope is very steep with some spruce, juniper, and pink wild roses. At times Joe gives me a helping hand while pebbles and sand roll down. From the top we can see the Great Kobuk Sand Dunes as a narrow light band at the horizon to the southwest. The dunes cover an area of 25 square miles. The mosquitoes are thick on the back of Joes' white bug shirt. They are less noticeable on Ben's red and Shirley's navy jackets. It is difficult to tell who attracts the most bugs.

As we continue paddling I am getting tired and often shift my paddle from side to side. We make a couple of stops to stretch our legs while looking for a suitable camping spot. Joe goes ashore to check out a sandy beach with willows.

"We are not that desperate," is his evaluation and we continue.

At six we find an expansive sandy beach with low sand dunes next to a creek. There are low willows to dry wet clothing and give privacy for nightly outings since it is light around the clock here above the Arctic Circle.

Alaska was photographed from the air and mapped in 1955. Joe and I study the maps and photos together and discuss our options. One problem is that the maps don't reflect the recent changes in the river's course.

It rains a little and the wind picks up during the night. My old tent shakes. How much wind can it take? I did reseal all worn seams before the trip so I don't worry and get a good night's sleep.

"Whoo whoo whoo," I hear again. "Is this an owl or a loon?" I ask Richard who knows birds and plants. Richard Beck is tall and heavyset with gray hair beneath his blue ABEC cap. While the rest of us normally wear jackets, Richard just wears a gray- checkered shirt and light pants. We were together on the John River but the only thing I remember about him is his silence. He is a retired mathematician.

"It's a snipe," Richard says. "The sound comes from the air flowing through its stiff tail feathers when it dives from high altitudes."

Today the river carries us along at 4 mph as we paddle leisurely.

At noon we pause on a beautiful beach with purple flowering chives and large bear tracks in the sand.

By now the mosquitoes have discovered us. We leave them alone and continue to a better place for lunch, a wide sandy beach without vegetation. Lunch 19 has a great tasty variety of goodies.

All through the day we see birds, Canada geese, a loon with young on its back, a Jaeger and terns.

"Where are we?" Joe wonders as we continue. "The GPS battery is dead. We cannot see the dunes from the river. We haven't seen any islands."

"The sandy beach where we had lunch could have been an island when the map was made 50 years ago," I suggest.

"The river will make a sharp bend to the left just before Kavet Creek. That's the closest access to the Great Kobuk Sand Dunes," Joe says.

We go ashore at the sandy beach before Kavet Creek to see if we can cross. Joe starts to sink. With a powerful jerk he saves his boots from being sucked down by the mud.

"Crossing on foot is not an option," Joe decides. "Let's empty one canoe and paddle across to explore. We need to find a place where a floatplane can reach us in five days. It's too shallow here."

We follow a game trail along the shore and get up on a steep ridge. Blackend remains of trees are left by an old forest fire. The sand dunes beckon at a distance. Tomorrow we will start out for them.

The wind picks up as we return, whipping the river into white caps. It is difficult to erect my tent. The sand whirls in although I point the back towards the wind. I strengthen the pegs with poles. Tired, I lay down in the sand to rest next to some bear and wolf tracks. My under lip is swollen from the sun. I should have brought Chapstick.

Joe is cooking beans and rice out of the wind behind a canoe on edge with the kayak on top. I am glad I don't have to cook.

In the morning we paddle to the west side of the Kavet and dismantle the canoes. I weed out everything I can live without for four days. Now my backpack weighs 40 lbs. That is what I trained with but the terrain here is a lot rougher. We hide our food and garbage in a pile among the tall willows, the canoe bags and excess gear in another pile some distance away.

"Let me help you get your pack on," Joe says and lifts it so I can stick my arms through the straps. We start walking along the beach, edged by tall willows. It is easy to follow behind Joe supported by my walking poles. It is as if some of his energy radiated to me. Today Joe finds a better route up to the ridge. At times we can follow caribou trails. Some of the old burn area is dry with almost bare ground, easy to walk on. Soon willows and dwarf birch take over interspersed with blooming cloudberries.

We stop for lunch 20 at an open place less favored by bugs.

"Look, there's a huge nest of dry branches in the top of a tall spruce," Joe points. Two large light birds with brown wings fly out. "They look like bald eagles," I say. "No, they are ospreys," Richard says.

We cross a couple of mushy streams and squeeze through dense growths of dwarf birch. I steady myself with my poles over the uneven ground. Suddenly I lose my footing. One pole bends under me as I topple into the bushes with my heavy pack. I am no longer in Joe's footsteps. No one is close by to help. The only way out is to release my pack, get up, and wrestle the pack up on my knee and from there to my back. "A Be Careful," Joe reminds us now and then. That's one of the many meanings of the company name ABEC.

When the brush thins a little we can see across a valley to the north edge of the dunes beyond a dense growing spruce forest with some taller dead trees. We continue until we are level with a small green valley into the dunes where we plan to camp. Kavet Creek is about 15 feet wide. The edges are solid with low brush and rocks. I take my hiking boots off.

"Let me take your pack and shoes," Joe says and steadies me as I cross in my socks through the pleasantly cool water. Maybe I should have worn my rubber boots as he and Greg but I left my Xtratufs as excess gear.

Big bear tracks and wolf tracks cross our camping area at the edge of the dunes. I set up my tent. The zipper along the lower edge of the mosquito net is stuck.

"Give me your water bottle," Joe says and flushes the zipper. It worked!

Greg joins us as we study the maps. "Ahnewetut Creek runs through the dunes. Could we make it there and back in one day?" he asks.

"It's about 6 miles one way. Let's start with a shorter hike tomorrow and see how it feels to walk on the sand," Joe says.

I wake up to 39 degrees in the tent and drizzle outside. We squeeze into the tepee-shaped cook tent for breakfast of multigrain porridge and cocoa. The rain stops and we start walking across the dunes towards the east along a spruce forested canyon. Gradually the sand dunes increase in size. There is a 20-foot high wave of sand with small dark crusted hills at the base filled with snow. Here the sand is gradually over taking the forest.

Joe lent me a reprint about the dunes yesterday. They are relics of glacial erosion of quartzose rock in the Brooks Range during the Pleistocene age and transport by winds and water to the Kobuk Valley. Some plants here are remnants from the glacial period. These dunes are actively moving westward as a result of strong easterly to northeasterly winds.

We hike up on the dunes. I am finally in physical contact with the Great Kobuk Sand Dunes I discovered on satellite imagery 28 years ago. The open, wide undulating fields remind me of skiing in Lapland.

Joe with a large green backpack normally marches ahead scouting out the terrain. He finds many polished skulls and bones of small rodents. Greg often sets up his tripod for serious picture taking. Bob is a professional photographer. Richard has big field glasses instead of a camera. He lags behind studying plants and birds. Walking the dunes is a good opportunity to talk to the others.

A tall sand mountain rises ahead. Without any reference it is difficult to tell how tall or how far away it is. Ben and Shirley reach it first. Others hold back for photography. A soft sand ridge leads to the top.

"This looks like an advancing ocean wave," I say.

Joe bends down with a measuring triangle.

"It's 30 degrees, just as the Parker and Mann reprint says," Joe confirms.

The other side slopes steeply to a deep dark floor of desert pavement, maybe 300 feet below.

We might have reached the eastern sand peninsula and turn around.

"This was a pleasant five hour walk," Joe says as we return to a sunny camp.

Slightly after seven next morning I hear Joe's wake-up call: "Water is hot."

"This is our big day of hiking lengthwise across the dunes to the creek that runs through them," Joe says and sniffs the air. "It is cool and windy, an excellent bug free day for hiking."

The dunes are generally bare but in places yellow chrysanthemums and arnicas, blue lupines and purple peas stick up in decorative clusters.

Kristina with 40-lbs pack and bug shirt on Kobuk Sand Dunes traversed by bear tracks.

We make good time and reach Ahnewetut Creek at lunchtime. Joe empties bag 22, for June 22, and starts to slice cheese as we sit down around the food. This is a unique setting among a few short spruce trees on the high bank of the creek. Steep sand dunes slope down into the creek on the other side. This should be a corridor for animals but we only see porcupine tracks.

"We don't have a group picture," I say and fiddle with the timer on my camera until I get one.

Richard, Shirley, Ben, Greg, Kristina, Joe, and Bob at the creek traversing the Kobuk Sand Dunes.

We follow a long high sand ridge like a snow crest. The wind is blowing.

The drizzle turns to rain. I get wet from condensation inside my Gortex jacket. Maybe that's why Richard never wears a jacket? My feet and legs are sore. I start to sag behind. It is frustrating not to be able to keep up with the group. They wait but take off as soon as I catch up without giving me a chance to recover. This is both physically and mentally exhausting. Towards the end Joe slows down. As I follow in his footsteps he turns around frequently to check. I feel like a dog he should have put on leash.

"How are you doing?" Joe asks each of us individually as we stop.

"Fine," is the positive answer. "Staying warm?"

"As long as we are moving."

Finally we walk side by side as the direction to camp is clear and those who want can surge ahead. As we start talking I forget how tired I am and feel renewed strength. My legs are stiff when we reach camp after an eight-hour walk of 13 miles but the experience was well worth it.

"There is ice on the riverbanks," Ben and Shirley report when they return with filtered water. There is fresh snow on the mountaintops to the north. It was 34 degrees in my tent last night. I am glad I had my heavy sleeping bag.

We hike out over the dunes as far as we can. It is easier walking than the brush.

"This is the last certified bug free zone," Joe announces as we reach the northern edge. We stop for lunch but the bear tracks discourage us from opening any smelly cans of sardines.

The water in the creek is a lot colder than three days ago I notice when I take my hiking boots off to cross it. There are dense willows on the other side, glowing green muskeg with red nagoonberry flowers and emerging iris leaves. It is difficult to walk through the brushy dwarf birch on wet muskeg. I stumble and fall on my knees. The pack is about to pull me over but I manage to steady myself. I do better walking today as I generally manage to stay behind Joe and Greg and so get a chance to rest when they wait for others to catch up.

"Well done," Joe says when we reach our cached gear on the Kobuk River.

Joe's praise feels good. I made it. I can still carry my personal gear for an over-night camp. Never could I imagine that I would actually walk for three days on the tiny hot spot on IR satellite imagery that I figured out was the Great Kobuk Sand Dunes.

38

Cape Krusenstern

Mosquitoes drown in my morning cocoa, faster than I have time to fish them out. They whine around my face netting that I lift just enough to take a sip. This last campsite among the willows on the Kobuk River was chosen for floatplane access. The 50-degree temperature feels pleasant with the sun warming my back. The river runs calm reflecting the short, struggling spruce on the opposite side. A Pacific loon with a white-and-black checkered back and pale gray head swims by. As we listen to the anticipated airplane noise, we hear a fluttering *who, who, whoo* as a Snipe swoops.

The red-winged, small plane makes a wide circle before landing on the river with the pontoons making impressive wakes. The pilot taxies to us, turns the plane around, and gets out on a pontoon in his hip waders. Joe, our leader in his white bug shirt, Richard, the silent one, and I can step on the pontoon. Inside, I have a good view from the seat behind Joe. The verdant vegetation is lush along the meandering rivers.

As we reach the coast of Kotzebue Sound, we fly a reconnaissance along the Krusenstern Lagoon. Our intention is to spend five days canoeing around it. The outside edge is unique with rows upon rows of furrowed land interspersed with ponds. What looks like furrows are old beach ridges.

The National Park Service (NPS) states that long shore currents have deposited sediments on this beach ridge plain, containing 114 discernible ridges. Cape Krusenstern National Monument contains archeological sites depicting every known cultural period in arctic Alaska over the past 6,000 years.

A 500-foot wide band of land, looking like a causeway, separates the western edge of the lagoon from the Chukchi Sea. Two groups of buildings occupy the two-mile-long strip where it widens into the ridged area.

We land on the southeast corner of the lagoon and bounce ashore over the choppy water. The pilot in his hip waders and Joe in his Xtratuf rubber boots step out first.

"The water is above your boots," the pilot tells me and offers me to "Piggy back!" I jump on his back. He sways a bit but both of us reach the shore safely. Maybe I weigh more than he expected?

"I'm going to check out the surroundings," Joe announces.

I change to warmer hiking boots.

"We have three hours until the next flight arrives," Joe says.

It is so cold and windy that even Richard puts on a jacket. We struggle up a willow-entangled slope to soft spongy muskeg with white cloudberry blooms on top. You have to step through water to reach a river with green edges. I let Joe and Richard check it out. The knolls on the uneven ground are shaking as we stagger ahead.

"You should be a moose or a caribou to keep your footing here," Joe says.

"Look, there's a Lapland longspur in that bush top. It's a redneck," Richard points.

Joe studies a light spot among willow bushes on a slope higher up. "It's moving, it's a grizzly!" He hands me his 8x40 binoculars.

We turn around when we hear the airplane and walk back along the beach covered with bear tracks.

Ben and Shirley arrive. The last planeload will bring Bob and Greg.

"We have to stay here tonight," Joe says. The wind calms down. I pitch my tent among forget-me-nots, caribou pellets, and sprouting iris at the edge of the willows.

Three cardboard boxes, sent by Ramona through Kotzebue, arrive on the last flight.

"Here's a shipment for you," Joe says and hands me a heavy package in bubble wrap.

"More film," I comment. Joe says nothing, doesn't even wink. Didn't Ramona tell him?

The next morning I wake up when the sun emerges from behind a mountaintop and hits the ridge of my tent. Birds are singing. The Ally Pack canoes are reassembled from the bags and loaded on the beach. By 8:45 a.m. we push off and paddle towards the northwest, closely following the shoreline on our right. A spit blocks our way.

"I wonder if we can portage across?" Joe says as a human approaches on the land. We pull ashore and Joe walks over to talk to the person while the rest of us wait in the canoes.

"It was a scientist from the NPS," Joe says when he returns. "She is camped out here with a graduate student to study raptors. There are 160 musk oxen in the area," she said.

We carry the canoes across the 70-foot wide strip. The wind is stronger, causing whitecaps on the other side that is the main body of the Krusenstern Lagoon. We paddle against the wind for a while looking for a river to replenish our water supply.

"No sense to push on to exhaustion. Let's stop for lunch," Joe declares as his standard solution to hardships. It is pleasant to sit down on the ground and dig into our new food rations: nuts, crackers, apricots, chocolate spread, summer sausage, hot Dijon mustard, two varieties of cheese, and creamed horse radish. The lunch packs are labeled by the current date, which serves as a calendar. Today, June 25, we eat lunch #25.

After eating, the wind and waves appear diminished. We paddle past a steep mountainside. Its continuation is flat and treeless.

"This is the best camp site in the vicinity. The ground is solid," Joe says.

We pull ashore and climb the highest hill, the Palisades. From the 900-foot top we can study the entire lagoon with its milky, mud colored water fringed by smaller lagoons in different shades of blue. Everything is flat except for our mountain. The blue-colored Chukchi Sea disappears into the horizon beyond the lagoon. The inside area to the southeast is a maze of low ridges, ponds and winding rivers.

The higher slopes of the mountain are rock beds any master gardener could be proud of. Most flowers are low to withstand the wind. The brightest blue forget-me-nots I have ever seen grow next to fireweed-red Siberian phlox and white mountain avens. Slightly taller yellow Arctic poppies shake their heads. Joe sits down leaning on his big green backpack and studies the panorama with his field glasses. Richard records every plant in his notebook. I use my camera. Greg continues to higher real estate and Ben takes a nap. The sun warms the air to 64 degrees according to my daypack thermometer. Life is good.

Walking down the rough rock covered slope covered with some grass is difficult. My knees start to hurt. I am glad I brought a walking pole for support.

"A B Extra Careful!" Joe admonishes us referring to the company name, ABEC.

We stop at a snow bank by the base of the mountain where we left two 5-gallon buckets on our way up.

When melted and filtered, this snow will be our drinking water. We fill two more buckets from a pond.

The June sun is still high in the sky north of the Arctic Circle when we eat a late dinner. An inflatable kayak on top of a canoe protects us from the wind. I pitch my tent in a field of rose-purple flowering wild chives on the beach.

June 26, I wake up to insects hitting my tent like raindrops although the sun is shining and the birds twitter. Outside, I notice a large black cloud of mosquitoes ascending from a bush. They are too busy to attack me, caught in rapture, a mating dance? What a birthday gift, non-biting mosquitoes!

Joe, who is still my paddling partner, and I reach Kasik, the first small lagoon we saw yesterday from the mountain, just in time to watch a grizzly bear walk away.

"Here we can easily filter water directly into our containers," Joe says and pulls out the pump. Gulls, a loon, three swans, and a merganser duck keep us company.

After an hour of paddling we stop at another small lagoon to give everybody a chance to catch up. The small lagoons concentrate a variety of birds. Joe identifies them through his field glasses: loons, an arctic tern, a golden plover, a northern pintail and a red-necked phalarope.

We have paddled around half of Krusenstern Lagoon and stop for lunch at the northern end. As we continue south along the narrow causeway like strip, I ask Joe; "Did you know what was actually in the heavy film-packet that came with the new food shipment?"

"Wasn't it film?" Joe replies surprised.

"Only part of it. There was a bottle inside the bubble wrap. Today is my 65th birthday. I want to have a small celebration after dinner."

Joe is continually alert watching everything. "Look at those three rocks on the strip," he blurts out. "The calm atmosphere is so strange, a *fata morgana* that it is difficult to tell size and distance."

"I think one boulder is moving. Could they be rolling stones?" I say.

"They must be grizzlies!" Joe says and pulls out his field glasses. "Oh no, they are musk oxen! Let's not disturb them. We'll continue to paddle well past them. Then we can go ashore, cross the strip and maybe sneak up on them from the other side," he says.

The low band of land is covered by grass and bleached pieces of wood. We see a sandpiper nest with four brown eggs; caribou hides; a caribou skull with horns; and the remains of an old driftwood shelter. This is an area of subsistence hunting.

The Chukchi Sea is as calm as a mirror. It feels pleasant at 55 degrees. We walk north along the beach covered with pea-sized brownish pebbles. Among them I find a two-inch long triangular shaped flat sandstone with a white quarts cross on both sides. I pick it up. *God's birthday gift to me!* "Fear not, I am with you," I interpret the message.

We take a peek along the causeway. The musk oxen are at a distance. As we return to the beach to get closer without being seen, one comes to the edge of the grass to look us over. The long brown outer fur moves as a hula skirt and the short horns rim the face as braids with the edges bent up as ears. What a treat to stand here nearby to a shaggy mammal from the Ice Age. Without the wind we can hear a whining and barking sound from ocean gulls and loons.

It is windier when we return to the canoes on the lagoon side. At 70 degrees, it feels hot. There is a seasonal fish camp at the southern end of the long strip.

"We better ask for permission to camp," Joe says and pulls ashore. I tag along. The camp consists of two cabins and a wall tent with a chimney. Buckets, boxes, split wood, a metal office chair, a homemade cutting table, a drying rack with two filleted salmon, a boat, a dogsled and the remains of a Skidoo snowmachine complete the surroundings. A white sign with red letters on the wall reads: WELCOME TO SNYDER'S CAMP. Joe knocks on the door.

"Maybe you can use a gallon of Coleman fuel?" Joe asks as Snyder opens the door. "Our trip is coming to an end, and we don't need it." Snyder invites us in. Two black-haired children sitting on a bunk bed eye us with shy curiosity in the cabin lit dimly through one small window.

"Could we camp at the beach tonight?" Joe asks. "It's OK as long as you don't leave any garbage," Snyder says. "I caught four salmon in a net this morning. Here's one for you," he offers.

"Thank you, that's wonderful since it's Kristina's birthday today," Joe says.

"How many are in your group?" Snyder asks. "We are seven."

"In that case I'll give you two fish. We'll go egg hunting tonight to the island in the lagoon. That's our grocery store. The small girls are good at collecting gull and eider eggs," Snyder says.

The rest of our crew is waiting in the canoes. We paddle some distance back and pitch our tents on a fragrant spot of spongy moss with dwarf birch and blueberry twigs. I put the secret champagne that was part of my film shipment in a 5-gallon bucket with water to cool while Joe starts to sauté the salmon with lemon pepper. What a meal! Afterwards Greg brushes out the plates in the lagoon and Shirley washes them in hot sudsy water.

Discreetly I take the black glass bottle with a golden bow from the cooler and give it to Joe.

"Kristina's birthday," he announces and opens the bottle. I play surprised and quickly catch some champagne in a cup as the bottle erupts. Everybody sings "Happy birthday."

"There's an honorary three-eider fly-by," Bob announces pointing at the ducks with black bellies and wings with white patches.

"How old are you?" somebody asks. Before I have time to answer, Joe says "35." I don't argue. Nobody comments.

While planning this trip I had wondered where we would be on my birthday. I had imagined us sitting around a campfire at the very cape. There had to be an observation tower I figured, and I wanted to climb it and have my birthday picture taken. From the air I had seen there was one.

"I want to hike to Cape Krusenstern," I announce after the toast. We have already had a full day by paddling eight miles and hiking four but I haven't yet reached my goal. Everybody is not as enthusiastic as I. Passing by Snyder's camp, we leave a 5-gallon bucket with excess food on his doorstep.

Richard trails behind studying everything. Joe keeps me company as we beach-comb towards the cape. The tower shouldn't be too far away, but it is hard to tell in this flat land.

"That's a walrus carcass," Joe points "but, unfortunately, the tusks have been sawed off. The ivory is valuable for carving."

The beach widens to the area with ridges we saw from the air but I have forgotten about them. Energized by my goal to climb the tower I surge ahead and reach the lookout tower at 11 p.m. I actually feel like 35. The tower is under repair. An aluminum ladder leans against it. Crows fly away as I reach the platform nine feet up it. Joe snaps a picture of me sitting in the tower looking out over the Chukchi Sea and tomorrow beyond the date line. What will my coming year bring? I wonder.

The light is airy with the sun behind cloud bands. I am getting exhausted. I can no longer pretend to be 35. It is past midnight. I no longer lead the hike. Anyway, it was a most memorable birthday.

The night rain stops by the time we launch the canoes, but the wind picks up. We try to ride the waves to get past a point and what we perceive as shallow water with small ripples and a darker color. The side wind increases. Waves break on the shore. Greg has a hard time steering his inflatable kayak alone. Joe throws him a towline.

"We better head towards the coast until the wind calms," Joe shouts.

We beach our canoes. Joe pitches the small red- and-white teepee-shaped cook tent. There is barely room for all seven of us around the center pole with the lunch bag spread out. At 41 degrees nobody minds the closeness in the tent. "Let's eat," Joe's solution for trouble doesn't work this time. It is still blowing too hard to paddle, but it doesn't rain and there are no bugs!

I am curious about the beach ridges I ignored yesterday, and decide to walk to the ocean I think I see in the distance. It is difficult to walk over the wet grassland and hummocky tundra. Two gulls dive towards me. I come to a large lake; it wasn't the ocean. The sandy shore has a high rounded edge around it. Part has exposed dark soil as if turned over by a giant plow. That must be a beach ridge. I look around for ancient cultural remains and find a caribou hide and some crushed aluminum cans. We don't leave traces like that. We bury our bodily waste, burn the toilet paper, and take everything else back with us.

I return to our emergency landing to wait out the wind. Joe has propped up a canoe on edge with a paddle and tied it with lines. In the lee of the canoe he cooks dinner of soup and pasta with dry tomatoes. We eat it in the cook tent.

Joe and Greg using an Ally Pak canoe as windbreaker by Krusenstern Lagoon.

Joe lends me two long plastic stakes to secure my tent. I strengthen the other pegs with pieces of caribou horns. My tent keeps a low profile with the inner lining almost touching the sleeping bag. The noise from the wind rippling over the nylon is louder than the waves when I fall asleep.

"Water is hot. Take your time, we are not going anywhere." Joe's late wake-up call this morning lacks urgency. The sun shining on the tent makes it pleasantly warm inside. The wind still whips up whitecaps in the lagoon and the waves break on the beach.

"If this wind keeps up, we cannot make it to the pick up point for the floatplane on the ocean side," Joe says. "Staying here isn't an option because the plane cannot land when the water is this rough."

"So, if we cannot go and cannot stay, what do we do?" I ask with curiosity, convinced that Joe has a plan B. My birthday rock reminds me that God is with us so I am not alarmed.

"If the wind doesn't permit us to paddle by tomorrow, the plane might be able to pick us up at a mile-and-a-half long lake," Joe says. "I'll go and check it out. Do you want to come along, Kristina?"

Caribou antlers are spread all over the tussocks that wobble as we step on them. We reach the calmer lake in 40 minutes. A merganser and a scoter duck greet us.

"It's possible that the plane could land here," Joe says.

"What about our gear and the canoes by the lagoon?" I ask.

"We'll deal with that tomorrow, maybe the wind has calmed by then," Joe says.

We walk back along the lagoon, fringed by a string of small lakes. We must lean into the wind with heads down and parka hoods tied tight over our caps.

When I look outside from the floppy tent the next morning there are serious whitecaps. It is 35 degrees and obviously too rough to launch canoes and too windy for the floatplane. Everyone else is inside his tent. I continue to pray for God to calm the waters. Joe still produces hot water in the lee of the canoe propped on edge.

"Our plan for today is to move to the 1-1/2-mile lake canoeing along some smaller lakes and portaging the rest of the way," Joe announces. "It's blowing 25 miles/ hour with gusts at 35 in Kotzebue."

Normally I pull everything out of my small tent and pack outside, but with this wind anything left unattended will fly away. I pack my personal gear weighing 60 pounds into two duffel bags. One I can carry on my back. The backpack is inside one of the duffels to stay dry.

We carry everything to the first pond along the edge of the lagoon and paddle. The second pond is too small to bother to reload so we portage around it. The third lake is a good paddle for half a mile. From here we have to go inland over the muskeg carrying the gear for a quarter of a mile. It takes many trips. I mark out the best route with caribou horns to avoid the mushy tussocks. The next lake is bigger. We reload the canoes and paddle. This lake is separated from the big lake by a two-foot wide sand spit that we drag the canoes across. By dinnertime we are set up at our new camp by the northern shore of the big lake. The wind is calmer here. It seems to be raining over the Palisades on the other side of the lagoon.

"We don't disassemble any canoes until we know that the pilot can land here," Joe says.

Seven eider ducks give us a good night fly-by as on my birthday.

The next morning the pilot finds us and lands successfully. Richard, Shirley, and Greg can step directly from the beach onto the pontoon.

"Kristina, Ben and Bob, be ready for the next flight. I'll stay behind with the gear," Joe says.

We start a frantic disassembly and packing of the canoes. By now the procedure is familiar. I walk over to Joe, planning to give him a hug, but he is busy packing kitchen gear. Suddenly, he puts his strong arm around me and gives me a squeeze.

"This was a good trip," he says. "Thank you for making it so," I reply.

Thanks to Joe's good leadership, we all end up safely in Kotzebue. If adventure is part of your enjoyment of life, an exploratory wilderness trip is a good choice. You don't know exactly what to expect. The unexpected is the norm. It tests you both physically and mentally. How you deal with it determines if you have a good trip. I am delighted that I am still strong enough to make it a memorable experience. I like visiting new places off the beaten track and to learn more about the life that inhabits them. Doing so with a positive congenial group is part of the enjoyment.

39

Addition with Running Water

It never occurred to me that I wouldn't have room for running water in my big cabin. The house is ten times larger than the 49-square-foot cache where I lived for four years. It is more than ten years since I last enjoyed the blessings of modern civilization, if the frozen pipes in the trailer I rented count for conveniences. Since I moved from my cache to the cabin in 1979, I have toiled with the choice between drilling a well or, getting a large water tank. The memory of the rusty water in the trailer definitely causes me to favor the tank. It would also be cheaper, for starters, but could I prevent the tank from freezing; could a water delivery reach me when I am out of water, and could I truly enjoy a shower when I know how much each gallon costs?

After careful consideration, I decide to take the risk and drill a well and become independent. The large red drill rig of Aurora Drilling carefully backs into my driveway in September 1989 while yellow birch leaves fall. Well driller Olin Patty rigs up his tall drill tower that can hold 20-foot long pipes. The clay that emerges from the frozen silt layer at a depth of ten feet smells rotten. I haven't dug this deep before, living in the hope that I don't have permafrost below my cabin. Now I know for sure that I do. Earlier I still took the precautions as if I did when building. The perennially frozen layer of silt is 64 feet deep. Below that is a 108-foot deep layer of soft schist above the bedrock. The well goes 200 feet deep with a submerged pump in the layer of schist.

When I get water after all these years I want to enjoy it thoroughly. It will be more than a toilet below the spiral staircase and a faucet over the kitchen sink as I originally planned. I desire a whirlpool bath, shower, washing machine, and of course, a sauna as my Finnish friends thought I should have built first.

There isn't room in my cabin to accommodate all my plans. The solution is to enlarge, but do I want to start a new 10-year project? I can scarcely count on the same volunteer work force as last time. Many have moved from the area, all are older and some have married. No one is curious about my activities any longer. The only solution is a bank loan and paid professionals. I continue to be the contractor who plans, orders materials and hires people. Cabin construction is continually on my mind. When I doodle, I draw visions of my finished cabin.

University Summer Programs offers a canoe trip on the Chena River through Fairbanks in June 1991. Inexperienced, I get to paddle with the instructor, Scott Olsen. Scott is very interested in all houses we pass.

"I am building an addition to my cabin," I say. "As soon as the ground dries I want to put down pilings. Do you know somebody who could help me with the foundation?"

"I can help you," Scott says to my surprise.

The ground behind the cabin is slightly higher. I do not want to disturb the permafrost by digging and there isn't room to add tailings, as I did with the original cabin. I decide to put the addition on pilings as my neighbors have done.

The addition will be 20 x 20 feet. The west side will butt into the existing cabin. The rest will be supported by 12 pilings in three rows of four posts each. I mark 12 large crosses with a can of red spray paint. My neighbors dug all their pilings with a posthole digger as I did my power pole. It is a big job. Experience has taught me to look for easier ways than sheer muscle power. Paying for technique is worth the time-savings. Joe Vargas, who installs fences, has a small 4-wheel drive drill car with a 16- inch auger on the roof. He arrives on June 27 and quickly drills a seven-foot deep hole in the center of each cross.

Sunday, June 30, I make detailed plans for the foundation of the addition. In the afternoon I call O.K. Lumber. Richard Kruckenberg, son of the owners, answers. It is a delight to talk to a professional who understands exactly what I need. O.K. has most of the material for the foundation and the floor.

"We can deliver your order today," Kruckenberg says after our efficient conversation. I feel a sense of pride and accomplishment after accepting a charge of $950 to my credit card. What a power words can have when backed up by a credit card! O.K. is out of 8 x 8-inch pressure treated timbers that I need for my pilings, but Northland Wood has them.

I have booked a week-long flight to Homer for the next day to see Vickey Hodnik, who has become my dentist, and Carol Hagglund, my best friend, who moved there from the Aleutians. My ticket cannot be changed and Scott doesn't have time to work when I return.

"I can put the pressure treated timbers in the holes, cut them to length and lay the 20-foot long 8 x 8-inch timbers across while you are gone," Scott says.

"I have a pile of pea gravel in front of the cabin. Pour two bucket-fulls into each hole. That will fill it to a depth of six feet and give the pilings a foot of gravel to stand on. Fill around the square pilings with pea gravel. Hopefully the gravel will not freeze to the posts and push them up as normally happens with frost heaving," I explain to Scott.

When I return, Scott has accomplished the work. "It rained before I could start the job and the holes got filled with water," Scott explains with concern. "Besides, two of the long timbers are twisted."

What do I do now? I think with frustration and consult anyone I can think of.

"Put weight on the beams," Dennis Gentleman, who showed experience when he helped with the cabin construction, says.

Doug Jenkins of Windy Creek sawmill promises to deliver 1800 linear feet of 6 x 8-inch dry fire-killed logs. These logs are two inches wider than the logs on the first floor of the cabin. This will help with insulation.

"You understand enough to appreciate good logs," Jenkins tells me. "If you are not pleased with one, send it back."

"This is a good warranty," I say. "I have checked out the log builders who advertise in the phone directory. They are all busy or uninterested in a small project like mine with three-sided logs."

"I'm interested in building for you in August, if I have time," Jenkins says.

"I believe you would do a good job," I reply happily.

A neatly printed card on the bulletin board of the health food store catches my attention. Simon is willing to work. I call him. A woman answers.

"Hello Kristina. I always recognize you by your voice. This is Sue, your previous neighbor. Simon is a good and dependable worker," Sue volunteers unsolicited testimony.

I take a day of annual leave on July 24 when Simon comes. "I think we can twist the beams straight," he says. "I have tried a little with your log- turner. Do you have a "come-along" hand winch to give us more prying power?"

Despite rain we work efficiently together for nine hours. Simon is one of those people who are fun and inspiring to work with. We get the beams straightened and anchor them to the pilings with railroad screws and steel plates.

"We have accomplished the impossible according to the lumber yard," he says with pride.

Simon comes back many times until he has glued and screwed all 12-1/2 sheets of 1-1/8-inch tongue & groove plywood in place. Sometimes he comes by bicycle. Other times he runs the six miles with a pack on his back. This is just a warm-up for this athlete. He carefully follows the instructions I leave him when I go to work.

"I would really like to work with the logs," Simon says "but it's time for me to return to New Zealand."

Doug Jenkins from the sawmill, doesn't have time to build for me but refers to his partner, Kent. The name is familiar. I bought skis at his mother's shop years ago. On August 25, Kent brings me a two-page handwritten proposal to build a two-story 20 x 20- foot log addition for $4,800. Page 1 lists 15 points that are included, page 2 lists 10 points not included; among them log peeling, painting, and oiling.

"Anything unclear will be up for discussion, work done outside of the bid I will charge by the hour," the dark-haired, trim cabinet builder says sincerely. I feel I can work with Kent and accept his bid with my signature and a handshake.

I consult Eugene Laitala, who taught me how to notch the ridgepole on the cache 16 years ago.

"I'm too old to do anything but I can come and look," Laitala says on the phone. I am surprised to see him get out of his car on crutches. He has lost a leg but it doesn't prevent him from jumping around the whole cabin including the 400-square-foot addition.

"Buy ready-made cement blocks and place them next to the pilings as added insurance," Laitala advises. "If needed, you can always put posts on them."

Kent and Eric start log course eight after the third day. We will soon run out of logs. I need four 21-foot long round logs as rafters for the first floor. When I arrive at the sawmill they are just starting to cut my logs. On September 2, Doug Jenkins backs down my driveway with a gigantic load, topped by four long natural logs. Alone, using experienced leverage he manages to get the logs rolled off alongside the addition. He tips the truck bed to unceremoniously flip the rest of the logs. I need more log peelers. The sawmill gives me some names.

On September 4 it is time to get the big logs up. It is comforting not to have to arrange it myself nor even have to worry about it. Eric knows my neighbor, Craig Van Amburg, who has an old gray winch truck. The windshield, including a lot of other parts, is missing but the initiated get it to work. It is no problem to winch up the heavy logs. The problem is to push them so the other end will extend over the opposite wall. Terrified I observe Kent and Eric standing on the high log wall handling them. There was no time to varnish them before they got up but I can do that from a ladder before the ceiling boards go on. Varnishing was not included in the bid.

The second story will be my bedroom and office. There I will have the green Whirl Bath, firmly anchored over one of the large rafter logs. To observe the Northern Lights from my bed, I plan a dormer window. It will create a few additional roof angles but it will be Kent's problem to solve. I just pay. The ceiling on the second floor will be lined by 1 x 6-inch T & G boards. Before the boards go up I take the time to sand them where necessary and varnish them.

The last log delivery arrives on September 18. Peter, a log peeler, helps Kent to lift the purlins. The operation to the second story goes in two steps. First, the log is lifted vertically with the tall triangular frame of the truck winch. Secondly, the iron chain is moved to the lower part of the log, which is then lifted along the wall to a low balcony, later to be covered for a greenhouse or solarium. Kent's and Peter's dogs thoughtfully keep out of the way. The second story is reached by a steep ladder through a hole in the southeastern corner of the floor. The ladder doesn't prevent Kent's dog from joining him for lunch in the solarium. Carpenters' dogs just learn to climb ladders, I suppose. On September 19, both the 24-foot long ridgepole and the purlin are in place on the second floor.

Fortunately we have an unusually long and warm fall, just as we did when I built my cache in 1975. My nasturtiums are still in bloom on October 4. It turns out to be a hectic day. Kent and Eric attach the last roof metal sheets above a foot-thick layer of fiberglass with an insulation value of R-38.

My two-story 646-square-foot addition is closed in when the first snowflakes fall on October 6. The addition is larger than my original cabin.

During the course of the winter I select my bathroom decor and negotiate with a plumber, carpenter, and electrician while analyzing my assets, job opportunities and loan. On November 13 it is - 15°F in the morning. The day proceeds as a well- rehearsed show. A man from Woodway arrives at 9

a.m. with a Monitor oil heater. I plug in a small electrical heater to help him keep his fingers warm while installing it. Greer Tank arrives two hours later with a 300-gallon fuel tank they place on a stand outside, so the oil can drain by gravity. While ordering an oil delivery from Aerofuel, a gigantic delivery van from Spenard Building Supply backs in with the front door for the addition. My professional builders have made the door opening in a standard size. When I built the cabin it didn't even occur to me that I could buy a ready-made door. In the twilight at 4 p.m. I see flashing red lights surrounded by ice fog as Aerofuel's red 4-wheel-drive tanker backs in. The #1 heating oil we use in Fairbanks stays liquid in colds down to -60°F so the storage tank can be outside. The oil heater makes it possible to continue work inside the addition.

Plumbing is started on December 6. On the 14th, the electrician pulls lines from the cabin to the fuse box in the addition. Early on a dark morning in the beginning of January 1992 the plumber, aided by three men, directs my whirl bath to the second floor through the hole in the corner of the ceiling. The log walls get covered by two sheets of 1-inch thick fiberglass covered foam boards with a layer of sheetrock on the inside. This makes the walls 10-1/2-inch thick. The sheetrock gets painted in a shade of rose, complimentary to skin tones.

The southeast corner of the addition next to the well settles during the winter. That's the hole Scott was most concerned about and didn't consider stable although he had poured lots of pea gravel into it. The advantage with a building on pilings is the possibility to make adjustments when something moves. Kent jacks up the corner in April and levels it with wedges.

In the end of April 1992, it is time to saw openings between the cabin and the addition. Until now they have had their separate entrances. The eastern wall of the loft is occupied by my bed and a long cloths rack. The wardrobe must be removed to make room for an entryway into the addition and a washing machine in the corner. I lose all my storage space for clothing. Everything must be moved into the cabin.

A long kitchen counter with cabinets above occupies the eastern wall of the cabin. The new entry into the addition will be sawed through the middle. Room must be made on the side for a pressure tank and a hot water heater. The entire L-shaped kitchen counter including all cabinets must be removed. All eight wall-cabinets must be emptied. How did I end up with so many cabinets?

When I moved into the cabin in 1979, I felt a need for kitchen cabinets but didn't want to take the time to survey the market and figure out what I needed. A trip to China was more important at the time than cabinets. They could wait.

One afternoon I suddenly remembered that Plywood Supply had a sale. Quickly I jumped into my car without taking too much time to brush the sawdust off my construction clothing. In a dark storage building I saw a sign for 13 kitchen cabinets in oak for a price you would normally pay for two or three. Everything was in boxes so I couldn't see them. I asked a sales man who judged me by my clothing.

"These cabinets are of such quality that you couldn't afford them for their normal price. This is a good buy even if you use them for fire wood."

In the haste I forgot to bring my money. While driving home I considered if I should return. I had no idea what kinds of cabinets I needed or had room for but this was a good deal. When I returned I planned to point out that the bath vanity that was included was too large for my outhouse. The persuasive sales man had completely changed his outlook. He didn't appear receptive to humor.

"God knows who priced these cabinets!" he exclaimed.

Silently I wrote my check. Maybe God really wanted me to have kitchen cabinets? To my surprise all fit as if they were ordered for me except for the bath vanity that has stayed in my woodshed until now.

On September 22, 1992 I can delight in running water in my kitchen and the downstairs toilet after 17 years without these conveniences. My joy, however, doesn't last long. All pipes are not insulated. Both water and sewer freeze and remain frozen for most of the winter. I used to pay rent for this in the trailer. Now I pay property tax and a bank loan. The plumber has more important customers and sends his less experienced workers to me. In the winter they get stuck in the snow, in the spring in the mud. Little gets done despite my reminders and complaints.

In February 1993 I bring my drinking water from the spring in Fox and melt snow to flush the toilet. I write an encouraging letter to the plumber listing the mileposts in his work. I also mention everything still to be done, including the inconveniences with frozen pipes and floods. I get sewer pipes connected under the shower. In May the washing machine gets installed. What a relief to be able to wash clothing at home when I want to without having to go to a Laundromat. In July I take my first bath. In August the whirl bath is operational. To prevent a repeat of the problems from last winter I call the plumber often and ask him to finish the plumbing below the house while the road is still good. He promises, as usual. I get heat tapes installed but many pipes are still un-insulated. I complain about the quality of the work but I have done that often. It has no immediate effect.

On the morning of September 25, 1993 it is 20 degrees. I light a fire in my cast-iron Jøtul-stove and jump into the shower, but—the water is frozen again. I connect the new heat tapes and go upstairs. Soon I notice a strange smell. I quickly dress and go downstairs to check the wood stove. It is OK. I go behind the addition and look under the house. The pipe insulation is on fire. Shocked, I rush in with a pounding heart and call 911. The University fire department is on its way. I snatch the fire extinguisher I never used before, direct the hose towards the flames and press the handle. To my relief, the fire goes out. I rush in again and call my friend Dennis Gentleman.

"The pipe insulation below the addition is on fire. Please pray for me, and fast!"

With my panic voice, which is the only one the plumber presently pays attention to, I call him.

"You promised not to burn down houses. The heat tapes have ignited the pipe insulation."

I exchange pressure tanks in the fire extinguisher and run out again. I thought the fire was out but the flames burn higher than before. The fire extinguisher doesn't work a second time. I used up all extinguishing powder in the first round.

What shall I save in my house? Panic stricken I cannot think logically. I am going to Scandinavia in three days. I grab my hand luggage with passport and tickets and throw it into the car that is parked some distance from the house. Next round I grab my entire traveling wardrobe from a pole in the cabin. When I rush out with the clothing, a hanger catches the 20-foot long phone line and pulls out the telephone. Embarrassed I wonder what the fire department would think if they came now but they don't. My thoughts continue to race with the pounding of my heart.

I pull in a 75-foot garden hose, open the bathroom window above the fire and throw out the end of the hose. Black smoke wells in. I attach the other end of the hose to the outlet of the hot water heater, but no water comes out. The last time I tried to get water from the tank the attachment came off and water poured out on the floor. That was another time I used my panic voice to call the plumber while I kept my finger in the hole. I pull in the hose and close the window.

Thick black smoke pours out from two sides below the house. It is a desperate feeling to see the results of almost 20 years of my labor including all my material possessions on the brink of oblivion. This cannot happen to me. I earnestly send up brief prayers to God for intervention. The Fire Chief comes running through the forest with a fire extinguisher. It doesn't work. The Fire truck is lost. They didn't listen to my instructions but followed an old outdated map. "Do you have a rake or some long item?" the Chief asks.

I hand him a shovel with a long handle. Why didn't I think of that? The fire truck arrives. Quickly the crew crawls under the house and hoses the pipes and foam insulation with water. They cut a hole in the metal netting that protects the fiberglass bats from squirrels. The floor joists are undamaged. Luckily, fiberglass doesn't burn. After the fire is out the fire chief gives me directions and asks questions.

"Turn off all electricity until an electrician has checked the wires. What kind of heat tapes do you have?"

The phone rings. It is the plumber.

"I couldn't get through," he says. "The road was filled with fire equipment and black smoke."

"The Fire Chief wants to know about the heat tapes. I'll let you talk with him," I say.

My electrician arrives and checks the wires.

"You can plug in the oil heater and the refrigerator but most of the wires on the north side and below the house must be exchanged," he says.

I have two days to interact with my insurance company and a business that will repair the damage. The plastic pipes have melted inside a wall. It must be opened and the pipes replaced. The outside back wall is black from smoke.

My neighbor, David Dausel, who recently shot a moose, brings a steak.

"I can keep an eye on your house while you are gone and see that it is warm when you return," he says.

"That's kind of you. A lot of people will be running in and out of my house repairing things while I am gone for three weeks."

When I return from Finland, I have reason to hire a new plumber who finishes the pipe work and exchanges all damaged foam insulation for fiberglass. The original plumber's insurance company pays for the repair. After three months of chaos, I can finally enjoy the blessings of running water in my own home after 18 years without. Now the pipes even work in the winter.

Gradually I can move my bedroom from the loft to the addition. On a balcony outside I can air my bedding. A sliding glass door leads to the solarium. My roll top oak desk with a computer stands by the door. The room with its large ridgepole and purlin, sloping plank ceiling, high window for viewing the Northern Lights and two glass doors is almost like an art studio. In the solarium I can give my plants an early start in the spring. In the fall I can take plants in to extend the joy of Alaska's short flowering season.

My new home that I have worked on for almost 20 years is finally completed with the exception of minor details. At last I am comfortable at home with heat and running water.

Life is directed by the choices we make. At times I have been at a cross road where I could have continued on the familiar path but chose to branch out on a new unfamiliar trail. My spirit of adventure and soul of an explorer urges me to visit new places, the more remote and difficult to get to the better. That's how I ended up in Alaska in 1969 and that's how I decided to move from Douglas to Fairbanks in 1971. When my rental-housing situation became unbearable in 1975, I decided to build my own. Never did I imagine I would live in a 49-square-foot cache for four years. Moving in 1979 into the down- stairs of my later to become 469-square-foot cabin was a great improvement in comfort. To finally achieve my dream housing of 1115 square feet has taken me 18 years of hard labor with the help of numerous volunteers.

Cabin with adition totaling 1115 square feet
finally finished after 18 years.

My job situation at the University of Alaska has been insecure. Due to temporary short-term grants, I have been blessed to work on the cutting edge of new research in fields ranging from the bottom of the ocean to the clouds. It is a miracle that I have been able to stay employed at the University for 30 years until my retirement in 1999.

Thanks to my jobs and despite their uncertainty, I have been able to see much of the state and to experience its culture and wildlife.

Fairbanks is the golden heart of Alaska that attracts a varied mixture of people from the Pope to the President. There is never a shortage of intriguing events to attend.

I have lived most of my life in Alaska and love the beauty and can-do mentality of the state. Here your dreams can come true if you dare to pray, believe and work.

Bibliography

Alaska News 1894, June 7: *How to Reach Alaska by Pacific Coast Steamship Co.* Scheduled sailings with two steamers from San Francisco and Seattle to Sitka, Juneau and Douglas.

Alaska News 1894, June 7: *Fashionable Dressmaking Parlor* advertisement

Alaska Northwest Publishing Co. 1974: *The Milepost, All-the North Travel Guide*

Alaska Northwest Publishing Co. 1983: *The Alaska Almanac* Anchorage, Alaska

DeGraf, Anna, edited by Roger S. Brown 1992: *Pioneering on the Yukon 1892-1917* Archon Books, Hamden, Connecticut

Federal Railroad Administration ca. 1950-1974: *The Alaska Railroad*; P.O.Box 7-2111, Anchorage, Alaska 99501

Inouye, Ronald 1986: *Starring and Slava: A legacy of Russian America.* Russian American Symposium II, Fairbanks March 7, 1986, in Bethel Cultural Center Kyuk Productions 1987: *Following the Star* video, in Bethel Cultural Center

Murphy, Claire Rudolf & Haigh, Jane G. 1997 *Gold Rush Women*, Alaska Northwest Books

Parker, Carolyn and Mann, Dan: *Floristics and Geomorphology of Active Sand Dunes in the Kobuk River Valley, NW Arctic Alaska*, University of Alaska Satterfield, Archie 1974: *Chilkoot Pass Then and Now*; Alaska Northwest Publishing Co.

State of Alaska 1968: *The Chilkoot Trail, A Guide to the Goldrush Trail of '98*; Division of Lands, Department of Natural Resources

U.S. Dept. Commerce, NOAA Environmental Data Service 1974, 1975, 1976: *Local Climatological Data, Fairbanks, Alaska*

White Pass & Yukon Train Trip Guide, 1971

Index

Aamodt, Patsy 100

Abel, Kaarina 135, 188, 189, 190, 191, 192, 196, 198, 199, 201, 202, 203, 206, 213, 215, 216, 220, 221

Alaska Highway 91, 93

Alaska Range 88, 135, 147, 158, 318 Alfven, Hannes148

Allen, Joyce 259, 263, 264

Alyeska 13, 28, 177

Ambler 345, 346

Anchorage 2, 3, 13, 14, 28, 35, 80, 86, 87, 88, 89, 118, 134, 136, 138, 158, 173, 226, 259, 262, 319

Anderson, Sven 32, 90

Asher, Robert 65, 66, 67

Aumiller, Larry 294, 295, 299, 301

Baldridge, Jim 183, 221, 267

Barrow 100, 102, 103, 104, 105, 254, 288, 292

Barter Island 288, 289, 290

Bears 293

Beaufort Sea 5, 159, 160, 271, 291

Beck, Richard 345, 350, 356

Bennett 83, 200, 208, 209

Bering Sea 2, 20, 23, 36, 138, 139, 161, 169, 170, 225, 229, 236, 238, 270, 271, 280, 322

Bethel 334, 339, 342, 385

Biedemeyer, Will 325

Blockcolsky, Bill 191, 192, 220

Boise, Tom 74

Bressler, Harte 60, 64, 66

Brickell, David 229, 230, 235

Brooks Range 2, 158, 160, 354

Burbank, David 98, 114

Burns, John 231, 233, 234, 235

Butterfield, Bob 345

Calvert, Marshall 51, 52, 67

Campbell, Bill 172

Cape Krusenstern 344, 358, 359, 365

Cape Prince of Wales 23

Carlson, Axel 183, 250

Cashen, Edla 7

Chapman, Tom – ST 227

Chastain, Charlette 3, 8, 37, 245

Chilkoot Trail 85, 196, 197, 198, 199, 209, 317, 386

Chukchi Sea 25, 359, 361, 363, 366

Clough, Al 61

Cook Inlet 138, 139

Dahl, Bernice 325

Dawson City 85

Day, Don – CS 227

DeGraf, Anna 315,
    316, 317, 323

Delta 94, 333, 335

DeWilde, Ray – Raven 324

Dickey, Terry 315, 321

Dilts, Bob 59, 60, 66, 67, 73

Dilts, Joan 59

Diomede Islands 22, 23

Douglas vii, 4, 5, 6, 7, 8, 9, 10,
    11, 13, 29, 37, 38, 40, 43, 46,
    47, 48, 51, 56, 57, 58, 59,
    79, 80, 81, 84, 90, 92, 94,
    96, 98, 104, 117, 123, 190,
    197, 200, 245, 322, 383, 385

Dow, Ralph 248, 263

Dow, Toni 249, 263

Durrenberger, Joe 345

Dyea 85, 198

Egan, William – governor 41, 274

Elborg, Margaretha
    183, 184, 185

Engles, David 329, 330

Ensign, Fred 188, 221

Epchook, Boris 337

Epchook, David – Aanaluq 334

Epchook, Jessica 336, 337

Epchook, Vanessa 336, 337, 339

Eriksson, Olle 90

Etholen, Adolph – governor 273

Fairbanks vii, xi, 4, 36, 42, 46,
    79, 86, 87, 88, 89, 90, 92,
    93, 94, 95, 96, 97, 98, 100,
    107, 108, 109, 112, 115,
    116, 117, 118, 119, 121,

124, 128, 131, 132, 134,
135, 136, 138, 147, 159,
160, 161, 163, 168, 174,
176, 179, 182, 184, 190,
209, 220, 224, 226, 243,
245, 251, 253, 262, 265,
270, 271, 274, 276, 278,
280, 282, 283, 284, 285,
286, 290, 291, 310, 312,
315, 318, 319, 323, 334,
345, 372, 378, 383, 384, 385

Ferrell, Jim 267

Ferrell, Sarah 333

Finland xii, xiii, xv, xviii, 1, 2, 3,
    10, 11, 27, 30, 33, 52, 79,
    96, 111, 118, 129, 131, 155,
    159, 162, 166, 181, 183,
    201, 210, 213, 214, 215,
    216, 218, 225, 238, 273,
    276, 280, 308, 319, 322,
    325, 339, 341, 382

Finnoff, Ramona 344

Fonselius, Stig 1

Garrison, Gerry 287, 290

Gentleman, Dennis 248,
    258, 374, 380

Gentleman, Marilyn vii, 249, 258

Gilkey Glacier 61, 68, 69, 72

Gothenburg, Sweden 1,
    2, 13, 163,

Granqvist, Eirik 276,
    277, 279, 281

Gudmandsen, Preben 152

Gulf of Alaska 33, 240, 244,
    271, 302, 305, 307, 308, 322

Guthrie, Dale 276, 279, 281

Guthrie, Mary Lee 381

Hagglund, Carol 181, 197, 213, 245, 253, 261, 293, 319, 373

Hagglund, Karen 194, 255

Haines 90, 91, 93, 197

Haines Junction 93

Hakkila, Jack 253

Hautala, Jim & Cindy 338, 339

Hegg, E.A.85, 204

Helsinki, Finland xiii, xvi, 2, 3, 276, 325

Henriksen, Kjell 171, 186, 215

Hodnik, Vickey 263, 373

Imamura, Ken 245, 246

Jayaweera, K.O.L.F. 112, 151, 155, 159, 178

Jenkins, Doug 374, 375, 376

John Paul II – pope 282, 285

Jøkulhaup 53

Juneau 2, 3, 4, 5, 6, 7, 8, 9, 10, 11, 12, 13, 28, 29, 32, 35, 36, 37, 40, 41, 42, 43, 44, 47, 48, 51, 55, 56, 57, 58, 59, 70, 79, 80, 85, 86, 90, 93, 94, 133, 134, 197, 201, 227, 245, 273, 274, 321, 322, 385

Juneau Icefield 43, 47, 56, 59, 70, 79, 134

Kalloch, Gina 323

Kaspsuk, Greg & Hedy 283

Kessel, Brina 147

Klondike 17, 82, 83, 84, 85, 197, 318

Kobuk River 344, 345, 347, 357, 358, 386 Kobuk Sand Dunes 158, 344, 350, 351, 354, 355, 356, 357

Kodiak 226, 240, 273, 281, 305, 307

Kotelainen, Erkki 214, 245

Kotzebue 25, 28, 158, 345, 358, 360, 369, 370

Kowalik, Zygmunt 271

Kurten, Björn 278, 280

Kuskokwim River 333, 334

Kwethluk 333, 334, 335, 337, 338, 339

Laitala, Eugene 190, 375

Lake Bennett 83, 207

Lake Linda 53, 54, 55, 66

Lamb, Rick 268

Leikas, Ailie 192, 215

Lewis, Roger 248, 251

Livingston, Arlo 58, 81

Llewellyn Glacier 64, 67

Lowe, Marieanna vii, 34, 37, 197

Lynn Canal 35, 58

Mackenzie River 289, 290

Marvil, Steve 159

McCarthy, Greg 345

McConnel, Dee 129

McKeoun, Patrick – ST 227

McNeil River 293, 294, 295, 298

Meyer, Craig 259

Meyer, Ken 157, 244, 246, 268

Miller, Adele 197, 198, 199, 200, 201, 202, 203, 206

Miller, Keith – governor 29, 32

Miller, Maynard 47, 72, 77

Moulin 65

Morey, Roy 248, 258, 262

Mount McKinley 60, 88, 147

Mt. Moore 62, 63, 72, 74

Kristina's Cache in Alaska

Mt. Roberts Muench, Robin (Bob)
155, 169, 170, 178, 191,
214, 225, 227, 270
Murphy, Claire 318, 319
Musk ox 99, 129, 130, 135,
164, 183, 246
Nayudu – Doc 3, 4, 33, 34, 35,
36, 37, 46, 47, 81, 94,
Nebert, David 226
Nestler, Ken 29, 31
Neuman, Karl 128, 194, 212
Newton, Carl 291
Nick, Barbara 267
Nome 16, 17, 19, 22, 24, 25,
27, 28, 105
Northway 94
Norway 29, 31, 186, 253,
264, 322, 340
Olsen, Scott 372
Palosuo, Erkki 162, 210
Palosuo, Maini 210, 213
Paluszkiewicz, Terri 270
Parke, Marianne 62, 63, 71, 74,
75, 76, 77, 78, 79, 80, 81
Peltz, Bob 116, 122,
183, 186, 192
Petersburg 29, 30, 31, 32, 276
Peterson, Dick 247, 257
Pierce, Walter 222
Pitsenberger, Barbara 331
Pribilof Islands 138, 140, 233
Prudhoe Bay 5, 108, 174,
176, 265, 290
Pyne, Kent 364
Ramsey, Guy 249, 252
Reagan, Ronald – President
282, 284, 285

Reckard, Matt 326
Reynolds, Eric 62, 74
Rice, Bob 38, 41, 46
Roelleke, Herman 195
Royer, Tom 244, 270, 307
Russia 5, 23, 30, 129, 273, 276
R/V Acona 33
R/V Alpha Helix 302, 306, 307
R/V Aranda xvi, xvii, 212, 225,
232, 233, 271, 304, 306, 307
R/V Surveyor 225, 226, 228,
235, 237, 238, 240, 248
Sackinger, Bill 265, 291
Schmidt, Ben & Shirley 345
Seppälä, Matti 79
Sharma 95, 98, 178
Shell, Ann Lillian 104
Sigman, Marilyn 226
Sitka 5, 29, 30, 91,
200, 273, 385
Skagway 35, 36, 82, 83, 84, 85,
197, 198, 322
Sorvoja, Martti 263
Spein, Elizabeth 340
St. John, Dan 217
Stevens, Eddie 328
Sullivan, Bob 118, 122,
185, 219, 241
Szafran, Ed 98, 108, 118, 247
Taku Glacier 48, 60, 61, 62,
73, 78, 80
Teller 22
Tetri, Eero 9
Thomas, Joe 249, 252, 257,
258, 349, 366
Thompson, Harry 60
Tobin, Carl 236

Tracy Arm 36

Unimak Pass 229, 236, 238, 240

Valdez 174, 308, 320

Vaughan-Lewis Glacier 61, 68

Van Amburg, Craig 376

Vargas, Joe 373

Warren, Dick 51

Waugaman, Candy 318

Wencker, Debbie – ST 233

*Wendler, Gerd 151, 155,
   159, 178, 270*

West, Helli 251

*White Pass & Yukon Rail
   82, 84, 386*

Whitehorse 82, 83, 84, 131, 209

Wienke, Sally 34, 37, 94, 104

Yukon River 82, 176, 318

www.ingramcontent.com/pod-product-compliance
Lightning Source LLC
Chambersburg PA
CBHW021605120626
46545CB00001B/78